Hanalei

A Kaua'i River Town

Hanalei

A Kaua'i River Town

Daniel Harrington

Mutual Publishing

The footnotes referred to in this text may be seen at www.hawaiianencyclopedia.com

Note: Hawaiian words in this book conform to proper Hawaiian spellings including the diacritical marks 'okina (glottal stop); and kahakō (macron). However, to preserve the authenticity of quotations, cited material is presented as originally written.

The image on page x is credited to the Bishop Museum. The image on pages 154, 171, and 172 are credited to the Hawai'i State Archives.

Library of Congress Cataloging-in-Publication Data

Harrington, Daniel.
  Hanalei : a Kaua'i river town / Daniel Harrington.
    p. cm.
  Includes bibliographical references and index.
    ISBN-13: 978-1-56647-847-2 (softcover : alk. paper)
  ISBN-10: 1-56647-847-2 (softcover : alk. paper)
    1. Hanalei (Hawaii)--History. 2. Natural history--Hawaii--Hanalei. I. Title.
  DU629.H225H37 2008
  996.9'41--dc22
                    2008037729

ISBN-10: 1-56647-847-2
ISBN-13: 978-1-56647-847-2

First Printing, October 2008
Second Printing, March 2010

Design by Wanni & Courtney Young

Mutual Publishing, LLC
1215 Center Street, Suite 210
Honolulu, Hawai'i 96816
Ph: 808-732-1709 / Fax: 808-734-4094
email: info@mutualpublishing.com
www.mutualpublishing.com

Printed in Korea

Table of Contents

Introduction

No place on this planet is so blessed by nature as Hanalei, the northern region of Kauaʻi which stretches from Princeville to Waikoko. Tucked beneath emerald green mountains, the fertile coastal plain known for its rich soils and agricultural bounty leads to golden-sand beaches and a bejeweled sea. Frequent rainshowers energize the streams and rivers and create rainbows that arc across the sky.

Hanalei names a valley, a town, a bay, and a river; it has been translated as "lei valley," referring to rainbows that color the sky like a lei of flowers, "wreath making," for the mountains that encircle Hanalei like a wreath, and "crescent bay," for the calm, protected waters fed by Hanalei River.

The story of Hanalei is one of a place and a people. Today the descendants of Hanalei's early residents carry on the culture of their forebears, making Hanalei seem almost timeless, an enchanted district that continues to cultivate a rich history.

Kauaʻi is set apart from the other Hawaiian Islands by a large ocean channel, which thwarted even the powerful armies of King Kamehameha I. Its relative isolation created a society distinct from the rest of the island chain, and the remote north shore of Kauaʻi was often among the last areas to feel the effects of Western influences and changing world events.

Still, Hanalei was well-populated in ancient times, supporting a thriving native population and producing bountiful food supplies including taro, bananas, breadfruit, sweet potatoes, yams, and coconuts. Hanalei Bay teemed with fish caught with hook and line, nets, and spears.

British explorer Captain James Cook established Western contact with the Hawaiian Islands in 1778. As ships found their way to Kaua'i in the following years, foreigners spotted opportunity in her rich, wet soil. During the first half of the 1800s Hanalei became the site of various agricultural endeavors that produced significant harvests of mulberry leaves, coffee, tobacco, cotton, rice, sugarcane, citrus fruits, peaches, pineapples, bananas, dates, tamarind, guavas, potatoes, plantains, yams, cabbage, and lettuce.

In the 1840s American Joseph Gardner began raising sheep and other animals; by 1848 he established a mill and loom with several spinning-wheels that manufactured wool and cotton cloth. Cattle ranching became another major land use in the Hanalei region beginning in the late 1800s and continuing into the next century.

Sugar was an important export as well, and in 1862 the construction of the Hanalei Sugar Mill was completed on the banks of the Hanalei River. The building of the mill was coupled with further attempts to grow and mill sugarcane in Hanalei Valley and on the Princeville plateau.

By the 1870s the well-irrigated Hanalei Valley lands formerly used for taro were converted to grow rice, as the Chinese, Japanese, Filipino, and Portuguese plantation workers, who ended their contracts on the sugar plantations, attempted new endeavors. The rice farmers also built homes, schools, stores, rice mills, churches, and temples as they settled and raised families in the Hanalei region.

Appreciated for her sheer beauty, Hanalei was also visited by many members of Hawaiian royalty including King Kamehameha II (Kalaninui 'Iolani Liholiho) in 1821; King Kamehameha III (Kauikeaouli) in 1852; and King Kamehameha IV (Alexander Liholiho) with Queen Emma in 1856. Alexander Liholiho and Emma visited again in 1860 with their young son Crown Prince Albert, who inspired Hanalei plantation owner R. C. Wyllie to name his growing estate "Princeville."

Princess Ruth came to Hanalei seven years later to enjoy the sights on the north shore of Kaua'i, and King Kalākaua came into Hanalei Bay in 1874, to be greeted by a "21-gun salute" fired from improvised cannons made from hollowed trunks of native 'ōhi'a lehua trees. His sister Princess Lili'uokalani followed in 1881, traveling to Kīlauea to drive the ceremonial first spike at the Kīlauea Sugar Plantation. She returned to Hanalei as Queen Lili'uokalani in 1891.

Since the 1950s Hanalei has been the scene of many a Hollywood film, and more recently has become a favorite retreat of the wealthy. Hanalei Bay's pristine waters attract many visitors to the island, and waves off the northern shore are some of the world's best, ridden by renowned locals such as famed Hawaiian waterman Titus Kinimaka, multiple world surfing champion Andy Irons, and his equally amazing brother Bruce Irons.

Hanalei has always been enjoyed for its rich and varied beauty and appreciated for its agricultural capability. People from all corners of the globe have fallen in love with her mountains, valleys, beaches, and bay; people have invested in the land and carved out fields, cultivated farms, built churches, ranches, and homesteads, and erected bridges and piers. People have made Hanalei home.

This book is also about the stories and traditions of these people, in this place, and the enduring aloha of Hanalei's residents today.

> At the time of my visit it was the rainy season. More than a score of cascades were leaping down the perpendicular steeps of those mountains, whose rugged summits, clad with a dense foliage, pierced the clouds at a height of four thousand feet. The valley itself was covered with plantations and pasturelands, dotted with groves of tropical trees. In the distance stood the Mission church and the other buildings comprising the station. Here and there the grass huts of the natives were sprinkled over the open tracts, or half concealed among the foliage. Beyond all, and forming the mouth of the valley, was the peaceful little harbor revealing its fair sandy beach, with the white foam of the surf defining its limits. The final touch to the picture was the beautiful river that meandered through the valley, kissing the wild flowers that clustered on its banks, or bearing a solitary canoe on its bosom, now losing itself among the dense foliage, and now bursting on the vision like a rich vein of silver stealing its way through the perpetual verdure.
>
> —Bates, 1854

Author's Note

While attempting to write a general history of the Hanalei region, I confronted the problem of telling a story of a place's past when it was glaringly noticeable that most of the available written history involved not natives but immigrants—and so I was left with many questions, particularly about the original Hawaiian people that lived in Hanalei before Western contact, and their stories.

The more I researched, the more I realized that an underlying story exists, one that is difficult to tell: the untold history of a vanishing culture dispossessed of their traditions, the transformation of the native landscape, and the decimation of the indigenous people.

What was it like more than a century ago as wave after wave of diseases killed many thousands of Hawaiians throughout the Islands? How did the natives cope as their communities were devastated by epidemics that emptied whole villages?

From 1835 to 1860, the population of the Hanalei district decreased by half even as the non-native population increased. Less than forty thousand native Hawaiians remained in the Hawaiian Islands by 1890, down from a native population at the time of Western contact estimated to have been more than a quarter million, and possibly more than three times that number.

All but lost to history are the stories of many of these native Hawaiians who perished in the wake of Western contact. Beyond the statistics of population decline, dates of epidemics, and names of foreign-introduced diseases, many details remain a mystery (though more historical information about this era has recently been made available through new access to Hawaiian language newspapers from the 1800s and early 1900s).

Each new epidemic, each new wave of foreign influences, furthered the inexorable unraveling of an ancient cultural fabric, the rich and complex culture of a self-sufficient people living on the planet's most isolated archipelago for more than one thousand years before Western contact.

To address these difficult questions—the subtleties of political events, issues of land ownership, and the complex human issues involving an indigenous culture and native landscape irretrievably changed—would require many more pages and need to range over all the Hawaiian Islands. This book is just the story of one area of one island, yet it was written with an awareness of, and sensitivity to, these complicated issues.

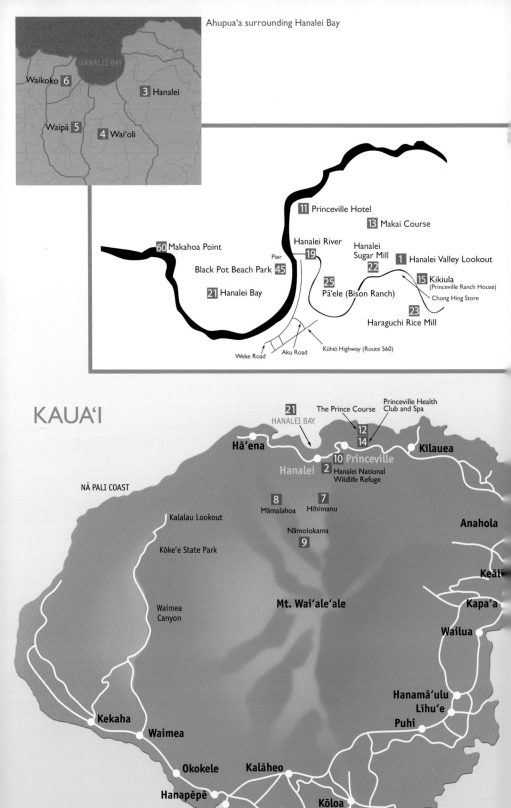

Ahupua'a surrounding Hanalei Bay

Waikoko **6**

3 Hanalei

Waipā **5**

4 Wai'oli

HANALEI BAY

Princeville Hotel **11**

13 Makai Course

60 Makahoa Point

Hanalei River

Hanalei Sugar Mill

1 Hanalei Valley Lookout

Pier

19

Black Pot Beach Park **45**

22

15 Kikiula
(Princeville Ranch House)

21 Hanalei Bay

25

Pā'ele (Bison Ranch)

Chong Hing Store

23

Haraguchi Rice Mill

Weke Road   Aku Road   Kūhiō Highway (Route 560)

KAUA'I

21
HANALEI BAY

The Prince Course

Princeville Health Club and Spa

12

14

Hā'ena

10 Princeville

Kīlauea

Hanalei

2 Hanalei National Wildlife Refuge

NĀ PALI COAST

8
Māmalahoa

7
Hīhīmanu

Anahola

Kalalau Lookout

Nāmolokama

Kōke'e State Park

9

Keāli

Kapa'a

Mt. Wai'ale'ale

Waimea Canyon

Wailua

Hanamā'ulu

Līhu'e

Kekaha

Puhi

Waimea

Okokele

Kalāheo

Hanapēpē

Kōloa

Port Allen

Po'ipū

A Drive Through
One Thousand Years of History

"As a scene of beauty, it is almost peerless."
—Theophilus H. Davies, 1862

When you approach Hanalei by car, pause first at the **Hanalei Valley Lookout** [1], located just above the eastern edge of Hanalei Valley alongside Route 560 (Kūhiō Highway) near the Princeville Shopping Center. The scenic overlook provides expansive views of Hanalei's coastal plain, including the taro patches of the 917-acre **Hanalei National Wildlife Refuge** [2]. Interpretive signs at the lookout provide information about the region's endangered waterbirds.

Hanalei's coastal plain spans the lower regions of four separate ahupua'a (watersheds)—**Hanalei** [3], **Wai'oli** [4], **Waipā** [5], and **Waikoko** [6]—all of which flow into Hanalei Bay. The massive mountains rising up from the coastal plain are, from east to west, **Hīhīmanu** [7], **Māmalahoa** [8], and **Nāmolokama** [9].

Above the lookout are the nine thousand immaculate acres of **Princeville** [10], Kaua'i's most famous resort, located on the coastal plateau known in ancient times as Pu'u Pehu, above the eastern side of Hanalei Valley. The **Princeville Hotel** [11] is terraced into the oceanfront hillside of Pu'upōā Ridge overlooking Hanalei Bay. Princeville's two golf courses—the **Prince Course** [12] and the **Makai Course** [13]—are consistently ranked among the best in the nation. On the hilltop above it all is the **Princeville Health Club and Spa** [14].

Along the eastern edge of Hanalei Valley once stood three of Hanalei's most historic post-contact homes: **Kikiula** [15], a two-room stone plantation home built in 1845 (later known as Princeville Plantation House and then Princeville Ranch House); the **Kellett**

HISTORIC HANALEI MAP*

*not drawn to scale

This map represents Hanalei in the early 1900s. Many buildings shown on this map are no longer standing.

Slogett Beach House 54 Mahamoku (1914) Lota House (1915) 53 Fayé Beach House (1915) 52 San

WE

Princeville Pla

'ANAE ROAD

MAHI MAHI ROAD

MĀLOLO ROAD

Nishimura Family

56
Waipā Bridge (1912)
(location off map)
←

59
Waikoko Bridge
(location off map)
←

• Waikoko Chock Chin Rice Mill
• Waipā Hiramoto Mill
  formerly Hee Fat Rice Mill

• Charlie McKee residence

• Masada family • Jail
• District Courthouse
• Judge Aarona's House
• Dispensary

• Old Post Office

• Chock Chin Store (1901)
  later C. Akeoni, Hanalei Store

• Chock Chin residence

37 Japanese Language School
   now St. Williams Catholic Church
• gas station • Hanalei Shingon
• John Lee's family
• Kam and Au families
• Nagaoka cafe
• T. S. See Wo Store
  now Church of Latter Day Saints

55 Wai'oli Bridge (1912)

ROUTE 560/G

Fish Peddler Morimotos
Hiramoto's Kogas

Robert Wong family
Hashimoto family
Kobayashi family
Edith Wong family

Azeka Farm
Matsuda Farm
Zaima family

Nakatsuji Rice Mill
formerly Hop Chong Wai

Tadao Nakatsuji family

30 Hanalei School

41 Old Wai'oli Church (1841)
   now Wai'oli Mission Hall

40 Wai'oli Hui'ia Church (1912)

Takahashi's Garage
and Repair Shop

• Tasaka's Coffee S

35 Lily Pond

34 33 3

Hanalei Poi Company

Say Dock House (1895)

KUMU ROAD

OLD SCHOOL HOUSE ROAD

42 Wai'oli belfry (1841)

43 Wai'oli Mission House
   (1834-1837)

36 Lily Pond House (1933)

Wai'oli Park 38

↖
Lumaha'i
Harada 'ohana
(location off map)

Japanese cemetery

57

39 Hale Hālāwai 'Ohana
   'O Hanalei Community

Other area residents:
Birkmeyre, Conant, James and Abraham Lota,
Gardners, Pauole, Pa, Kuehu, Kealoha

51 Hanalei Pavilion

44 Hanalei Pier (1892)

Kamoʻomaikaʻi Fishpond
Hanalei Sugar Mill (1862)
Birkmyre Estate
Hanalei Plantation Hotel

22 **17** **18**

(locations off map)

AKU ROAD

• Rice Warehouse

• Carpenter's Shop
• Alfred ʻAlohikea
• Hoe family
• Nakatsuka General Store
  now part of Tahiti Nui Building
• Mr. Shiraishi's barber shop
• Hanalei Liquor Store
• Bobby Tasaka's residence
• Shak family
• Ho family
• Trader Building

28

26

• Nakatsuka family home

49 Kauikeolani (1899)

50 Kanoa Pond

• Hamamura Store

45 Black Pot Beach Park
Roman Catholic Chapel
Rectory
Belfry

46 **47** **48**

Kellett House
(location off map)

16

25 Pāʻele
*Shing Kon Rice Plantation
formerly Soy Sung Wai,
now Hanalei Gardens Farm
and Bison Ranch*

Ching Ma Leong Store
*Originally called Ah Hoy Store
Later relocated to the Trader Building*

Hanalei Bridge (1912)

20

AD (now called Kūhio Highway)

, Residence

27 Hongwanji Japanese Buddhist Temple

Takahashi Farm

Miiki Farm
Liu Farm
Takenaka Farm
Ueda Farm

Ching Hing Store

Old Hanalei School Building (1926)

Haraguchi Farm

Princeville Ranch House
(location off map)

Lum Farm

Haraguchi House

Haraguchi Rice Mill (1930) **23**
former site of Man Sung Mill

Hanalei Chinese cemetery **24**

Yee Hing Society
Community Home

Atuck Wong Farm

Chinese temple

In area:
• Mal Quick House, 1925
  (on 1910 rice mill site)
• Mike Fitzgerald House, 1925
• Jed Mamaril House, 1930s

Chinese Clubhouse and
Social Hall (Yee Hing)

More Farms

Man Sung Wai Rice Mill

Pisante family

ʻŌHIKI ROAD

House [16], once home to Captain Kellett, Hanalei's "Pilot of the Port"; and the **Birkmyre Estate** [17], used as the French planter's home in the 1957 movie *South Pacific*.

The **Hanalei Plantation Hotel** [18] was built on the former site of the Birkmyre home, which later became a Club Med before eventually being torn down. For a few years in the mid-1970s a riverboat shuttle provided transportation across the Hanalei River from the resort to Black Pot Beach Park.

Traveling west from the Hanalei Valley Lookout on Route 560 leads you into the valley and across the **Hanalei River** [19]. At the bottom of the hill is the historic **Hanalei Bridge** [20], built in 1892 and replaced in 1912. The wagon road leading down to Hanalei Bridge was so steep that extra horses were required to help carriages up the hill or slow their descent.

Before the bridge was built, travelers were taken across the river on a ferry pulled on a cable. A legend from ancient times tells of a lizard dragon named Kamoʻo-o-kaumuliwai who guarded the rivermouth and required a gift to pass. When Hiʻiaka, the younger sister of the volcano goddess Pele, became angered that a torrent of water was blocking her path, she turned the lizard dragon to stone. Beyond Hanalei Bridge, fields of taro span the landscape from the base of the mountains into Hanalei Valley. Archaeological studies have traced agricultural activity back to at least 1200 A.D., though it probably began much earlier. In ancient times, native Hawaiians built their thatched homes along the Hanalei River and on the hillsides above the valley's taro patches, as well as along the shoreline.

The river runs to **Hanalei Bay** [21], where many ships sank as they carried armies, makaʻāinana, and royalty across the large and unpredictable Kaʻieʻiewaho Channel from Oʻahu.

British explorer Captain James Cook first established Western contact with the Hawaiian Islands in 1778 when he landed at Waimea on Kauaʻi's southwest shore. It would not be long before the population in the Hanalei region began to feel the wide-ranging influences of contact, including the effects of the sandalwood trade, whaling, and the arrival of American missionaries, who established the first permanent mission station in the region in 1834.

Other industries followed suit: in 1840, the lands just past Hanalei Bridge were the site of mulberry orchards that supplied food for a silkworm enterprise that manufactured fine silk sold in

Mazatlan and Mexico City. Just two years later the first commercial coffee plantation in the Hawaiian Islands was established, and downriver, the **Hanalei Sugar Mill** [22] was completed in 1862 with $40,000 worth of machinery from Scotland. The mill's 110-foot smokestack stood until 1919.

From the late 1800s to the early 1900s, Hanalei was a checkerboard of rice paddies, with numerous rice mills and stores operating throughout the region. Still standing just upriver from the Hanalei Bridge on the Haraguchi taro farm is the restored **Haraguchi Rice Mill** [23], originally built in 1930 and now Hawai'i's only surviving rice mill from the historic rice-farming era. Nearby is the **Hanalei Chinese Cemetery** [24], also known as Ah Goong San (Grandfathers' Mountain).

The road from Hanalei Bridge to Hanalei town meanders between fields of taro and the Hanalei River. Across the river a herd of bison roams on the marshy grasslands that were known in ancient times as **Pā'ele** [25], now the site of the Hanalei Garden Farms and Bison Ranch.

As Route 560 enters Hanalei town, makai of the road is the **Hanalei Liquor Store** [26], for many years owned and operated by Dora Ching Morishige, a descendant of an early rice farming family that still runs the store today.

Across the street is a former **Hongwanji Japanese Buddhist Temple** [27] that was built in Līhu'e in 1901 and moved to Hanalei in 1985, where it now is home to a bed and breakfast. Further west is another local landmark, the **Tahiti Nui** lounge [28], renowned for its classic, local-style musical performers and authentic Hawaiian hula.

In the center of town is the **Old Hanalei School Building** [29], built in 1926 and then moved a half-mile east from its original site, where the new **Hanalei School** [30] now stands. Also, the old **Ching Young Store Building** [31], constructed in 1905, houses several shops alongside the newer Ching Young Village Shopping Center, and is still run by the Ching family.

Across the street is the **Hanalei Center** [32] in the Wailele Building, which house various businesses and restaurants. The Hanalei Center was built and continues to be run by descendants of early Hanalei missionaries Abner and Lucy Wilcox.

Just west of the Hanalei Center is the **Say Dock House** [33], a private residence built in 1895 and now one of the oldest rice-farmer homes still standing in the Hawaiian Islands (please do not go on the property).

Further west is the **Hanalei Poi Company** [34], which processes local taro into poi, and the **Lily Pond** [35], dug in the early 1900s by Chinese rice farmer Chock Chin, who also ran a store and rice mill.

To the west of the Lily Pond is the **Lily Pond House** [36], built in 1933 near the shoreline of Hanalei Bay and later moved on coconut tree rollers to its current site. Next door is another rice-era home that once served as a Saimin and Pool Hall and is now a private residence.

St. Williams Catholic Church was built in 1955 at the corner of Mālolo Road and Route 560 on the former site of a **Japanese language school** [37] that began operating around 1903, and the Hanalei Shingon, a Japanese Shingon temple built on the site in 1934.

The Shingon hosted various local events, including weddings and the Obon Dori celebration held each July as part of a Japanese Buddhist holiday honoring the departed spirits of ancestors. The Japanese language school was closed after the Japanese attack on Pearl Harbor on December 7, 1941, which resulted in the internment of Japanese teachers and ministers throughout the Hawaiian Islands.

Hanalei's **Wai'oli Park** [38] is now the site of many local soccer games and craft fairs as well as the Hanalei Taro Festival. A weekly farmers' market is held Saturday mornings near the **Hale Hālāwai 'Ohana 'O Hanalei Community Center** [39] on the east side of the park.

At the west end, just behind **Wai'oli Hui'ia Church** [40] is **Wai'oli Mission Hall** [41]. Built in 1841, it is Kaua'i's oldest surviving church building, and served for many decades as the original Wai'oli Church. Next to the old church is the **Wai'oli belfry** [42], the only surviving example of a bell tower structure in the Hawaiian Islands. Tucked back behind the trees is the **Wai'oli Mission House** [43], built in the 1830s, completely restored in 1921, incorporated as a museum in 1952, and now offering free guided tours.

Hanalei Pier [44] is located at the eastern end of Weke Road near the Hanalei rivermouth. Originally built in 1892 to serve the region's thriving rice industry, the pier was rebuilt in 1912 and again in 1992 after Hurricane 'Iniki. Today the pier is a popular place to fish, swim, and enjoy views of the mountains rising up behind Hanalei town and the bay. To the east of Hanalei Pier is **Black Pot Beach Park** [45], named after a big iron pot used to cook fish during a hukilau, the traditional practice in which everyone cooperates to spot, net, and gather fish.

On the west side of the Hanalei rivermouth once stood a **Roman Catholic chapel** [46], established in 1864. A **rectory** [47] was built next to the chapel to provide housing for the priest, and around 1900 a slender, wooden **belfry** [48] was built on the site. The original church bell now hangs in front of St. Williams Church in Hanalei town.

Along Weke Road—beginning on the western end and going east—are several historic structures including **Kauikeōlani** [49], the 1899 home of Albert Spencer Wilcox and his wife Emma Kauikeōlani Napoleon Mahelona. Nearby is the historic **Kanoa Pond** [50].

On the shore of Hanalei Bay is the **Hanalei Pavilion** [51], built to replace the Old Hanalei Pavilion which was destroyed in the 1957 tsunami (tidal wave). The **Sanborn Beach House** [52], the first Western-style "beach house" on the bay, was built in 1910; in the 1957 tsunami the entire home was moved ten feet, and then reposted in its new location. In 1915, the **Fayé Beach House** [53] was erected by Norwegian Hans Peter Fayé, who managed sugar plantations on Kaua'i's west side.

Also on the shoreline of Hanalei Bay is the spacious, wood-framed home called **Mahamoku** [54], which means "island of peace." Mahamoku was built in 1914 under the direction of Mabel and Charles Wilcox, and is notable for its steep roof and cantilevered loft balconies.

Just west of Hanalei town, but still within the Hanalei region, are **Wai'oli Bridge** [55] and **Waipā Bridge** [56]. The two concrete, cast-in-place structures were built in 1912 after horse-drawn wagons that were heavily loaded with crushed rock for road construction caused the collapse of the wooden bridges in place at the time. An additional span was added to the Waipā Bridge after the 1946 tsunami altered the course of the Waipā Stream. Just past Waipā Bridge is Kumu Road, which leads to the **Japanese cemetery** [57].

The ahupua'a (watershed) of **Waipā** [58] is being restored by a community group called the Waipā Foundation. They utilize the valley as a "living classroom" that includes taro patches and an ancient fishpond, teaching children, residents, and tourists the history of the land.

After passing Waipā, the road crosses **Waikoko Bridge** [59], which collapsed in the 1946 tsunami. It was hastily repaired by stacking rocks atop the fallen structure, and it remains in use today.

Route 560 follows the sandy shoreline before climbing a hill to Hanalei Bay's westernmost point, Makahoa, "Friendly point." The road then winds around a bend towards the valley of Lumaha'i and out of our story.

More information about these Hanalei locations is provided within this book along with information about many more historic Hanalei sites not mentioned in this brief driving tour.

Chapter 1

First Settlement to Western Contact
Ancient Times–1778

In the Beginning

Eighty million years ago, a stationary plume of erupting lava called the Hawaiian magmatic hot spot broke through the Pacific seafloor to begin the formation of a volcano. This volcano, located along a moving piece of the Earth's crust called a tectonic plate, shifted northwest several inches each year, leaving the hot spot to create yet another volcano.

To date the Hawaiian magmatic hot spot has created 107 volcanoes, including all of the Hawaiian Islands as well as the Emperor Chain to the northwest. Collectively these volcanoes are called the Hawaiian–Emperor Chain, and they span the Pacific seafloor for more than 3,100 miles.

Except for the Hawaiian Islands, all the volcanoes of the Hawaiian–Emperor Chain are completely submerged. The North-

The trail of underwater mountains, created as a tectonic plate moved across the Hawai'i hotspot over millions of years, is known as the Hawaiian–Emperor seamount chain, or the Emperor Seamounts. **National Geophysical Data Center**

western Hawaiian Islands, which consist of 124 small islets and atolls, begin hundreds of miles northwest of the eight main Hawaiian Islands and are now part of the newly designated Papahānaumokuākea Marine National Monument.

Kaua'i is the oldest of the major Hawaiian Islands, formed roughly five million years ago. The island grew eight thousand feet above sea level before its volcanoes became dormant and then extinct. It is currently four hundred miles northwest of the actively erupting lava.

Today the lava plume of the hot spot sits just southeast of Hawai'i Island, where the newest volcano, Lō'ihi Seamount, has grown nine thousand feet from the sea floor. While Lō'ihi's summit is still three thousand feet from the ocean's surface, it should rise above the water in about one hundred thousand years to become the next Hawaiian island.

Life Takes Hold—Colonization and Evolution

Over millennia, the Hawaiian island of Kaua'i continued to change. The island's summits eroded from eight thousand feet above sea level to five thousand feet, and the harsh volcanic landscape was overlaid with soil. As the terrain became lush and green, plant and animal species began to take hold.

As the tropical Hawaiian Islands sat more than 2,400 miles from the nearest continental land mass, relatively few species made the journey across the Pacific Ocean. Yet species that did survive adapted to the variety of island habitats and food sources, evolving into unique Hawaiian species.

One example of this type of evolution is found in the case of the single type of finch bird that arrived in the Hawaiian Islands and eventually evolved into more than fifty endemic[1] species and subspecies of Hawaiian forest birds. Their fascinating array of beak shapes revealed their favored food sources: insects, seeds, and fruit.

Other species were able to survive because of the wide diversity of habitats in the Hawaiian Islands. Stout koa trees and tiny forest birds found refuge in the mountains, while koloa ducks and black-necked stilts thrived in wet lowland areas.

As coral reefs built up around the islands, they created areas of ocean habitat that allowed fish and other marine species to establish populations and evolve into unique Hawaiian species. Well known are the Hawaiian species of nai'a (spinner dolphins), 'īlio-holo-i-ka-uaua (monk seals), and honu (green sea turtles).

The island's geography also continued to change, as erosion carved out deep valleys from Kaua'i's landscape and the active volcano built upon existing land. The canyon of Hanalei Valley was about two thousand feet deep when lava from eruptions known as the Kōloa lava flows filled it entirely, creating the broad and relatively flat plateau lands on the peninsula now referred to as Princeville.

The Kōloa flows also changed the route of the Hanalei River, moving it further west. In its new location, the streambed eroded basalt lava from earlier, thinner flows known as the Nā Pali flows to create the modern Hanalei Valley. Today the eastern ridge of Hanalei Valley is a basalt mold of the ancient canyon.[2]

The abundant rains of the Hanalei region also caused constant erosion and intermittent landslides. During the last four millennia the rains washed volcanic earth down from the surrounding mountains, depositing rich soils on the valley bottoms and over the broad, open plain along Hanalei Bay.[3]

The coastal area also changed about four thousand years ago, as steadily decreasing sea levels revealed a part of the island which Hanalei town occupies today.[4]

The Polynesians Arrive

Hanalei's human history reaches back nearly two thousand years to when the first Polynesian settlers arrived on Hawai'i's shores in their double-hulled voyaging canoes, known as wa'a kaulua.[5] Sailing over the enormous Pacific Ocean, the Polynesians were guided by the sun and stars, prevailing winds and ocean currents, flight patterns of birds, and other clues of nature.

The ancient Polynesians were master navigators who inhabited hundreds of Pacific islands over a span of thousands of years before discovering the Hawaiian Islands.[6] The first human arrivals in the Islands likely occurred around 300 A.D., although the exact date of the first inhabitation remains uncertain, and might have been much earlier.[7]

Amazingly, settlers discovered the remote island group despite the fact that the Hawaiian Islands add up to less than 6,500 square miles of land in an ocean that covers 70 million square miles, nearly one-third of the Earth's surface.

After Polynesians settled in the Hawaiian Islands, it is believed they continued to sail back and forth to the islands of southern Polynesia until around 1250 A.D. At that time, contact with southern Polynesia ceased or significantly decreased and the settlers no longer pursued long-distance, open-ocean voyages. Thus a unique Hawaiian culture began to develop, and continued to evolve during a period of isolation that lasted until British Captain James Cook arrived in the Hawaiian Islands in 1778.

By the time of Cook's arrival, Hawaiians possessed a culture that utilized the unique natural resources found in the islands, such as colorful bird feathers and durable native hardwoods. Hanalei was already known as a prime agricultural region, with fertile soils and plenty of water. As an important center of food production, Hanalei was likely a bountiful bread basket for the entire island of Kaua'i.[8]

The Development of a Unique Hawaiian Culture

Hawaiians made use of hundreds of native species for food, shelter, and tools as well as for medicine, religion, and ceremony. They also employed the plant and animal species they had brought with them on voyaging canoes, including dogs, chickens, pigs, and more than two dozen species of plants that were important for the Hawaiian people (see *Appendix I*).

One of the most fundamental plants the early Polynesian settlers brought with them was kalo, or taro. They ate the plant's heart-shaped leaves and mashed the underground corm with water to make poi, a main staple in the Hawaiian diet. They also used taro to make kūlolo, a pudding-like dessert, by sweetening the grated flesh and water of coconut with sugarcane then blending it with the grated corm of taro. The mixture was wrapped in ti leaves and baked in an imu (underground earthen oven).

Aside from food, taro was used as a dye for kapa barkcloth, an adhesive, and as bait for 'ōpelu fish. Additionally a mixture of taro corm with the nut sap of kukui was used as a medicinal purgative, and the sap of the taro leaf stem was applied to cuts to stop bleeding.

Beyond utilitarian purposes, kalo also held spiritual significance. Hawaiians consider the plant their direct ancestor, and "staff of life." According to legend, the first son of Wākea, god of the sky, was Hāloa-naka, "long, trembling stem," who died at birth. From his burial place a taro plant grew. Wākea's second son, the human child

Preparing taro. **Kauaʻi Historical Society**

Hāloa-naka-lau-kapalili, "long-stalk-quaking-trembling-leaf stem," is considered the ancestor of all Hawaiians.

The manner in which kalo grew functioned as a strong metaphor for the extended Hawaiian family, or ʻohana. In fact, the word for family is derived from the name of the offshoots of a mature taro plant, known as ʻohā. The ʻohā grow in a circle around the parent plant, and as they mature produce their own circle of shoots. In this way, a single taro plant may eventually fill a taro patch, as a family grows with the maturing of each child.

Polynesians also brought wauke, or paper mulberry. The plant's bark fibers were beaten and used for clothing, bedding, and wrapping. Oftentimes this barkcloth, known as kapa, was colored and scented with dyes and fragrances derived from native plants.

Polynesians, in particular Hawaiians, produced some of the finest kapa in the Pacific. The high quality was in part due to a unique fermentation process the Hawaiians used during the kapa-making process.

Unique to Hawaiian kapa was an imprint design, much like a watermark, which was pounded into the wauke sheet during the second beating. When held to light, these designs would reveal an additional dimension to the painted, stamped, and lined surface designs of the barkcloth, creating artifacts found nowhere else in Polynesia.

Settlers also brought ipu (bottle gourds) that were used to make containers, bowls, and musical instruments. The kukui (candlenut tree) had a multitude of uses as well, as the tree's oily nut provided light and food, and the wood was carved into small canoes to be used in nearshore waters.

Prehistoric agricultural activity in Hanalei Valley included irrigated pondfield technology (taro patches) consisting of large ponds, usually square or rectangular in shape, separated by earthen banks and irrigated by 'auwai (earthen and stone irrigation ditches). Today the floodplain of the Hanalei Valley floor is again covered with taro patches, and some ancient 'auwai are still used to irrigate the fields.

Subsurface excavations have shown that taro was cultivated not only in the river valleys but also on agricultural terraces built into the hillsides above the valley floor.[9] Some of these ancient taro sites were irrigated by natural springs flowing out from the mountainsides. Dryland taro was also cultivated.

Various native Hawaiian birds were hunted for food, including Newell's shearwaters, petrels, and wedge-tailed shearwaters. Also captured and eaten were large flightless geese such as the moa nalo, a now-extinct bird notable for its tortoise-like jaws.

Some native bird species, such as the prized 'i'iwi, 'ō'ō, and mamo, were valued for their colorful feathers that were woven into royal capes and cloaks known as 'ahu'ula, and feather-crested helmets called mahiole. Feathers from both the red-tailed tropicbird and white-tailed tropicbird were utilized to make royal feather standards called kāhili, symbols of chiefly rank that consisted of feather clusters attached to long poles.

Ancient Hawaiians used no written language aside from the petroglyphs they etched into stones. Remnants of Hanalei's earliest human history include ancient fishponds and 'auwai (agricultural irrigation ditches).

Other archeological artifacts from ancient times include stone adzes that were used for wood carving, and also stone poi pounders. Scientists investigating the past also rely on other clues found in ashes, bones, pollen, and other materials. Preserved now in various forms are the ancient stories, legends, and sacred chants that were passed down orally from one generation to the next.

Heiau (sacred places of worship) also stand as records of the past. A prominent heiau in the region, and one of the largest on Kaua'i, is Poʻokū, located atop a hill on the eastern side of Hanalei Valley. Another important Hawaiian cultural area still revered for its place in Hawaiian history and its mana, or spiritual power, is located just west of Hanalei at the base of the cliffs above Kēʻē Beach. Hula dancers and chanters came to the site from throughout the Hawaiian Islands, and perhaps from throughout Polynesia, to receive intense training from a kumu hula (hula teacher) in the sacred art of hula and mele, the chanting that often accompanies hula.

Hula and mele chants, as well as oli (chants not accompanied by hula) are used by Hawaiians to tell their stories, pay reverence to nature, and give thanks for the natural wonders that enrich their world. Performed by those who are trained in the arts, hula, mele, and oli are infused with all the power and history of the Hawaiian people, telling tales of migrations, genealogies, legends, and traditions.

With their spoken words Hawaiians passed on their beliefs, recounting the complex genealogies of their ancestors, carrying on their oral traditions, and perpetuating an extensive knowledge of their natural world.

Nā Pali coastline. **Douglas Peebles**

One of the two heiau at Kē'ē is Ka-ulu-Paoa, "the inspiration [of] Paoa,"[10] referring to a legend about the Kaua'i chief Lohi'au and his friend Paoa, who trained in the art of hula at the site beneath the lava cliffs. A structure where hula was performed, called a hālau, was formerly located on the uppermost of the stone terraces beneath the mountain peak called Makana (gift)."[11]

Nearby to Ka-ulu-Paoa is another heiau, known as Ka-ulu-o-Laka (the inspiration of Laka),[12] and is dedicated to the hula goddess Laka, who was said to have begun her hula at this location. According to legend, this is also where the volcano goddess Pele first fell in love with the Kaua'i chief Lohi'au.[13] These heiau sites are extremely sacred to the Hawaiian people and should not be disturbed.

Beyond Kē'ē is the spectacular Nā Pali coastline, which spans the next fifteen miles of rugged shoreline to Polihale on Kaua'i's southwest side. Nā Pali means "the cliffs," and is a fitting name for this region of steep seacliffs rising thousands of feet and becoming pointed spires, sharp ridges, and volcanic pinnacles that stand sentinel over deep, ancient valleys.

> Here nature has wrought with bold hands and on a large scale, gouging profound valleys out of massive mountains, scoring them deep with gorges and buttressing them thick with ridges, and then throwing over them a veil of tropic verdure that half reveals and half conceals and wonderfully softens, the bold hard features of the geologic. Nature has contributed the magnificent semi-circular bay with its fine beach and swimming, a succession of splendid cliffs and broad level fertile valley, bounded by mountain walls down whose sides leap numberless thread-like waterfalls which now and again lose themselves in the foliage.
>
> —J. M. Lydgate [14]

The Moku (Chiefdom) of Halele'a

In ancient times, each Hawaiian island was divided into numerous moku, or chiefdoms. Each chiefdom was under the control of an ali'i 'ai moku (high chief). Most of Kaua'i's north shore, including Hanalei, fell within the moku known as Halele'a, which means "joyful house,"[15] or "house of happiness."[16]

At sea level, Halele'a is bordered on the east by the moku of Ko'olau, and on the west by the moku of Nā Pali. In the higher mountain regions, the Makaleha mountain range forms a natural border between Halele'a and the moku of Puna.

> Halele'a is cooled by the Kaiāulu, the pleasant and gentle trade wind. Sometimes the Hao-Ko'olau-o-Halele'a, 'Ko'olau trade winds coming with force,' blows, an unfriendly reminder of the power of nature.
>
> —*Kaua'i: Ancient Place-Names and Their Stories* [17]

Each moku, or chiefdom, is divided into many ahupua'a, the natural watershed land divisions that extend from the mountains to the sea, including the offshore coral reefs. Within the moku of Halele'a are nine ahupua'a. In order from east to west, the nine ahupua'a of Halele'a are Kalihiwai, Kalihikai, Hanalei, Wai'oli, Waipā, Waikoko, Lumaha'i, Wainiha, and Hā'ena.

Hawaiians maintained a system of communal subsistence based on the natural boundaries of the ahupua'a, which contained all of the resources necessary for survival. It was a tradition that "the farmer gave to the fisherman, the fisherman to the farmer," as conveyed in the saying, "O kau aku, o ka ia la mai, pelā ka nohona o ka 'ohana" (From you and from him—so lived the family).[18]

Ancient Hawaiians lived within a fairly rigid caste structure, including ali'i (royalty), kāhuna (priests and experts in a given profession), maka'āinana (commoners, who were mostly farmers), and the kauā[19] class, who were the lowest outcast members.

A system of kānāwai, or laws, determined if something was kapu, meaning it was sacred or forbidden. Commoners fell prostrate to the ground in the presence of high-ranking chiefs, who possessed mana, or divine power.

Each of the nine ahupua'a of Halele'a were traditionally under the control of a konohiki, the headman of the land division under the chief. Hanalei is one of Halele'a's largest ahupua'a, encompassing Hanalei River's vast watershed that extends from the highest reaches of Mt. Wai'ale'ale to the ocean at Hanalei Bay.

Many of the early Polynesian settlers of the Hanalei region built their homes near the shore, where the climate was warmer and drier than inland at the base of the mountains or up in the valleys. They fished the ocean and gathered shellfish, and some traveled from the shoreline into the valleys during the day to farm taro, and then returned at night to their settlements near the sea.

Groups of thatched homes formed small villages, mostly near the water but also inland, scattered throughout the valleys and on the hillsides, particularly above the taro patches. Homes were thatched with pili grass, fronds of coconut palms, or lau hala (leaves of the hala tree).

> [Hanalei] was a region of many rivers and heavy rainfall, its great dark mountains crowding close to the sea. Both rivers and ocean furnished good fishing. Most of the numerous thatched houses were clustered makai, near the sea in the curve of the great bay, where less rain fell and yet where there was a luxuriant growth of bananas, breadfruit, sugarcane, sweet potatoes, yams, squashes and pia, or arrowroot.
>
> —Koamalu[20]

The Mountains of Hanalei

The coastal plain of Hanalei includes sections of four separate ahupua'a—Hanalei, Wai'oli, Waipā, and Waikoko—all bordering Hanalei Bay. Towering up behind these river valleys are three monumental mountains: Hīhīmanu, forming the west side of

Waterfalls line Nāmolokama, which towers up behind Hanalei Town. **Dave Cunning**

The expansive sands of Hanalei Bay with Nāmolokama and Māmalahoa mountains in the background. **Dave Cunning**

Hanalei Valley; Nāmolokama, rising up behind Wai'oli Valley; and Māmalahoa, rising up to the west side of Wai'oli.

In the lower western reaches of Māmalahoa are the ahupua'a of Waipā and Waikoko. These mountains are often lined with dozens of waterfalls that encircle Hanalei Bay and the whole coastal plain.

At the very top of the ahupua'a of Hanalei Valley is the 5,148-foot peak of Mt. Wai'ale'ale, more than ten miles from the sea and not visible from the shores of Hanalei Bay. Wai'ale'ale means "rippling water," and is said to refer to the lake that sits atop the plateau at the volcano's summit where the Hanalei River begins.

Mt. Wai'ale'ale is located at the center of the island of Kaua'i, and is said to be "the wettest spot on Earth." Average annual rainfall on Wai'ale'ale is more than 450 inches, the highest in the world.[21]

On the western side of Hanalei Valley are the twin peaks of Hīhīmanu, which rise to 2,487 feet and form the border between Hanalei and Wai'oli.[22] Hīhīmanu has several translations, including "beautiful,"[23] "manta ray,"[24] and "great ray fish."[25] The two peaks of Hīhīmanu are said to resemble the appearance of a ray's fin tips

The Menehune

According to some, Hanalei's history includes an ancient race of Kauaians who were reputed to be very small but very skilled and supernaturally strong. This race, called Menehune, was said to have numbered about a half-million, and they built irrigation canals, heiau, roads, and dams. Each of the Menehune's projects would be accomplished with great precision and expertise, and would all be completed within a single night. If they failed to complete the project, it would be abandoned.

There remains some mystery surrounding the exact origin of the stories about Menehune. Early Westerners seeking information about various structures on Kaua'i might have been told that "Menehune" were responsible, referring to an old meaning of the word "manahune," which is "common people" (common laborers), likely indicating the early Marquesan settlers of Hawai'i.

The Marquesans might have been dominated by the later Tahitian settlers and made to perform the hardest work, including stonework. In other words, the term "Menehune" might have been a reference not to the Marquesan settlers' small size but instead to their lower status in the social system after the arrival of the Tahitians.

Confusion over the origins of term Menehune might have led to a myth about a small race of people, and the myth might have been compounded over the years. This is one possible explanation of the mysterious story of the Menehune.

poking above the water when it glides along near the ocean's surface.

According to legend, a "Ka-ua-hā'ao, 'gentle rain,' fell over Hīhīmanu, so-called because its showers follow one another like members of a chief's retinue that came in procession in sections or divisions."[26] Anyone who has seen the tradewind showers marching across the north shore mountainsides can relate to this description.

> Fall after fall of shining water hastens down green, abrupt slopes and across brief shore lands to the sea held within the broad curving arms of Hanalei bay. To the south of this green valley of Waioli stand its three peaks, Namolokama at the center,

flanked on the west by Mamalahoa, on the east by Hihimanu. Eastward still further, wandering in wide bends to the sea, lies the more open valley of Hanalei, largest river of all the islands and drawing its source direct from Waialeale's summit lake. Halalea, Place of Rainbows, the district was anciently called.

—Ethel Damon [27]

Nāmolokama is the massive mountain rising up at the back of Wai'oli Valley. Nāmolokama means "the interweaving bound fast,"[28] perhaps referring to the intermingling waterfalls that pour from the mountain's summit. Nāmolokama is also interpreted to mean "long rock clefts."[29] From Hanalei town, Nāmolokama's peak is often seen only through wisps of distant fog as frequent north shore rains send torrents of water plunging from the mountain's regal summit.

According to tradition, the first rainbow came to the Hawaiian Islands when Ānuenue, the goddess of rainbows (ānuenue means

Kāne and the Legend of Ānuenue. **Mark Daniels**

13

Kauahoa: The Handsome Hero of Hanalei

A famous and proud warrior of Hanalei in ancient times, according to legend, was Kauahoa. His name means "the friendly rain," and he was known as Ka meʻe uʻi o Hanalei, "the handsome hero of Hanalei."

Kauahoa was known, however, for an unfriendly act: blocking the headwaters of the Hanalei River because he was angry that the chief ʻAikanaka did not utilize his fighting skills. When Kauahoa was finally called to battle he pulled up a large koa tree to use as a war club. As he held the club aloft, birds were still singing in the tree's branches.

"rainbow"), hid on Kauaʻi while calling to the god Kāne through her dreams. Kāne came to search for her, and when he arrived at the Waiʻoli rivermouth he met several women falsely claiming to be Ānuenue. Each woman gave him a piece of colored kapa cloth. Finally Kāne reached the pool at the base of Nāmolokama's precipitous waterfall, where he threw all the kapa pieces into the water. There the kapa pieces joined together to form the first rainbow, and it was then that Ānuenue rose up from the water.[30]

Located nearer to the shoreline of Hanalei Bay is a mountain ridge called Makaihuwaʻa ("eyes for the canoe prow"[31]). Makaihuwaʻa is said to be the site of the first "lighthouse" in the Hawaiian Islands because a platform was built halfway up the mountain by Menehune so they could place large torches there to guide the fishermen back into Hanalei Bay at night.[32]

Māmalahoa rises up from the floor of Waiʻoli Valley to a height of 3,745 feet. Some say the mountain's name comes from Kānāwai Māmalahoe, or "law of the splintered paddle."[33] The law was declared in 1797 by King Kamehameha I to protect weak and innocent people from injustices imposed by those who were stronger and more powerful.[34]

The declaration stemmed from an event that had occurred years earlier when Kamehameha had attacked a man without provocation, and the man hit him back and fled. When he was later brought before

Kamehameha to be punished, the man was instead pardoned by the monarch, who gave him land and set him free.

It is perhaps more likely, however, that the name of the Hanalei mountain called Māmalahoa predates Kamehameha's encounter with the fisherman, and instead refers to the god Kāne's wife, also named Māmalahoa.[35] In ancient chants the name Māmalahoa describes a strong 'awa (kava) drink used for medicinal purposes.

The eastern edge of Māmalahoa is a sheer cliff that drops straight down for more than one thousand feet and forms the boundary between the valleys of Hanalei and Wai'oli. The two watersheds join on the broad plateau above Māmalahoa.[36]

The southernmost tip of Māmalahoa forms the back of the valley of Wai'oli, about five miles from Hanalei Bay. Above the western side of Hanalei Bay is the peak called Pu'ukamanu (the bird hill), traditionally used as a vantage point to spot fish in Hanalei Bay.

Four Ahupua'a of Hanalei Bay

The upper portion of the ahupua'a of Hanalei is deep but relatively narrow. The extremely mountainous terrain includes a massive gorge through which the Hanalei River descends as it makes its way down from the summit of Mt. Wai'ale'ale to Hanalei Bay.

At lower elevations the Hanalei River winds its way through a broad valley and flows across the Hanalei coastal plain for the last four miles of its length, then empties into the ocean on the east side of Hanalei Bay.[37]

Ka ua Noelehua o Wai'ale'ale

The Misty-lehua rain of Wai'ale'ale

The rain of Wai'ale'ale that moistens the lehua blossoms there.[38]

From atop Mt. Wai'ale'ale the border of the ahupua'a of Hanalei extends past Hīhīmanu along the ridge of Kamo'okoleaka and then across the coastal plain to the ocean.[39] A channel in the reef forms the ocean boundary between the ahupua'a of Hanalei and Kalihikai. This boundary continues across the coastal plain to Kapaka, "the raindrop,"[40] and eventually to the summit of Mt. Wai'ale'ale where the ahupua'a of Hanalei borders the ahupua'a of Lumaha'i.

The ahupua'a of Wai'oli is bordered on the west by Waipā and on the east by Hanalei. These three watersheds, along with the ahupua'a of Waikoko, merge on the broad coastal plain bordering Hanalei Bay.

The 3,350-acre ahupua'a of Wai'oli has a width of only about half a mile on the coastal plain along Hanalei Bay, but inland the width of Wai'oli Valley increases to about two miles and forms a massive amphitheater-like area that encompasses the waters of three separate streams and many smaller tributaries. The ahupua'a of Wai'oli culminates about five miles from the sea at the southernmost tip of Māmalahoa.

Wai'oli was probably home to a large Hawaiian population in ancient times, and may have been generally better suited for taro farming than Hanalei Valley. Taro grows best when cool river water surrounds the plants, and Wai'oli's gradual slope allowed the water to flow continuously through the fields.[41]

> On the opposite side to us there stretched from the sea, where it terminated in a bold headland, a lofty range of deep purple mountains, the highest part immediately before us. Fronting this were two lower ranges, the nearest of which rose abruptly from the flat, through which the river wound like a snake. A waterfall of immense height streaked like a broad ribbon the huge purple mass behind: beginning at about 1,000 feet from the summit, its course was visibly unbroken for 2,000 feet at least, when it was lost to view. From other points, smaller cascades of equal height but more slender in width were plainly seen...no less than nineteen streams cast themselves down the huge front presented to us.
>
> —Miss Sophia Craycroft, 1861[42]

The ahupua'a of Waipā is located along the shoreline of Hanalei Bay just west of Hanalei town beneath the majestic 3,745-foot summit of Mt. Māmalahoa. Waipā means "touched water,"[43] or "request; prayer, as to gods."[44]

The name of the ahupua'a was sometimes written as Waipa'a, which translates as "dammed-up water,"[45] possibly referring to the large sand bar that often builds up at the mouth of the Waipā Stream and blocks the water from flowing directly into the sea. This often causes the stream to run along the beach for a ways before flowing into Hanalei Bay.

Legends tell of a boy named Lauhaka who was raised by his uncle, a bird catcher in the hills of Waipā. On a steep trail, Lauhaka confronted and killed two bird catchers who were hunting protected petrels,[46] and the bodies of the slain bird catchers fell into the river where they formed a dam that blocked the water.

Since ancient times the ahupua'a of Waipā was used by Hawaiians for growing taro and for raising fish in fishponds. It was also the site of heiau dedicated to Kāne, the god of fresh water and life, and the leading god of the four primary Hawaiian gods: Kāne, Kū, Lono, and Kanaloa.

Located on the western end of Hanalei Bay, the ahupua'a of Waikoko consists mostly of low, marshy plain. Wai means "water"; koko means "blood" or "rainbow-hued."[47] The name Waikoko has many possible origins. It translates literally as "rainbow tinted mist,"[48] "blood water,"[49] or "bloody stream,"[50] possibly referring to the legend of Lauhaka mentioned above, when the blood of the slain bird catchers at Waipā flowed into the neighboring ahupua'a of Waikoko.

The name Waikoko has also been attributed to a red-colored algae said to have once grown plentifully in the Waikoko Stream before rice-growing became a prominent land use in the area.[51]

Hanalei in Ancient Times

By the thirteenth century, perhaps much earlier, Hawaiians began cultivating taro in Hanalei Valley and on the slopes above the valley floor. A 1980 study claimed to have found evidence of agricultural activity (taro patches) from around the seventh century, the oldest date found in the Islands, but subsequent analyses failed to replicate the results, and only thirteenth-century dates have been confirmed.[52] Also located in Hanalei Valley were many living sites as well as heiau.

The rich bottom lands of Hanalei Valley, irrigated by the Hanalei River, were eventually filled with hundreds of taro patches stretching from the sea up into the valley and on the surrounding hillsides.[53] An extensive irrigation system was developed on the valley floor for the cultivation of taro.[54]

Many farmers of Hanalei lived near the coast and traveled daily to their inland farms. Others lived in the valleys and on the surrounding hillsides. Living sites and stone enclosures were often located above and overlooking agricultural terraces.[55]

"According to old residents," wrote Ethel Damon in 1931, "the natives would go into the valleys to mahiai [mahi 'ai], or farm, during the day, and return at night to their homes on the beach. Remains of these terraced taro-lands are still to be found far up in the valleys where no one now lives."[56]

In addition to the irrigation ditches in Hanalei Valley, there were stone walls, tool manufacturing sites, and imu. Ancient construction methods documented at the archaeological sites include rock-lined terraces that incorporated flaked and modified basalt. Set into one rock alignment was a basalt adze blank, a tool traditionally used for wood carving and tool making.[57]

A 1995 scientific study by Lisa and William Shapiro on an agricultural site discovered on a southwest hillside of Hanalei Valley revealed "a large complex of platforms, enclosures, waterworn rocks and upright stones that incorporated both agricultural and habitational features." To the east, researchers discovered "an upright stone and platform feature...suggesting a religious aspect to this large agricultural and occupational site."[58]

Concentrations of cultural artifacts were also located at two nearby sites along the irrigation channel known as Kuna Ditch, which runs north to south on the eastern edge of the valley. The other primary irrigation canal of Hanalei Valley is the China Ditch, running south to north along the western margin of the lower portion of Hanalei Valley.

An extensive network of smaller ditches connects to the two primary ditches, Kuna Ditch and China Ditch, and these 'auwai form a complex irrigation system designed to bring water to the many taro patches on the alluvial floodplain of the Hanalei River.

The China Ditch is cut about six feet deep into the hillside slope, and is almost three miles long with an intake on the west side of the Hanalei River.[59] An earthen berm reinforces the downslope side of the ditch, whose path crosses several small streams that in turn contribute to the water flow. Today only parts of the China Ditch remain, and much of the watercourse has been abandoned and is overgrown.[60]

In the post-contact era, new irrigation channels have been built along the former course of the China Ditch.[61] Two dam-type devices on the Hanalei River are constructed of boulders and stacked rocks, and extend into the river to control the flow of water. Flow control devices, such as hand-controlled wooden boards in the irrigation canals, divert water into smaller ditches.[62]

The Kuna Ditch is on average about seven feet wide and five feet deep,[63] running north-south for about two miles along the east side of Hanalei Valley.[64] Some portions of the Kuna Ditch are no longer in use, including the northern section. Like the China Ditch, the Kuna Ditch is mostly an earthen channel without rock reinforcement.[65]

One of the largest heiau on Kaua'i is called Po'okū or upright head,[66] and is located atop a hill on the eastern side of Hanalei Valley, on the plains of Princeville near a grove of hala trees that was one of the largest hala groves in the Islands.

Hanalei Bay

The broad, curving coastline of Hanalei Bay is about five miles long and lined with a sandy crescent of golden-sand beaches. The horseshoe-shaped bay is more than two miles across at the mouth, making it one of the largest bays in the Islands.

The warm, turquoise waters of Hanalei Bay are the final destination of the streams and rivers of four ahupua'a: Hanalei, Wai'oli, Waipā, and Waikoko.

Hanalei Bay. **Douglas Peebles**

> The view from the anchorage has been pronounced by travelers
> as one of the finest in the world.
>
> —Whitney, 1875 [67]

The eastern point of Hanalei Bay is known as Puʻupōā; puʻu means "hill" or "peak," and pōā means "robber, pirate; to rob, plunder."[68] The western point of Hanalei Bay is Makahoa, which means "friendly point."[69]

Ironically, Makahoa was said to be the home of an ʻōlohe, or robber, named Ka-puaʻa-pilau and his two friends who were trained in the ancient warrior skills of bone breaking known as lua. They attacked people passing by and placed the bodies in caves at the bottom of Makahoa Ridge. The robbers were finally dealt with by the konohiki (headman) of the ahupuaʻa of Wainiha.[70]

Chapter 2

Western Contact to the Great Māhele
1778–1850

Thousands of thatched huts dotted this land of rainbow and stream, of frequent rain and fertile soil. Beat of tapa mallet and poi pounder echoed abroad by day, thrum of hula drum by night.

—Ethel Damon[1]

British explorer Captain James Cook reached Kauaʻi in 1778 and established the first documented Western contact with the Hawaiian Islands.[2] Cook was on a voyage of discovery for England and in command of two ships, the HMS *Discovery* and the HMS *Resolution*.[3]

In the decades after the arrival of Captain Cook, explorers, fur and sandalwood traders, whalers, and missionaries began to arrive, bringing significant changes to Hawaiian culture. Beginning in the late 1800s, immigrant laborers arrived to work on sugarcane plantations, and later rice and pineapple plantations.

Hawaiians had lived in relative isolation for many centuries before Western contact, thus had little or no immunity to foreign diseases. Measles, smallpox, Asiatic cholera, whooping cough, scarlet fever, diphtheria, influenza, bubonic plague, dysentery, and numerous other maladies decimated the native population, which declined from an estimated three hundred thousand[4] people in 1778 to forty thousand in 1890.

The high death rate left many empty villages and abandoned taro patches throughout the Hawaiian Islands. Though the Hanalei region continued to farm taro longer than other areas in the Islands, it did not remain unaffected.

Beginning in the mid-1800s, Hanalei Valley's rich bottomlands, traditionally used for taro, began to be used to farm coffee, tobacco, sugarcane, and rice. By the end of the century, rice farming and cattle ranching dominated the region's landscape, and taro agriculture steadily diminished until residents of Hanalei were forced to import poi from Kalalau Valley along the nearby Nā Pali coastline.

Kamehameha and the Treacherous Kauaʻi Channel

Kauaʻi is the northernmost of the eight main Hawaiian Islands. Between Kauaʻi and its neighbor, Oʻahu, is the longest and most treacherous of the inter-island channels. This channel, known as the Kaʻieʻiewaho Channel or the Kauaʻi Channel, kept Hanalei relatively isolated from Western influences.[5] Also keeping the Hanalei region remote were the large waves that arrived on Kauaʻi's north shore every winter.

The channel proved daunting to King Kamehameha I in his efforts to establish a united Hawaiian kingdom. In 1795, he led an estimated 16,000 soldiers with 960 canoes and 20 armed foreign ships to victory over Oʻahu, gaining control of all of the Hawaiian Islands except Kauaʻi and Niʻihau. Spurred on by his success, Kamehameha immediately began preparations to cross the Kaʻieʻiewaho Channel to invade Kauaʻi.

Kamehameha's impressive invasion fleet set sail for Kauaʻi in April of 1796, leaving Oʻahu at midnight with an estimated eight hundred or more canoes and more than eight thousand soldiers. A storm over the ocean channel brought tempestuous winds and violent seas that forced Kamehameha's warriors to turn back.[6]

Undeterred, Kamehameha continued making plans to attack Kauaʻi. He built his fleet to include twenty-one armed schooners, many double-hulled canoes, forty swivel guns, eight cannons, and an estimated seven thousand warriors. Among Kamehameha's forces were about fifty Europeans, most of them armed with muskets.[7] Preparing his warriors for battle, he pronounced,

> Let us go and drink the water of Wailua, bathe in the water of Nāmolokama, eat the mullet that swim in Kawaimakua at Hāʻena, wreathe ourselves with the moss of Polihale, then return to Oʻahu and dwell there.[8]

His second attempt to conquer Kauaʻi was stalled due to an epidemic[9] that infected thousands of native Hawaiians, even himself. Many warriors died, including one of his most prominent warriors, Keʻeaumoku Pāpaʻiaheahe, father of Queen Kaʻahumanu.

Kamehameha began to plan yet another invasion, unwilling to give up the idea of a united kingdom. For this large-scale attack he employed foreigners to construct an armada of sailing ships in Waikīkī. This third planned invasion never took place, however, because Kauaʻi's King Kaumualiʻi ceded the island in 1810 and pledged his allegiance to the powerful ruler. Kaumualiʻi was allowed to remain Kauaʻi's vassal ruler.

King Kamehameha's reign over the Hawaiian Islands marked a new age of Hawaiian government. Establishing a Western-influenced system, he appointed a council of advisors, a treasurer, and a prime minister, as well as a governor for each island.

Taxes were levied and could be paid with handicrafts or produce. King Kamehameha also instituted a fee for licensing trade and wharfage.[10]

A bustling trade with China in Hawaiʻi's native sandalwood began in 1791 when it was discovered that the fragrant wood could be sold for a high price in Canton. The sandalwood trade brought a steady stream of foreign ships to the Hawaiian Islands. Extensive groves in the mountains above Hanalei were harvested and shipped to a nearly insatiable Chinese market.

The sandalwood trade had profound effects on native ways of living as the growing demand for wood led to the abandonment of taro patches and other traditional food-producing activities. Commoners were ordered by chiefs to travel high into the mountains to harvest the sandalwood, valued by the Chinese for making fine furniture, boxes, chests, carvings, perfume, and incense.

The wood was sold or traded for Western products, including ships, clothes, furniture, weapons, food, and liquor. In 1820 King Kamehameha II traded $80,000 worth of sandalwood for an elegant, ocean-going yacht named *Haʻaheo o Hawaiʻi* (*The Pride of Hawaiʻi*). The vessel served as the monarchy's official ship until it sank in Hanalei Bay in 1824.

Due to intense harvesting, virtually all of the large, marketable trees were logged by 1840. Only small, young groves remain today.

Whaling, which began in 1819, was another industry that brought in money and visitors to Hawaiʻi's shores. During the industry's zenith, Kōloa on Kauaʻi's south side was the third biggest port in the Islands.

In the 1830s as many as sixty whaling ships arrived in Kōloa each year. A smaller number of ships visited Hanalei to trade for supplies and restock their provisions. The presence of whaling crews and the associated trade in Western goods furthered the change to traditional ways of life.

Missionaries Come to Hanalei

Hawaiian society continued to change after the death of King Kamehameha I in 1819. When King Kamehameha II ate with the dowager queens Keōpūolani and Kaʻahumanu, the eating kapu (law), which had prohibited men and women from sharing meals, was broken. Kapu were thought by Hawaiians to be governed by the gods; thus when the kapu was broken without repercussion, traditional Hawaiian religious beliefs began to erode.

Just a few months after the breaking of the kapu, the First Company of American missionaries arrived in the Hawaiian Islands, known at the time as the Sandwich Islands. They sailed to Hawaiʻi from Boston aboard the *Thaddeus* with the task of converting native Hawaiians to Christianity.

Between 1820 and 1848, twelve separate companies of Protestant missionaries would make the journey to Hawaiʻi under the auspices of the American Board of Commissioners for Foreign Missions (ABCFM).

A total of 180 American missionaries arrived, exerting wide-ranging influences on native ways of life. They built churches and schools, developed and taught a written Hawaiian language, and ran the Mission Press that printed millions of pages, many in Hawaiian.

Earlier degradations of traditional culture by visitors from the sandalwood and whaling eras and the decimation of the Hawaiian population due to disease were only small signs of the change that was to come. The missionaries' words and work would transform the Hawaiian culture.

Among the first missionaries to arrive in the Hawaiian Islands were Samuel Ruggles and Samuel Whitney. They docked at Waimea, Kauaʻi, aboard the *Thaddeus* on May 3, 1820, and soon visited the Hanalei region.

Also arriving on Kauaʻi in 1820 on the *Thaddeus* was George P. (Prince) Kaumualiʻi, also known as Humehume. Humehume was the son of Kauaʻi's ruler, Kaumualiʻi, and had been sent to the United

States when he was a child. He had not returned to Kaua'i until arriving with Ruggles and Whitney.

Joyous at his son's return, Kaumuali'i placed him second in command and rewarded the captain of the *Thaddeus* by giving him a valuable cargo of sandalwood. The missionaries Ruggles and Whitney were welcomed by the elder Kaumuali'i, and were given land and a residence.

Ruggles and Whitney established Kaua'i's first mission station at Waimea. They were also instrumental in establishing new mission stations in other areas including Hanalei. Whitney served his entire missionary career on Kaua'i, primarily at the Waimea mission station.[11]

The Alexanders at Wai'oli

On July 15, 1834, Reverend William Patterson Alexander and his wife Mary Ann, along with their young son William DeWitt, arrived at Kaua'i's Waimea Bay. William and Mary Ann, who were Presbyterians, had just finished serving in the Marquesas Islands.

William Patterson Alexander was the son of James Alexander, a Kentucky Presbyterian elder and "one of the early settlers in the blue grass state."[12] William had graduated from New Jersey's Princeton Theological Seminary.

> William Patterson Alexander, a tall Kentuckian with aquiline nose and very blue eyes, had just had his twenty-ninth birthday... Mary Ann, who as a young bride three years earlier he had brought around Cape Horn from Harrisburg, Pennsylvania, was now twenty-four. She 'was beautiful to look upon' at this time, wrote mother Parker, one of their co-workers at the Marquesas. Mary Ann wore her hair in the curls of that day. She too had blue eyes, and perhaps she had not yet entirely lost her rosy cheeks of Harrisburg. Their seventeen months' old baby they had named William DeWitt after Mary Ann's pastor who had introduced them to each other and also married them.
>
> —Mary Charlotte Alexander[13]

On July 19, 1834, William Alexander traveled from Waimea to Hanalei in anticipation of establishing the Wai'oli mission station, the first permanent mission station on Kaua'i's north shore. Two months later, the Alexanders left Waimea accompanied by about seventy-five people, including Davida Papohaku (David Stonewall) from the church of Father Whitney at Waimea.[14] In a double-hulled canoe belonging to Kaua'i's Governor Kaikio'ewa they sailed for eight and a half hours along the Nā Pali coast, arriving at the mouth of Wai'oli Stream in Hanalei Bay.

> At early dawn a canoe passing into the bay over the wave called Mano-lau touched the beach at Wai-oli, the valley of "Waters-singing-praises"—of waterfalls singing over high wooded cliffs, of streams singing along fern banks, of 'wreath-making' Hana-lei river singing through flowering lowlands, and of waves singing as they thrum on an ivory shore:—Waioli in Hale-lea, 'House-of-joy.' To Mary Ann, with perils over, it seemed like heaven.
>
> —Mary Charlotte Alexander[15]

William Alexander, his wife Mary Ann, and their son William DeWitt were among the first "outsiders" to settle in the Wai'oli area. During the following decades several different missionary families ran the church and school, and these families were some of the first Caucasian residents of the region.

In anticipation of the Alexanders' arrival, the Hawaiians at Wai'oli had built a fifty- by twenty-foot grass-thatched dwelling.[16] This structure served as the Alexanders' residence for about three years before a more suitable building was constructed.

> Natives thronged the shore to help beach the canoe and thus have first sight of the strange white woman and child [the Alexanders] who had come from so far. And crowds accompanied the little family to the new thatched house which during preceding weeks the dwellers in this northern valley had gladly made ready for their kumu [teacher].
>
> —Ethel Damon[17]

The Alexanders soon added various improvements to their home. They used stalks of native ferns to partition the house into three rooms including a sitting room and dining room, both of which had lau hala mats on the floor, and a bedroom, which had boards on the floor, a rarity at the time.

"It was a good sized house," wrote Mary Alexander. "We made partitions of the stalks of uluhi [uluhe] ferns…for 3 rooms—bedroom, dining room, and sitting room. Lumber was scarce in those days so we had but one room with a board floor—our bedroom. The rest of the house was covered with lauhala mats."[18]

In the Alexanders' first grass-thatched mission house dwelling at Waiʻoli, they had two more sons: James McKinney, born January 29, 1835, and Samuel Thomas, born October 29, 1836.

Their neighbor, Joel P. Dedman, a carpenter, made the Alexanders' doors, windows, and furniture which included "a study table, trundle bed, two settees and a high chair."[19] With his construction skills, Dedman made plans to build his own house, and constructed the first large-scale sugar mill in the area.[20]

In 1834, after receiving a land grant from Kauaʻi's Governor Kaikioʻewa and permission to cultivate sugarcane, Dedman began construction. His mill, built with wood bought by the governor, was comprised of wooden rollers placed on end and turned by horse power. The cane was fed in from the side and crushed by the rollers, extracting a sugary juice that was then boiled down in a whaler's trypot.

Despite his efforts, Dedman's plan to run a sugar mill for Governor Kaikioʻewa was unsuccessful, and the mill was soon abandoned.

Difficulties at Waiʻoli

In the early years at Waiʻoli, the comforts of home to which the missionaries were accustomed were difficult to come by. The Alexanders made do with whatever materials they could acquire. Mary Ann Alexander wrote: "Glass too was very scarce then. We oiled paper and used that instead for some of our windows. We commenced housekeeping without furniture, no cooking stove, no cupboard for our dishes, only a pine dining table and a few chairs that we had brought with us from the states and an ironwood settee that a carpenter made for us, but we were content."[21]

Despite the hardships, there were many joys in which to delight. "We lived three years in the native house," recalled Mary Ann. "I was never happier. It was delightful to live with my doors open, and have no fear of the people around me. James and Sam were born in that house."[22]

In 1834 the Alexanders built a study and a cookhouse that would later become part of a large mission home (the Waiʻoli Mission House). Coral limestone blocks were cut from the shallows near the mouth of nearby Waipā Stream for use in the foundation of the cookhouse as well as for the front steps and chimney. Alexander described the structure as "a substantial native building, thatched with grass, 50 feet long and 20 feet wide."[23]

That same year the Alexanders received land from Governor Kaikioʻewa for a school and church. The establishment of the church was assisted by Kauaʻi's dowager queen, Kekaihaʻakūlou (Deborah Kapule), a Christian convert.[24] The Waiʻoli Church was officially established on October 19, 1834, with just ten original members.

> The mission center of church and school and home pitched its tent a little further mauka near the Waioli river and in the very shadow of the three mountains, Hihimanu, Namolokama and Mamalahoa, on whose precipitous sides waterfalls were almost constantly splashing out of the clouds or the deep blue of distance into the dense green of trees and ferns below. Namolokama, the middle peak, rises more than three thousand feet toward Waialeale, the center of the island, but so close did the Waioli mission houses cling to the base of the mountains that the blue ridge of Namolokama seemed to be the very summit of the island.
>
> —Koamalu[25]

About 700 people attended worship at the Waiʻoli Church on the Sabbath. The population of the Haleleʻa district at this time was estimated by the missionaries to be 3,107 people.[26]

In April of 1835 at Waiʻoli, Reverend Alexander oversaw the construction of a new pole-and-thatch meetinghouse. It was an open-sided structure thatched with lau hala, and was built on the same site as the previous meetinghouse that had burned down.[27] The building took about three months to complete, and the finished structure measured about ninety by forty feet.

Reverend Alexander wrote: "Since the meeting house was erected, the congregation, Sabbath forenoons, has usually amounted to 800 to 1,000."[28] Those who attended the church meetings left a variety of contributions, including fresh chicken as well as "fish, a canoe paddle, the handle for the spade used in cultivating taro, and very rarely a piece of money."[29]

At the beginning of 1836, the new meetinghouse at Waiʻoli was officially dedicated, with Reverend Samuel Whitney of the Waimea mission in attendance.[30] More than one thousand Hawaiians regularly attended Alexander's mission gatherings.

Other Missionary Influences

Aside from preaching, the missionaries felt it their duty to aid the Hawaiian people in various capacities. The Alexanders often acted as doctors, administering treatments such as castor oil, and providing toast and coffee for the ailing.

They also introduced Western-style methods of schooling. With land and wood grants from Governor Kaikioʻewa, the Alexanders constructed schoolhouses, and by August of 1836, Reverend Alexander had established five schools, with over ninety children in his newest school.[31]

The missionaries also sought to spread literacy among all Hawaiians. In 1836 Alexander reported that "over one thousand adults out of the whole population had some knowledge of reading the Hawaiian language."[32] This high literacy rate was in part due to the assistance of five graduates from Maui's Lahainaluna Seminary, where many native teachers were being trained at the time.[33]

Other less overt changes were happening as well. While Hawaiians maintained many traditional customs in the Hanalei region, they were intrigued by the new styles of dress and Western habits they observed. Often they wove small changes into their lifestyle.

"The people...had cloth of their own manufacture, tapa made out of the bark of a shrub. They had learned from the first missionaries to make holokus [Mother Hubbard wrappers], and to braid hats; they still wore the pau [pāʻū] [skirt made of a long length of bark cloth wound around the hips]."[34]

As the Alexanders' mission continued on Kauaʻi, their thatched home deteriorated. In January of 1836 Reverend Alexander began acquiring logs of native ʻōhiʻa lehua timber from the nearby mountains. By November of that year the frame of a Western-style home had been erected.

The two-story, four-room home at Waiʻoli was finished in April of 1837 for a total cost of about $2,000. The house was built with a gable entrance and a front lānai on both the first and second stories. The outside of the house was originally yellow. The color was most likely chosen because "yellow ochre was the only paint available."[35]

The dwelling was built about twenty-one feet from the cookhouse that Alexander had erected in 1834. The cookhouse would later be connected to the main house by the addition of a dining room/pantry. This home would eventually be known as the Waiʻoli Mission House.

Waiʻoli Mission House, built 1834–1837. The closest section in this photo is the cookhouse, built in 1834 using coral limestone blocks from the nearby reef for the foundation and chimney. **Kauaʻi Historical Society**

Interior of the house. **Kauaʻi Historical Society**

More Missionaries Arrive

From 1836 to 1838 a religious revival known as the Second Great Awakening took place in the United States, boosting interest in mission membership throughout the Hawaiian Islands. Alexander noted that there was "a general religious excitement all around Kauai."[36] The new wave of missionaries would help not only the church but also the schools, which at the time were inundated with students.

Reverend Alexander had been teaching 120 children for five days of the week, and Mrs. Alexander had been teaching girls in the subjects of "geography, arithmetic, writing, & sewing; a weekly meeting with 70 or 80 women to read the scriptures & converse on religious subjects; and a semi-monthly meeting with mothers to teach them their duty to their children and urge them to perform it."[37]

Support in the form of Mr. and Mrs. Edward and Lois H. Johnson arrived at Wai'oli from New Hampshire, to assist the Alexanders and direct the schools of the mission station. On their way to Wai'oli they stopped at Kalalau Valley, where they were struck by the beauty of the land, and the eagerness of the Hawaiian people to learn.

"Brother Alexander and Husband took a walk back among the inhabitants," wrote Lois, adding that "[t]he shore where we landed is overhung by an immense ledge of rock affording a shady resting place underneath its own overhanging summit for two or three hundred... In the meanwhile, the people assembled, being marched on to the ground in regular order by one who seemed to act as a captain and apparently felt as much pleasure and pride as a General would in marching his regiment on to the field. Brother Alexander proceeded to examine them and preach to them."[38]

When the Johnsons finally arrived in Hanalei Bay they were greeted at the shore by Hawaiians. "We arrived safely at Waioli, the place of our destination," wrote Lois Johnson, "and were welcomed by multitudes of natives on the shore, anxious to see their new teachers. Glad was I after being tossed about for six months to set my foot upon the spot which is to be the field of our labours, and a delightful spot too in prospect; here perpetual spring smiles and the luxuriant soil spontaneously yields her increase."[39]

The Alexanders had successfully established the Wai'oli Mission more than three years earlier, and finally, in November of 1837, they were getting some help. "We are not so lonely as we were the last three years," wrote William Alexander, adding, "we have been singularly favored in getting associates. Brother and Sister Johnson, who were part of the large reinforcement who arrived last Spring, are located with us: and we find them true yokefellows, amiable, affectionate, devoted and active."[40]

With the work of the missionaries, devotion to Christianity continued to grow.

> I have just returned from an excursion to Kauhakake in Koolau where I preach every Thursday under the shade of a large kukui grove to an attentive audience of 400. It is about 10 miles distant up hill and down. I preach 5 or 6 times a week to an audience of about 1000 here at the station, give out medicine to many 'impotent folk'—spend as much of the forenoon in my study as the sick will allow, and afternoons converse with those who come in crowds to enquire about the way to heaven. We have cheering evidence that the Holy Spirit is moving on the minds of many... The little church here now consists of 38 members.
>
> —William Patterson Alexander, in an 1837 letter to his brother James in Tennessee[41]

Funding for the breadth of their mission, however, did not come easily. An 1837 report by William Patterson Alexander to the *Missionary Herald of Boston* stated, "The people in our vicinity are now planting cotton, with the governor's approbation, for the purpose of raising funds to build a permanent schoolhouse and church and get a bell."[42] Seven acres of sugarcane were also planted to raise money, although only crude methods of sugarcane juice extraction were available at the time.[43]

Despite their efforts, raising money to support the mission continued to be a challenge. "Our common schools taught by native teachers are in a languishing condition," wrote Alexander in 1838. "This arrives mainly from the want of means to support the teachers."[44]

The missionaries of Waiʻoli also endured the hardship of living far from their mainland homes and families. On November 10, 1841, Mary Ann Alexander wrote to her mother: "O how I do want to see you, my dear mother, my heart does agonize to see you...Jane tells me that you indulge the hope of seeing me yet once more in this world...Still, dear mother, much as I want to see you, I could not go

The Wai'oli Lease

"I, Kamehameha III, lease out to William P. Alexander a certain parcel of land at Waioli, Kauai. On the East of said land the river of Waioli is the boundary; on the North and the West the mountain between Waioli and Waipa is the boundary; on the South the pond called Momona is the boundary...said land is William P. Alexander's and his heirs or his assigns, for twenty-five years, for a cattle pasture...he is to pay to Kamehameha III one-half of the cattle born on said land, female and male; and he is also to see that they are cut and branded before being delivered into the hand of Kamehameha's man...and on the expiration of aforesaid term of years he is to restore the land, together with the houses and fences and all the property attached to the land to Kamehameha III or his heir, the owner of the land."

Lease signed by Kamehameha III, William Patterson Alexander,

and G. P. Judd on October 12, 1841, in Honolulu.[45]

home now with an easy conscience, and take my husband away from the great work he is engaged in."[46]

Still, the Alexanders were committed to staying and continued to expand their home. In 1840, William Alexander added a dining room and pantry to the Wai'oli Mission House (built in 1837), connecting the structure to the cookhouse (built in 1834). By 1841, the Alexanders had five children: William DeWitt (8); James McKinney (6); Samuel Thomas (5); Henry Martin (2); and one daughter, Loise, who was born at the end of 1840.[47]

A lease for the Wai'oli Mission lands was signed by King Kamehameha III and William Patterson Alexander in 1841.

A storm in 1837 brought gale force winds that knocked down the pole-and-thatch meetinghouse at Wai'oli. The structure was repaired, but plans were begun for a more substantial and durable building.

Seven acres of sugarcane were planted and a horse-powered sugar mill was constructed to raise money to build a new church as well as a schoolhouse. The $413 earned from the sugar enterprise was put toward the construction of the schoolhouse and church.[48]

In 1840 King Kamehameha II signed legislation establishing a public school system throughout the Kingdom of Hawai'i. All children from the ages of four to fourteen were required to attend school. Meanwhile, plans progressed for the new church meetinghouse at Wai'oli.

In 1841 William Alexander wrote: "Our present tabernacle was overthrown by the winds last winter and is now unsafe when the wind is strong."[49] The new Wai'oli Church was completed in November of 1841, constructed in the Western style, timber-framed, using logs of the native 'ōhi'a lehua harvested from the hills rising up behind the Wai'oli mission station.

In a memoir, Reverend James M. Alexander recalled his father, William Patterson Alexander: "It was an exciting time in Waioli, when the whole population, with long ropes, with shouts and chanting, dragged the heavy timbers into place for the church, and also for a house for Mr. Alexander. Coral stone was obtained by divers from the sea, and made into lime for the masonry."[50]

In November of 1841 the new church building was completed,[51] with a main interior space of thirty-five by seventy feet, and plastered on the inside and outside. The church was thatched with lau hala.[52] The hipped, thatched, split-pitch roof and four-sided lānai made the structure a blend of Hawaiian traditions and American architecture.[53]

The Wai'oli belfry was built next to the new church in the tradition of English and Colonial American missionary churches. Like the church, the belfry also used structural beams made from 'ōhi'a lehua, and had a thatched exterior.

In a letter to her mother, Mrs. Alexander describes the new Wai'oli Church as "a frame house covered with grass. It is neatly plastered inside, and on the walls outside as we could not afford to clapboard it. As we have no pews, most of the people sit on settees of their own making, and some on the floor. The preacher has a stand with a table before him. We are obliged to adopt this plan as lumber is very expensive out here. When the house is finished the people will try and raise money to buy a bell."[54]

Funds were indeed raised to purchase a church bell, including eighty-eight dollars contributed by natives. The bell arrived by ship from Boston in 1843. Ethel Damon noted that the bell "seemed almost a personage of distinction in its village, its arrival at the

Waiʻoli belfry and Waiʻoli Mission Hall. **Bob Waid**

beach greeted by the entire congregation...as a special guard of honor, certain men were appointed to raise it on a frame of poles and bear it proudly to its thatched belfry,"[55] with "the bearers and accompanying throng moving as in a royal procession."[56]

The building of Waiʻoli Church was a significant accomplishment in terms of architecture and construction at such an early date in the region's history, as was the construction of the Waiʻoli Church belfry.

Mary Charlotte Alexander wrote: "The greatest material achievement of the people at Waioli during Mr. and Mrs. Alexander's nine years there had been the earning of funds and the building of their own new frame church, accomplished in 1841 after five years of united effort on the part of the whole populace."[57]

Church membership at Waiʻoli rose from 27 in 1837 to 180 in 1843,[58] when Reverend George B. Rowell arrived with his wife, Malvina. George had previously graduated from Amherst College and Andover Theological Seminary, and he took over the ministerial duties of Reverend Alexander at Waiʻoli.

In 1844 students from the Waiʻoli Select School worked on the nearby coffee plantation of Charles Titcomb, earning a total of about $500. They also cultivated beans for their own use.[59] The Waiʻoli Church was re-thatched with lau hala in 1846, and shingles were installed on the roof in 1851. About ten years later, a board floor, seats, and a pulpit were installed in the church.

Abner and Lucy Wilcox

Abner Wilcox married Lucy Eliza Hart on November 23, 1836. They were both district schoolteachers in Connecticut before volunteering for missionary work. Just three weeks after being married, the newlyweds left Boston Harbor and sailed for Hawai'i with the Eighth Company of American Protestant missionaries, the largest of the twelve missionary groups.

The Wilcoxes, along with thirty other volunteer missionaries, sailed around Cape Horn aboard the 228-ton barque *Mary Frazier* on a 116-day voyage—the fastest of all the ABCFM journeys. After teaching in Hilo from 1837 to 1844, Abner and Lucy Wilcox were transferred to Waialua, O'ahu, where Abner was placed in charge of the Manual Labor Boarding School. Lucy led weekly prayer meetings for women.

On July 15, 1846, the Wilcoxes boarded the schooner *Emelia* with their four young sons—Charles Hart, George Norton, Edward Payson, and Albert Spencer—and sailed for Kaua'i to teach at the Wai'oli mission station. The next day they sailed into Hanalei Bay where a large group of native Hawaiians awaited them at the landing. Also greeting the Wilcoxes were the Reverend George B. Rowell, his wife Malvina, and a small number of other Caucasian residents.

On the same day the Wilcoxes arrived at Wai'oli, they moved into the Mission House and the Rowells were transferred to the mission station at Waimea, Kaua'i. For the next twenty-three years—from 1846 to 1869—Abner and Lucy Wilcox and their growing family lived in the Wai'oli Mission House. Abner Wilcox taught at the Wai'oli Select School for Hawaiian boys, and preached on Sundays.

The Wai'oli Select School was a thatched house with desks constructed of boards and blocks, and floors of woven lau hala. It taught the brightest and most promising students of the various schools on Ni'ihau and Kaua'i, and the finest of these students were in turn sent to the Lahainaluna Seminary on Maui.

Wilcox taught reading, writing, mathematics, geography, moral philosophy, and church history. His classes were attended by forty-eight native Hawaiian boys ranging in age from twelve to eighteen.

Classes were taught in the Hawaiian language using Hawaiian language materials.

Waiʻoli Select School students lived with local families, and some of the students worked at coffee plantations in the area. Students also worked on the school's four-acre farm, growing a variety of produce including corn, beans, potatoes, yams, and bananas. They also farmed a large patch of taro. Much of this produce was sold to whaling ships that arrived in Hanalei Bay hoping to restock provisions.

In 1846 the Hawaiian Kingdom established a Department of Education and adopted the missionary-funded common schools as public schools. At this time twenty former Waiʻoli students were running common schools on Kauaʻi. The mission district schools were present in at least twelve different north shore settlements, with more than four hundred children of the Haleleʻa district (about one-sixth of the total population) in attendance.[60]

The curriculum had grown as well, and by 1848 included geography, arithmetic, geometry, astronomy, algebra, moral philosophy, church history, sacred geography, and chronology. Classes in reading, writing, penmanship, public speaking, and English were also taught.[61]

The Select School continued its efforts into the 1850s, but lack of funding from the government hindered the Wilcoxes' efforts to provide books for the children and expand the school. Around that time, the Hanalei English School, the first English school in the Haleleʻa district, was founded, broadening the scope of education on Kauaʻi.[62]

A fire in 1863 burned down the Waiʻoli schoolhouse. "At about 10 o'clock in the evening of Monday the 2nd of March, the alarm of fire was given which proved to be our schoolhouse," recalled Abner Wilcox. "Being covered with thatch, the flames spread with great rapidity, and very little could be saved."[63]

Salvaged were some large timbers, which were later used to start the foundation of a new schoolhouse. Additionally, "a few books and slates were snatched from the flames by those who first arrived," recalled Abner, "[and] my writing desk escaped...with only three legs."[64]

Undaunted, Abner continued his mission to educate the children at Waiʻoli. With assistance from the Board of Education, Wilcox was able to build a new schoolhouse. "On obtaining the materials," recalled Abner, "we commenced as soon as possible to prepare the foundation and build a house 32 by 21 feet. My second son, with a native carpenter, undertook the work."[65]

Next Generation

Abner and Lucy Wilcox had four sons before arriving on Kaua'i, and then four more sons in the twelve years following their arrival at Wai'oli.[66] The Wilcox boys were known as mischief-makers on the island among the Wai'oli Hawaiians, and easy to spot as there were few other Caucasians in the area.

The boys grew up with privilege not afforded to their predecessors. The Wilcox family maintained contact with their relatives in Connecticut, and sent their sons to visit when they had the means. Sam recalled seeing his maternal grandmother: "And that Grandmother Hart! Did I ever tell you that I actually saw her when I went East as a boy? She was ninety-five years old, but so spry she could sit on a small milking stool—and so I saw her sitting one day milking a cow and smoking her corn cob pipe while she milked."[67]

Young George was given a pet Galapagos turtle in Hilo by a sea captain named Pitman. "When Captain Pitman gave George that baby turtle for his own," recalled Samuel Wilcox, "George was the happiest little fellow alive…[O]nce we found [the turtle] way across the Waioli river." When the yard of their mission home was flooded during rains, Samuel recalled, "…we often used to stand on [the turtle's] back, three or four of us, and ride across the water."[68]

The Wilcox boys also befriended a dog that would occasionally wander back to its original owner. "Our Smut was just a dog, but we boys liked him," recalled George, adding, "Old Titcomb gave him to us. Then Smut had two homes, because he would run over to Titcomb's when he felt like it."[69]

The boys were sent to O'ahu for education at Punahou School, and would later travel off-island for college. George, the Wilcoxes' second son, attended Sheffield Scientific School at Yale from 1860 to 1862, earning his engineering certificate. When he returned, his first job was planting sugarcane on his parents' land at Wai'oli. He later worked as a luna (foreman) on the Princeville sugar plantation of R. C. Wyllie before building Grove Farm in southern Kaua'i into a major sugarcane plantation.

By mid-century the Wai'oli Mission House and adjacent mission station pasturelands included a total of thirty-nine acres.[70] Missionaries estimated the population of the Halele'a district to be about two thousand people, with about seven hundred included in the congregation.[71] In 1854, Reverend David Nuuhiwa was chosen as Assistant Minister, becoming the first native Hawaiian to serve in such a post for the Wai'oli Mission.

The change of hands furthered the integration of the Western system of religion into the Hawaiian culture. More over, the missionaries were assimilating into the populace, learning and developing a new Hawaiian language and culture.

In 1861 Abner Wilcox was advised by his sponsors, the ABCFM, that continued support for the mission was doubtful.[72] Two short years later all mission lands in the Hawaiian Islands, including the Wai'oli mission, were divided among Hawai'i's missionaries as pension. The Sandwich Islands Mission became independent, and was no longer supported by the American Mission Board. The Wai'oli Mission House was deeded to Abner Wilcox.

Reverend Johnson passed away in 1867, and the pastorate at the Wai'oli Mission was taken over by Reverend Adamu Pali, a native Hawaiian from South Kohala on Hawai'i Island.

In 1869 Abner and Lucy Wilcox made their first visit back to their home in Connecticut since they left for the Hawaiian Islands thirty-three years prior. Accompanied by their youngest son Henry, Abner and Lucy crossed the mainland from California via the new transcontinental railroad. They left Henry in California with oldest son Charles and continued their journey.

The new rail system was not lavish by any means, and was actually quite arduous.

> No luxuries such as Pullman sleepers and diners existed on this first trans-continental railroad...Abner and Lucy carried baskets of food for the week's wearisome journey over a rough roadbed, and sat up all night on the hard seats of draughty, dusty day coaches. Hold-ups by Indians were not infrequent.
>
> —Ethel M. Damon [73]

Tragically, both Abner and Lucy contracted malarial fever during the overland journey, dying soon after they reached their New England home.[74] Even after their death, however, their sons continued to work and live in the Islands.

The eldest, George, built Grove Farm Sugar Plantation on Kauaʻi into a massive and profitable enterprise, becoming one of Kauaʻi's most generous philanthropists. George was also a member of every Hawaiian legislative body from 1888 until 1898, and served as King Kalākaua's prime minister in 1892.

Samuel Wilcox became sheriff of Kauaʻi in 1872, and served in that capacity for twenty-five years. He was a member of the House of Representatives from 1901 to 1902 and a senator from 1903 to 1907.

Albert was a member of the House of Representatives of the Hawaiian Kingdom in 1891 and 1892. He helped found the Samuel Mahelona Memorial Hospital at Kapaʻa with the daughters of Samuel and Emma Wilcox, Mabel and Elsie.

Mabel was selected by the Territorial Board of Health as Kauaʻi's first public health nurse in 1913, and Kauaʻi's Territorial Board of Health Tuberculosis Nurse from 1914 to 1917. Elsie served as Chairman of the Kauaʻi Board of Child Welfare and Commissioner of Education for twelve years, resigning to take a post as the first woman senator in the territorial legislature.

The Wilcox Family left a legacy on Kauaʻi in their enduring mission work and their dedication to education. For generations to come, their offspring would go on to leave their own legacies as children of the Islands.

Russian Forts in Hanalei

Western presence on Kauaʻi wasn't confined to visiting sailors and American missionaries. As various trading prospects developed in the Hawaiian Islands, several major countries began to take an interest in establishing a presence and securing future trading opportunities.

The 210-ton, three-masted *Behring* anchored at Kauaʻi's Waimea Bay early on the morning of January 31, 1815. It was under the command of Captain Bennett, and carried cargo of sealskins and otter pelts bound for headquarters at Sitka, Alaska, the capital of Russian-America. After Bennett went ashore, southwest winds intensified rapidly and pushed the *Behring* onto the beach.

King Kaumualiʻi, Kauaʻi's vassal ruler who had ceded Kauaʻi to King Kamehameha I in 1810, seized the *Behring*'s cargo and had the valuable pelts taken to his home near Makaweli in west Kauaʻi. After hearing of the seizure, Alexander Baranov, the Russian-

American Company's governor, sent German-born Georg Anton (Egor Nikoloaevich) Schäffer[75] to Hawai'i to retrieve the cargo.[76] If Schäffer could not retrieve the cargo, he was to seek a fair amount of the native sandalwood as payment for the furs.

In his initial adventures on the islands of Hawai'i and O'ahu, Schäffer angered American traders when he began building a blockhouse on the Honolulu waterfront (the location of the site is near what is now the intersection of Fort Street and Queen Street). John Young ('Olohana) persuaded King Kamehameha to halt the work on the fort, and Schäffer was soon forced to leave.

Schäffer then traveled to Kaua'i, and in the spring of 1816 two Russian ships, the *Otkrytie* and *Ilmena*, carrying forty Aleuts and several Russians, arrived to support Schäffer's mission.

Schäffer's luck changed on Kaua'i, as he quickly gained favor with the vassal ruler when he cured Kaumuali'i of dropsy and then cured the fever of Kaumuali'i's wife. Kaumuali'i returned what was left of the *Behring*'s cargo. Schäffer then managed to convince Kaumuali'i that the strength of Russia could be used to throw off the rule of King Kamehameha. Such an offer had not been authorized by anyone in Russia.

Schäffer's offer appealed to the chief, who had long been unhappy with Kamehameha's domination, and saw an association with Russia (Schäffer) as a chance to reclaim his own independence as ruler of Kaua'i.

Schäffer promised Kaumuali'i an armed Russian warship to lead an attack on Kamehameha's forces. Unaware that Schäffer was promising more than he could deliver, Kaumuali'i agreed to the arrangement.[77] On May 21, 1816, without the knowledge or approval of Czar Alexander Pavlovich, Kaumuali'i signed a document that put Kaua'i under the protection of the Russian Empire.

On September 12, 1816, Kaumuali'i's men and a few hundred Aleut Indians began building a lava-rock fort on the east bank of the Waimea River, at a sacred site on Waimea Bay known as Pa'ula'ula o Hipo (red enclosure of Hipo). The fort was built in the design of a six-pointed star, and included thirty-eight cannons to protect trading vessels arriving at the important anchorage. Schäffer raised the Russian flag and named the fort Elizabeth, in honor of Empress Elizabeth (1779–1826).[78]

Schäffer then took possession of the Russian–American Company's ship, *Lydia*, by sending the captain off to Sitka for an imaginary payment, and promptly gave the *Lydia* to Kaumuali'i. In turn, the chief granted Schäffer ownership of the valley of Hanalei, which at the time included at least thirty families. Schäffer was to assume the traditional role of konohiki, or headman of the Hanalei ahupua'a, and control the accompanying land and fishing rights.

With the encouragement of Kaumuali'i, Schäffer renamed Hanalei Valley, calling it Schäfferthal ("Schäffer Valley" in German), and reputedly gave Russian names to some of the Hawaiians living there. A formal transfer of ownership took place on October 6, 1816, "with the Russian flag flying, a twenty-one gun salute, and toasts."[79]

Schäffer began to build two earthen fortresses in Hanalei: Fort Alexander, named after Czar Alexander and built on the bluff above the Hanalei River near the current location of the Princeville Hotel; and Fort Barclay, named for Russian general Barclay deTooly and built nearer to Hanalei River.

Unfortunately for Schäffer, rumors of his activities filtered back to the czar's court. On November 21, 1816, Lieutenant Otto von Kotzebue arrived in Hawai'i on the Russian Navy brig *Rurik* to inform King Kamehameha that Russia supported neither Schäffer nor Kaumuali'i.

A few weeks later natives killed a Russian and set fire to some buildings near Fort Alexander. Aleuts from Russian Alaska carried water from the marsh below in an attempt to extinguish the flames.[80]

In May of 1817, Kaumuali'i was falsely informed that Russia and America were at war, as part of a plot by Americans in Hawai'i to weaken the alliance between the chief and the Russian. The implication was that by coming under Russian protection, Kaumuali'i had declared himself an enemy of the United States. Fearing reprobation, Kaumuali'i promptly renounced the deal with Schäffer, who was run out of Waimea.

Hoping to find refuge, Schäffer sailed to Hanalei on the *Kodiak*, which was leaking badly. He arrived at Fort Alexander, fired a three-gun salute, and raised the Russian flag. Hawaiians had just killed two Aleuts, and this show of Russian control further angered Hanalei's natives, who attacked the fort and wounded a third Aleut. Russians began to fire their six-pound cannons.

Unprepared for war and anxious to flee, many of Schäffer's men abandoned the fort for Sitka. Schäffer himself sailed for Honolulu on the *Kodiak*, which at the time was taking on two feet of water per hour. It took five days to reach Honolulu, whereupon Schäffer was greeted by a command to stay offshore unless he wanted to surrender all arms and be taken, as prisoner, to Hawai'i Island.

Fortunately for Schäffer, the American vessel *Panther* happened to arrive at O'ahu under the command of Captain Isaiah Lewis, who had been treated medically by Schäffer a year earlier. On July 7, 1817, Lewis provided Schäffer with safe passage from the Hawaiian Islands.[81]

Though Schäffer escaped unscathed, he did not leave without regret. Sailing away, one imagines he may have glanced back, trying to save images of the islands in his mind.

> Westward of [Hanalei Valley] there is a region of mountains, slashed by deep ravines. The upper ridges are densely timbered, and many of the ohias have a circumference of twenty-five feet three feet from the ground. It was sad to turn away forever from the loveliness of Hanalei, even though by taking another route, which involved a ride of forty miles, I passed through and in view of, most entrancing picturesqueness. Indeed, for mere loveliness, I think that part of Kauai exceeds anything that I have seen.
>
> —Isabella Bird Bishop, 1873[82]

The Sinking of *Ha'aheo o Hawai'i*—*Cleopatra's Barge*

The elegant royal ship *Ha'aheo o Hawai'i*, originally known as *Cleopatra's Barge*, was perhaps the most famous sailing vessel ever owned by the Hawaiian monarchy. It was purchased by King Kamehameha II in 1820 for a lot of sandalwood.

Cleopatra's Barge was built in a Salem, Massachusetts, harbor, as commissioned by George Crowninshield Jr., heir to a shipping fortune. It would cost $50,000 to build and another $50,000 to furnish, and would be the first ocean-going yacht in the United States built for pleasure rather than commerce or war.[83]

The ship's name found inspiration from the famous William Shakespeare play *Antony and Cleopatra* in a description of how a barge appeared as it carried Cleopatra on the river of Cydnus:

"The barge she sat in, like a burnish'd throne,
Burn'd on the water: the poop was beaten gold;
Purple the sails, and so perfumed that
The winds were love-sick with them; the oars were silver,
Which to the tune of flutes kept stroke, and made
The water which they beat to follow faster,
As amorous of their strokes."[84]

Thousands came to see *Cleopatra's Barge* as it was being built. It measured one hundred feet along its deck and eighty-three feet long at its waterline. The extravagant vessel was known as a hermaphrodite brig and had five staterooms, a large forecastle, and mahogany paneling inlaid with bird's-eye maple and other fine woods.

In April of 1817 George Crowninshield Jr. journeyed on *Cleopatra's Barge* to sixteen southern European and Mediterranean ports to show off his ship. When George Jr. passed away suddenly, however, the ship's expensive furnishings were auctioned off, and in July of 1818, *Cleopatra's Barge* was sold to the Boston merchant firm of Bryant and Sturgis for $15,400.[85]

Cleopatra's Barge (Haʻaheo o Hawaiʻi), the monarchy's royal ship now buried beneath the sands of Hanalei Bay. **Peabody Essex Museum**

Cleopatra's Barge was then sent to the Hawaiian Islands in the hopes that it could be traded for fragrant and valuable sandalwood.[86] The ship made the voyage in 1820 under the command of Captain John Suter and sold to King Kamehameha II (Liholiho), the twenty-four-year-old son of King Kamehameha I, who had begun his reign just one year prior.

Cleopatra's Barge cost Liholiho a cargo of sandalwood of eight thousand piculs, which could in turn be sold for $80,000 in China. This trade yielded a significant profit for the Boston merchant firm.[87]

Liholiho renamed the ship *Haʻaheo o Hawaiʻi* (*Pride of Hawaiʻi*), and used it as a royal pleasure craft, merchant vessel, and for interisland travels that included transporting American missionaries.

On July 21, 1821, the king sailed to Kauaʻi on his royal ship to meet with Kaumualiʻi to confirm the vassal ruler's allegiance to the monarchy. Despite his covert plans to overthrow the monarch with the help of Georg Schäffer, Kaumualiʻi pledged his allegiance.

Yet the second Kamehameha, unimpressed by Kaumualiʻi's show of loyalty, invited the chief to join him aboard the *Haʻaheo o Hawaiʻi*. Kaumualiʻi jumped at the opportunity, and Liholiho then set sail for Oʻahu, with Kaumualiʻi as prisoner.

The powerful kuhina nui (premier) Kaʻahumanu, who had been queen as the wife of King Kamehameha I, married the captive Kaumualiʻi on Oʻahu to ensure the monarchy's control over Kauaʻi. Kaʻahumanu also married Kealiʻiahonui, the son of Kaumualiʻi, in an attempt to solidify the monarchy's power. Kaumualiʻi passed away on Oʻahu in 1824.

The sinking of the *Haʻaheo* occurred in 1824, when the king traveled to England with Queen Kamāmalu. Left to investigate a possible insurrection on Kauaʻi, a royal crew sailed the *Haʻaheo* into the mouth of the Waiʻoli River and became shipwrecked at Hanalei Bay.

In a written account, missionary Hiram Bingham blamed the shipwreck of the *Haʻaheo o Hawaiʻi* on a drunken crew. Others blamed the inclement weather, and still others blamed Kauaʻi's natives, who were angered that Kaumualiʻi was being held in Honolulu as a prisoner of King Kamehameha II.

A few days after the shipwreck, an attempt to salvage pieces of the stately treasure was witnessed by missionary Reverend

Hiram Bingham. His account states: "After the people had, with commendable activity, brought on shore from the wreck, spars, rigging, and other articles they attempted to draw up the brig itself. This furnished one of the best specimens of the physical force of the people, which I ever had opportunity to observe for more than twenty years among them—indeed the most striking which I ever saw made by unaided human muscles."[88]

Bingham tells of how the natives wove rope from the bark of hau trees, "and with their hands without any machinery, made several thousand yards of strong rope...twelve folds of this they made into a cable. Three cables of this kind they prepared for the purpose of dragging up the wreck of the *Cleopatra's Barge* on shore."[89]

Three ropes were attached to the ship's mainmast, and the men were directed by an older man named Kiaimakani (wind watcher) who "passed up and down through the different ranks...the old chieftain, with the natural tones and inflections, instructed them to grasp the ropes firmly, rise together at the signal, and leaning inland, to look and draw straight forward, without looking backwards toward the vessel."[90]

Unfortunately the ship's main mast snapped and the huge vessel rolled back, ending the salvage efforts. Bingham, however, had seen with new eyes:

> ...the ancient meles of Hawaii, prayers for divine aid and means of infusing the swing of rhythm into prolonged muscular effort, old songs of an almost vanished folk disappearing before the steam-roller, as it were of civilization which would iron every folk out on the same model. Such a prayer of olden days was heard there at Hanalei, chanted by one trained in the art, to swing the waiting multitude into the rhythm of concerted action. It was an ancient and popular song, used when a tree for a canoe was to be drawn from the mountains to the shore, rehearsed with great rapidity and surprising fluency.
>
> The multitude quietly listening some six or eight minutes, at a particular turn or passage in the song indicating the order to march, rose together, and as the song continued with increasing volubility and force, slowly moved forward in silence; and all strained their huge ropes, tugging together to heave up the vessel. The brig felt their power, rolled up slowly towards the shore, upon her keel, till her side came firmly against the rock [reef], and there instantly stopped: but the immense team moved unchecked; and the mainmast broke and fell with its shrouds,

being taken off by the cables drawn by unaided muscular strength. The hull instantly rolled back to her former place, and was considered irrecoverable.

—Reverend Hiram Bingham, 1824[91]

Kamehameha II and Queen Kamāmalu never learned of the demise of the *Haʻaheo*. On their tour of Europe, a change of plans led them to sail on the whale ship *L'Aigle*. Both contracted the measles, and died within a week of each other in 1824.

Throughout history, the *Haʻaheo o Hawaiʻi* has sustained interest in the revolving populations that learn of the shipwreck in Hanalei Bay. In the 1850s, the builders of a small vessel at Waiʻoli paid native Hawaiians to retrieve an iron gun from the wreck, as well as an oak capstan (much decayed) and the iron post upon which it revolved.

In the 1900s, George Norton Wilcox recalled diving down to the wreck when he was a boy: "The natives told me it was five fathoms deep there where it lay....Some divers went searching there to find a brass cannon that was said to be on it. But it must have been taken off long before. I tried to dive with the natives, but it was so deep I had to come up, couldn't stand the pressure. The natives brought up some bolts encrusted with coral."[92]

Researchers from the Smithsonian Institute later rediscovered the shipwrecked *Cleopatra's Barge* buried beneath the sands of Hanalei Bay, and many historic artifacts were recovered (see *Chapter 5*).

The Kauaʻi Rebellion

In 1824, after the death of Kaumualiʻi, his son Humehume challenged the rule of the monarchy, attacking the fort at Waimea while King Kamehameha II was visiting England. Kaʻahumanu, the kuhina nui, sent the well-armed troops of her principal counselor, Kalanimoku,[93] whose warriors easily defeated Humehume's meager and ill-prepared forces.[94]

Many of the dead were left on the battlefield to be eaten by pigs, and thus the event became known as ʻAipuaʻa, meaning "pig eater."[95] Kalanimoku further avenged Humehume's rebellious attack on the fort by searching out and slaughtering any suspected accomplices to the failed rebellion, including many Kauaʻi chiefs.[96]

Kaʻahumanu arrived on Kauaʻi on August 27, 1824, to replace virtually all of Kauaʻi's chiefs with chiefs from Oʻahu and Maui, most of whom were relatives of King Kamehameha I.

The only exception was Kealiʻiahonui, son of Kaumualiʻi, who was kept in control of the ahupuaʻa of Kalihikai.[97] Kaikioʻewa, a cousin of King Kamehameha I, was appointed governor of Kauaʻi and Niʻihau, replacing Governor Kanoa. Humehume was imprisoned on Oʻahu until his death of influenza on May 3, 1826.

Captain Kellett—Hanalei's Pilot of the Port

One of the first Caucasians to settle in Hanalei was Englishman Captain John Kellett, who first arrived in the Islands in 1825 and came to Hanalei in 1836. Kellett served for many years as Hanalei's harbor pilot, overseeing the movement of ships at Hanalei Bay. Kellett also kept a warehouse for produce exported from Hanalei.[98]

He built his home on a bluff called Lanihuli overlooking the ocean near the mouth of the Hanalei River. The Kellett house was often referred to as the Lanihuli home, or simply Lanihuli, the name of the area where it was built.[99] The makai side of the large home was rented to numerous Hanalei families including the Dudoits, Rhodes, Wundenbergs, and Princeville Plantation owner Robert Crichton Wyllie. These wealthy families would often rent half the house, employing Kellett's servants while he was away.

The daughter of the Princeville Plantation manager recalled: "Our servants were all Hawaiians with the exception of Koka...a Chinese steward, who was a very superior man...and kept a store on the hill near Lanehule [Lanihuli]."[100] Koka's younger brother, Ah Poi, came from China to run the business with him, "and they were most successful."[101]

Captain John Kellett passed away in 1877 and was buried at Lanihuli.[102] By the early 1900s the Kellett House fell into disrepair, and soon was beyond reclamation. "On the bluff of Lanihuli, overlooking the ocean," wrote Ethel Damon in 1931, "lived for forty years Captain Kellett, an Englishman...He built the quaint, rambling house at Lanihuli, now, alas, almost in ruins..."[103]

The First Charting of Hanalei Bay

The first official survey and charting of Hanalei Bay was done in July of 1837 by the crews of the *Sulphur* and the *Starling*, the first two British ships of war to visit Hanalei. At that time the Hawaiian Islands were known by Westerners as the Sandwich Islands, having been given that name by Captain Cook in honor of his patron, the Earl of Sandwich.

Hanalei farmers and ranchers supplied the crews of the *Sulphur* and *Starling* with a variety of food products, including beef. "Our object in coming hither was to embark bullocks," wrote Belcher, "which, we were assured, were better and cheaper than at Oahu; and we were fully repaid for the trouble; we obtained noble animals." [104]

Belcher also noted that "large quantities of meat had been salted, and much butter cured...the cattle we embarked twelve, having already experienced their superiority over any I have met out of England." [105] The ships' crews also acquired "vegetables of the finest quality...fruits, poultry, turkeys, &c., cheap and in abundance. Water can be filled in the boats, by sending them into the river." [106]

Silk, Coffee, Sugar, and "Emmasville"

Hanalei's ready water supply, fertile soils, and warm climate made it the site of many agricultural endeavors in the early 1800s. An American named Charles Titcomb, by profession a watch-maker, was one of Hanalei's first foreign agricultural entrepreneurs, and perhaps also the most persistent.

His first venture, begun in 1836, was to build an extensive silk cocoonery in Hanalei. His silkworm operation extended along the banks of the Hanalei River, about one mile up from the ocean, on ninety acres of land leased from King Kamehameha III (Kauikeaouli).

Titcomb initially planted about twenty-five acres of mulberry trees, and by 1840 he had about one hundred thousand of the trees growing to provide food for an estimated five hundred thousand silkworms imported from China and America.[107]

The Chinese-American silkworm produced a pale yellow silk (sometimes straw-to orange-colored), and the American silkworm produced a coarser, white silk. About 5,500 silkworm cocoons were required to produce one pound of reeled silk, with one acre of trees producing about fifty pounds of raw silk. Hawai'i's rich soil and

Hanalei rice fields on the former lands of Charles Titcomb's silk plantation. **Kauaʻi Historical Society**

warm, moist climate allowed the mulberry trees to grow extremely fast—up to one inch per day.

Titcomb was said to be the first person to export silk from the Hawaiian Islands, producing several high-quality crops that he sold for a high price to companies in Mazatlan and Mexico City.[108] He also employed many native Hawaiians and considered the Hawaiian women "skilful [*sic*] in the art of reeling the delicate threads from the tiny cocoons."[109]

Despite some initial success, Titcomb's silkworm enterprise suffered numerous setbacks due to droughts, insect pests, and strong seasonal winds that stripped the trees of their leaves.[110] Another obstacle was the fact that the worms needed daily care, but missionaries discouraged work on the Sabbath, traditionally a day of rest.

By 1844 Titcomb had transferred his energies to the production of coffee after "securing berries from the Kona fields of Messrs. Hall and Cummings."[111] Titcomb's coffee plantation put him in direct competition with his neighbors, Englishman Godfrey Rhodes and Frenchman John Bernard, who had started their coffee plantation in Hanalei in 1842.

Titcomb hired children of the nearby Select School at Wai'oli to tend to his thousands of coffee plants growing near the Hanalei River. He provided the students with hoes and also allowed them to plant beans between the rows of coffee for their own use.

In return for the work, Titcomb wanted to offer paper money to the students, but the Hawaiian Kingdom had not yet developed currency. Eventually, Titcomb and other early immigrant agriculturalists convinced Judge Lorrin Andrews to "engrave small currency for the settlers, Bernard, Titcomb and Kellett, of Hanalei."[112]

In 1844 the students of the Select School earned "about $500.00 in paper currency or trade for cultivating [Titcomb's] thousands of coffee plants on the Hanalei River, after the young plants were set out."[113] By 1846, coffee trees on the plantations of Titcomb and his neighbors John Bernard and Godfrey Rhodes totaled one hundred thousand. Titcomb also milled coffee, using a mule to move a perpendicular post and a cog wheel that turned a flay wheel connected by bands to the milling machinery.[114]

Like his silk endeavors, however, his efforts to produce coffee in the Hanalei region were unsuccessful. Eventually, the loss of laborers to the California Gold Rush in the 1840s, floods in 1847, a drought in 1851, and blight due to the white hairy louse (an aphid species) crushed his hopes of successful coffee production.

The sizeable coffee plantations of both Titcomb and Wyllie—who had purchased Rhodes' plantation for $8,000 in 1855—soon succumbed to the various problems, and both men took to growing sugarcane.[115] By 1862, the uprooted coffee trees were being used to fuel sugar boilers.

> The coffee blight has already covered the two Hanalei plantations which in the spring of 1857 we saw in full and successful culture, yielding 200,000 pounds of excellent coffee. The scores of women and children were busy picking the ripe berries and depositing their gathering at night at the overseer's office, but now all is silent. Not a gatherer was abroad and we saw laborers bringing in coffee trees upon their shoulders, to heat the sugar boilers of Mr. Titcomb.
>
> —Reverend Samuel C. Damon[116]

Determined to utilize the fertile soils, Titcomb planted sugarcane and built a crude sugar mill that used five horses to turn the rollers. Titcomb's mill, according to Hanalei resident Josephine Wundenberg King, "had no centrifugals to dry his sugar but his golden syrup was beautiful."[117]

Hoping to boost production, Titcomb asked the captain of a whaling vessel to bring him new varieties of sugarcane. This whaling ship, the *George Washington*, under the command of Captain Pardon Edwards, returned to Hawai'i from Tahiti in 1854 with new sugarcane varieties, but Edwards sailed to Lahaina instead of Hanalei and Titcomb never received the samples.

The new varieties were propagated by United States Consul Chase who found that both the Tahitian and Cuban sugarcanes flourished in his garden.[118] The lush growth attracted the attention of Hawai'i's sugarcane farmers, and within a few years cuttings were being widely planted. The Tahitian variety eventually came to be known as Lahaina cane, and was preferred because it grew fast and had high yields as well as a hard rind that deterred rodents and other pests.[119]

In 1856, after King Kamehameha IV married Emma Na'ea Rooke at Kawaiaha'o Church, the royal newlyweds visited Kaua'i as part of a "Royal Progress" through the Hawaiian Islands, staying at

Titcomb's coffee plantation in Hanalei. To honor the Queen, Titcomb changed the name of his plantation to "Emmasville."[120]

On February 5, 1863, 750 of the 956 acres that made up Emmasville were purchased by Princeville Plantation owner R. C. Wyllie for $29,000. Titcomb retained ownership of his sugar and coffee mills. Titcomb then moved to Kīlauea, "where he had already, on January 27, 1863, secured from Kamehameha 4th for $2000 the Grant to the Ahupuaa...."[121]

Kaua'i's First Cattle Ranch

Another significant foreign influence on Kaua'i's north shore in the early 1800s was Englishman Richard Charlton's cattle ranch, which was founded on August 27, 1831. Charlton was the British consul for Hawai'i in Honolulu at the time, and he started the ranch after securing a twenty-year lease from Kaua'i's Governor Kaikio'ewa for a portion of Hanalei from the eastern side of Hanalei Valley to Kalihiwai.[122]

With longhorn cattle brought from "Norte California,"[123] Charlton started one of the first cattle ranches in the Hawaiian Islands, and the first on Kaua'i. By 1840, Charlton had about one hundred head of cattle. Charlton's fee for use of the Hanalei area land was paid with 560 boards of lumber,[124] which were to be cut by Charlton and used by King Kamehameha III to build a house. The fee was never paid by Charlton, yet he retained use of the land until the lease was purchased by Captain Jules Dudoit in 1845.

Dudoit, who moved to Hanalei after serving as French consul to Hawai'i from 1837 to 1848, lived in the Kellett House and expanded the cattle trade. Conveniently behind the Kellett home was an area where cattle were slaughtered.[125] Dudoit would manufacture and export butter, as well as pack salt beef for whaling ships.

Then, Dudoit began to trade cattle and salt beef from Hanalei to Honolulu in exchange for household supplies. Gaining ownership of the brigantine *John Dunlap* and frequently navigating the Ka'ie'iewaho Channel between the islands, Dudoit became the chief supplier of goods to the island of Kaua'i.

The Great Māhele

On January 27, 1848, a new system of private property ownership was instituted by King Kamehameha III. Known as the Great Māhele ("māhele" means division), the king divided land between himself and 245 of his chiefs in an event that would eventually lead to the loss of land by the Hawaiian people.[126]

On March 8, 1848, any unclaimed land was divided between the king and the government. Thus, 24% of the land in the Hawaiian Islands was owned by the king (crown lands); 37% was owned by the government; and 38% was given to the ruling aliʻi (chiefs).[127]

Makaʻāinana (commoners) were able to apply for title to lands they cultivated, referred to as kuleana. In 1850 the Kuleana Act was passed to define owner rights; additionally, a Land Commission was created to grant land titles.[128]

Throughout the archipelago, 11,000 makaʻāinana were granted 28,600 acres of land.[129] The Indices of Awards in the Māhele recorded seventy kuleana grants in Waiʻoli, fifty-five in Hanalei, and nineteen in Kalihikai.[130] The Legislature also passed a law in 1850 allowing non-Hawaiians (resident aliens) to own land in the Hawaiian Islands. By 1890, more than seventy-five percent of the land in the Hawaiian Islands that had been granted to chiefs in the Māhele was owned by non-Hawaiians.[131]

After the Great Māhele, Hanalei was considered crown land,[132] Waiʻoli was considered government land, and Waipā was owned by Princess Ruth Keʻelikōlani, great granddaughter of King Kamehameha I.[133]

Names of native Hawaiians living in the Hanalei region in the 1800s may be found on documents such as the Māhele records,[134] and historical maps from that time reveal specific boundaries of ancient living and farming areas as well as the locations of important cultural sites. Some names listed in the *Hanalei Land Commission Awards* included: Kalawakea, Keala Iki, Keka Uaniu, Kahio-Keahi, Kahue, Hanaimoa, Ikuwa, Ielemia, Kalalaweikeau, and Kalakala.[135]

An 1893 map[136] showed the following Hawaiian names on lands near the Hanalei Bay shoreline: Koenepuu, Kiolea, Nunu, Kuheleloa, Timoheo, Papa, Makole, S. Kawainui, Kealaiki, and Kahui. Near the current Hanalei town area were Hanaino, Kahanuala, Kahilina, Kamaiwa, Kamakaulii, Kamohaiwa, Kaunahi, Kuaua, Mahuahua, Makole, Naiwi, and Wahineiki.

Some Hawaiian names of people in the Hanalei region listed in the 1914 *Polk-Husted Directory of Honolulu and the Territory of Hawaii* include: Ho, Hookano, Kaakau, Kahai, Kaheleiki, Kaiawe, Kalani, Kamoa, Kaneole, Kauhaahaa, Kaui, Kaumealani, Kelau, Keolewa, Kuapuhi, Mahanaumaikai, Mahilahila, Maka, Maluna, Pa, Pauole, Puulei, and others.[137]

Chapter 3

Royal Visits and the Story of Princeville
1850–1900

By the mid-1800s, visits to Hanalei Bay by sandalwood traders and whalers decreased significantly, and the Hanalei region returned to relative isolation. The peak years of the sandalwood trade were from 1810 to 1840 as sandalwood forests were logged at a rapid pace to meet China's growing market. By 1840, nearly all of Hawaiʻi's sandalwood trees of marketable size had been cut down.

Around this time, the whaling era, which had begun in 1819 when the *Equator* and the *Balena* approached waters near the Hawaiian Islands, began to pick up. The peak year for whaling ship arrivals was 1846, when at least 596 ships crowded Hawaiian ports, including Kōloa on Kauaʻi's south side. Like sandalwood, however, the whales were taken in excess, and whale populations diminished rapidly. Within the decade oil was discovered in Pennsylvania, and the new source of industrial lubricants brought an end to Hawaiʻi's whaling profits.

The end of the sandalwood and whaling eras caused problems for anyone needing off-island products. In 1857, a *Pacific Commercial Advertiser* article stated: "The trade of the port [Hanalei Bay] is now very limited and is confined to a few coasting vessels, which supply the wants of the natives and the coffee plantations."[1] Carrying goods, the steamer *West Point* stopped in Hanalei Bay as it made regular trips around the Hawaiian Islands, but the untimely sinking of the ship ended its visits to the increasingly isolated region of Hanalei.

Without regular access to imported goods, various crops were planted to provide for local demand. Cotton was grown at Waiʻoli in 1848 to supply a small cloth factory run by Joseph Gardner, and many fruits and vegetables were grown in the Hanalei region throughout the 1800s including significant quantities of oranges, lemons, peaches, pineapples, tamarinds, mulberries, guavas, and plantains.

Samuel Whitney Wilcox recalled that during his childhood in the mid-1800s "we did have oranges at Waioli! Right there on our own place, and hundreds of trees in the valleys. Wainiha was full of such oranges, the sweetest and juiciest I've ever tasted."[2] Species introduced by Polynesians before Western contact also continued to be grown, including bananas, breadfruit, and coconuts.

Hanalei also experimented in agricultural and cattle ranching endeavors: "The two largest coffee plantations on the islands are located here [Hanalei], producing annually 150,000 to 200,000 lbs. of coffee. In the neighborhood of the port several thousand head of cattle run wild, and in former years considerable quantities of beef were packed here, but owing to the poor and irregular facilities for sending it to market, it has been entirely broken up."[3]

Princess Ruth Visits Hanalei

Members of the Hawaiian monarchy paid numerous visits to Hanalei for relaxation as well as business. King Kamehameha II took a forty-two-day tour of Kaua'i in 1821, and King Kamehameha III came in 1852 with a large entourage. King Kamehameha IV and Queen Emma visited Hanalei in 1856 and returned in 1860 with their two-year-old son, the Crown Prince Albert Kauikeaouli, inspiring Hanalei plantation owner R. C. Wyllie to name his growing estate "Princeville." Princess Lili'uokalani sailed into Hanalei Bay in 1881, returning ten years later as queen.

Princess Ruth Ke'elikōlani arrived in Hanalei in 1867 on the U.S.S. *Lackawanna*.[4] On board were Captain Reynolds, Reynold's wife, Mrs. Anna Dudoit (the wife of Jules Dudoit), Emily Corney (the wife of Hudson Bay Company employee and author Peter Corney, who wrote *The Early Voyages of Peter Corney*), and Princess Ruth's two white poodles. The *Lackawanna* engaged in several days of target practice in north shore waters, and invited prominent local persons aboard "to luncheon and to witness the exercises."[5]

During her visit, the princess stayed at the Wai'oli home of Judge Wana. Josephine Wundenberg King, who was a child at the time, recalled seeing Princess Ruth "lounging on the beach with her retainers and her two little white poodle dogs of whom she was very fond. The other ladies visited at Princeville, and John Low the manager entertained the party quite extensively, getting up a large picnic and fish or 'Kahe' drive on the Hanalei river near Kuna."[6]

> The Kahe was built in the middle of the river near the rapids by a fine kukui grove where the ahaaina ['aha'aina] or feast was spread. When school was out Julia Johnson and I rode up the river bank to the rendezvous, and as we neared the spot where the fish were being driven down and caught, we saw [Princess] Ruth in a pink Muumuu [mu'umu'u] having a bath and finally getting into the 'Kahe' [run of fish] and catching the mullet herself, beheading and enjoying the tid-bits that she found. When she emerged later from her dressing room in the guava bushes in her black silk holoku [holokū][7] she looked quite regal and happy as she embraced her lady friends and saluted them in the usual Hawaiian manner.
>
> —Josephine Wundenberg King[8]

When Princess Ruth passed away in 1883 she bequeathed the ahupua'a of Waipā to Princess Bernice Pauahi Bishop, the great granddaughter of King Kamehameha I, and potential heir to the throne. Pauahi died just a year later at the age of fifty-two, leaving her land in perpetual trust to assist in the establishment of Kamehameha Schools.

Coffee and Tobacco

On September 8, 1842, British sea captain Godfrey Rhodes and Frenchman John Bernard obtained a fifty-year government lease of ninety acres of land on the east side of the Hanalei River and sixty acres on the west side of the river. On this land, Rhodes and Bernard began the first commercial coffee plantation in the Hawaiian Islands.[9]

Soon after, Gottfried Frederick Wundenberg, an agriculturalist from Hanover, Germany, and former secretary to Robert Crichton Wyllie, the Minister of Foreign Affairs for the Hawaiian Kingdom, partnered with Archibald Archer, "half-Scotch, half Norwegian, and an engineer by profession,"[10] to lease a portion of the Bernard/Rhodes plantation. Wundenberg and Archer also began growing coffee in an area on the east side of Hanalei Valley known as Kuna.

Rhodes left for Australia in 1844, selling his interest in the coffee operation to Bernard. The following year, Bernard traveled to Honolulu to deal with financial troubles, and on his return to Kaua'i on April 18, 1845, he boarded the schooner *Paalua*, which sank just a few hundred yards offshore of Hanalei. Bernard, along with several of his crew members, was killed.

> She was first struck by a heavy squall and then shipped a heavy sea which carried her under. The following persons were unfortunately drowned: Captain Bernard, Mr. Popelwell, and Mr. Higginbotham with his wife and two children. All the Hawaiians succeeded in reaching the land with the exception of a boy.
>
> —*The Friend*, May 1845 edition[11]

The estate was left unclaimed until Rhodes returned from Sydney a few months later. On June 16, 1845, he repurchased the estate with the help of his new business partner, John K. Von Pfister. Rhodes and Von Pfister created the Rhodes & Company Coffee Plantation, and along with Rhodes' brother-in-law, a horticulturalist named Thomas Brown, the company built a substantial coffee plantation of nearly 1,000 acres.

Settling back into Hanalei, Rhodes built a home he named Kikiula, atop a bluff near a bend in the Hanalei River.[12] The two-room stone plantation home was constructed with thick walls and deep-silled windows and was plastered both inside and outside. Kikiula enjoyed spectacular mountain and valley views.

On December 12, 1845, Gottfried F. Wundenberg married Ann Moorea Henry and they settled "in a small house on a little mound 'makai' of the Kikiula house, and the wedding took place there."[13]

> My mother came to Hanalei late in 1845 on a visit with her sister and brother in law the Joseph Smiths from Tahiti where she was born, she was the daughter of the Rev. Wm. Henry one of a band of English Missionaries who were sent out to Tahiti by the London Missionary Society in 1796, and met and married father on December 12, 1845 at Kikiula where Mr. Godphrey Rhodes lived and planted coffee. Their wedding took place under an orange tree in front of the house that the Joseph Smiths occupied, Mr. Rowell of Waimea, Kauai, performing the ceremony.
>
> —Josephine Wundenberg King[14]

As plantation owners settled in the area, the industry continued to boom. In October of 1845, Rhodes and Von Pfister formed a partnership with retired English Naval Officer Captain Henry Samuel Hunt. At this time, about 750 acres in Hanalei Valley were controlled by Rhodes and Von Pfister, and an estimated 1,000 acres of Hanalei Valley were cultivated in coffee.

The coffee mill of the Rhodes & Co. Coffee Plantation was built on Hanalei Valley's eastern slope, just above the current site of the Hanalei Bridge.[15] Together, the coffee plantation of Charles Titcomb and the neighboring plantation of Bernard and Rhodes had more than one hundred thousand coffee trees planted by 1846.[16]

Von Pfister left the Hawaiian Islands to participate in the California Gold Rush and was later murdered in San Francisco, leaving Rhodes as the sole owner of the coffee enterprise. Hindered by the loss of labor to the California Gold Rush, "two weeks of heavy rains"[17] and flooding in 1847, and epidemics that killed many Hawaiians,[18] the crops suffered. Four years later, in 1851, the plantations were put through the severe effects of "an unprecedented drought in the valley of Laughing Water."[19]

Rhodes, as vice president of the Royal Hawaiian Agricultural Society in 1851, reported: "The coffee plantation of Mr. Titcomb is in excellent order, the trees [are] healthy, and he expects a tolerably large crop from it. The plantation belonging to Mr. Hunt and myself and those of Messrs. Archer and Wundenberg, should, if in good order, yield at least seventy tons of coffee this year, but I am sorry to say that owing to the want of labor they are in a very bad state and the most we can expect from them is one third of that amount; and even this we shall not be able to collect if the Chinamen do not arrive, as the natives will not work."[20]

The situation disenchanted the entrepreneurs, and many abandoned their businesses for want of something easier. Rhodes' partner, Henry Hunt, like Von Pfister, left the Hawaiian Islands "and was never heard from again."[21]

The importation of Chinese laborers at the end of the drought helped to return the coffee fields of Hanalei to significant production, but a subsequent blight caused by a species of aphid known as the white hairy louse "affected the coffee trees on all the islands"[22] and soon ended commercial coffee production in Hanalei for good.

While many left the Islands in search of gold and riches, some entrepreneurs were drawn back to Hanalei in further attempts to mine the riches of the valley soil. Along with H. A. Wiedemann and Charles Titcomb, Gottfried Wundenberg had left Hanalei for San Francisco,

California, in November of 1848, seeking Gold Rush riches. In his absence, his business operations were run by Archibald Archer.[23]

Wundenberg, who lived at Kuna on the east side of Hanalei Valley until 1847, had always planned to return. Just a year prior to his Gold Rush venture, he had built a new home at Limunui, "in the valley just below Kikiula and across the river,"[24] below the cliffs Kuakea and Kaʻūpūlehu where the banks were "lined with weeping-willow trees."[25]

Wundenberg returned to Hanalei in September of 1849, and in 1851 began to grow tobacco in Kuna as well as at Limunui. At this time, another tobacco enterprise in Hanalei Valley had been started by two men named Bucholz and Gruben.

Prospects for tobacco in Hanalei appeared favorable for about two years, and by 1852 "the Hanalei planters were ready to manufacture 200,000 of the best Hawaiian cigars."[26] As history would have it, a cutworm suddenly devastated the tobacco crop, dashing hopes for the Hanalei tobacco industry.

Wundenberg moved to Honolulu in 1853, only to return to Kauaʻi two years later to manage the Princeville Plantation.

Princeville

At age twenty, Scotsman Robert Crichton Wyllie abandoned medical studies at Glasgow University to become a merchant in Mexico and South America, where he made a small fortune. Wyllie later came to Hawaiʻi and served as British proconsul before serving as Minister of Foreign Affairs from 1845 until his death in 1865.

Wyllie's work in the kingdom spanned the reigns of Kamehameha III, IV, and V. He was particularly concerned with having high officials in the kingdom follow proper etiquette, and "was held by a sense of chivalry that was centuries out of date if, indeed, it had ever existed at all."[27] Wyllie also strived to have other countries recognize Hawaiʻi as an independent nation.[28]

Even with his government position in the Hawaiian Kingdom, however, Wyllie was not powerless against the enrapturing beauty of Hanalei. Of Hanalei, Wyllie writes, "I never saw such a romantically beautiful spot in all my life time. Were I forty years younger…I would throw the Foreign Office with all its musty papers into the King's hands and spend the remainder of my life here."[29]

This 1890 photo shows residents posing in front of the renowned magnolia tree at Kikiula, the Princeville Plantation House. **Kauaʻi Museum**

On March 14, 1853, Wyllie paid $1,300 for the government (Crown) lands leased to the Rhodes & Co. Coffee Plantation. This marked the beginning of the acquisition of lands which would later become Princeville Plantation at Hanalei.[30] He would go on to purchase Godfrey Rhodes' business interest in his Hanalei Valley plantation for $8,000 on September 13, 1855,[31] eventually expanding his estate to include a great deal of land to the east and above Hanalei Valley.

Gottfried Wundenberg, who had tried his hand at coffee and tobacco interests in Hanalei before sailing to Honolulu for reprieve from the agricultural bouts, returned to Hanalei to manage Wyllie's plantation.

Finding workers for Wyllie's plantation was Wundenberg's primary job. In the early 1850s some Chinese workers were hired, but Wundenberg preferred Hawaiians, as they were more readily available. "Many of them lived on the estate," recalled Wundenberg's sister Josephine, "and their wages were twenty-five cents a day. Our house women were paid three dollars a month...They got their fish from the river and the taro grew on the plantation."[32]

For mechanical and general utility work, Wundenberg hired Charley Griffiths, "...an old sea faring man... [who] did everything on the place that a mechanic was needed for." Griffiths "lived in a little two roomed cottage on the knoll over the river where the path passes on its way to the sugar mill...it was one of our delights to visit the old man in his den and have him tell us wonderful tales of his sea life."[33]

"Old Charlie Griffiths gave us a colored picture of the Virgin Mary in a frame that he had made," recalled Josephine Wundenberg, adding, "we hung it in our school room and shocked the Johnson girls by having a Catholic picture in our house...In 1857, Lizzie Johnson came to stay a few months with us to teach the young ideas, and give us some book learning, none of us had ever been to school."[34]

The Wundenberg family stayed at the Kellett house at Lanihuli before permanently moving into Kikiula, when the Rhodes family moved out. Wundenberg made significant improvements to Kikiula, including adding a wooden clapboard structure, as well as a top story covered with lath and plaster. His daughter recalled that the stone house "was painted white and the roof red, as were all the buildings that were shingled on the place. The red material was a clay found in the hills near by, which wore well when mixed with a little lime to make it stick."[35] Bamboo troughs were used to channel a nearby spring to the house. A tin-lined box above the bathroom was filled with buckets of water and served as a shower.

The house was fit for royalty. And, when King Kamehameha IV and Queen Emma visited Hanalei in 1860 with their son, the Crown Prince Albert,[36] they stayed with the Wundenbergs at Kikiula.

Wundenberg's daughter recalled that the royal guests "were both charming people and the little Prince a dear little boy of two years. Madam Namekaha was his nurse. She afterwards married Kalakaua and became Queen Kapiolani in 1875. She was a lovely sweet woman and we became great friends."[37]

As minister of foreign affairs, Wyllie was fond of entertaining guests at his Hanalei estate. Wyllie often brought a musician to entertain his royal visitors and provide music for dancing, which was a favorite activity of King Kamehameha IV and Queen Emma. The monarchs "were delighted with a pretty tyrolese waltz taught to them by Wyllie."[38]

The children of government officials also became close with the Hawaiian royal family. Recalling her youth, Josephine Wundenberg writes,

> [Queen Emma] ate her meals with the little Prince at the children's table, and was with us a great deal. She helped me

to make a little Hawaiian flag out of white and blue cotton cloth and turkey-red which I flew on my own flag staff and at the stern of our boat when we went rowing. I used to play tricks on her too, such as putting sand in her private bowl of pink poi and hiding her shoes up in a tree, where she could not get them until I was ready to give them to her, thereby gaining the name of 'Keike Mahine Kolohe' [Mischievous Child] which title she was pleased to remember after she became Queen of Hawaii and tease me with.

—Josephine Wundenberg King[39]

Both the king and the queen were not above mischief themselves. "Queen Emma went up stairs nearly every evening to have a romp with

Prince Albert. **J.J. Williams, Bishop Museum**

us girls when we were going to bed," recalled Josephine, "and loved a pillow fight as well as any of us. The King was a very entertaining man and loved to dress in disguises for the amusement of us children, he dressed up as a ghost once and gave himself quite a shock when he peered into a looking glass, in a partly darkened room."[40]

King Kamehameha IV was also an avid hunter, and traveled east to the valley of 'Anini to catch kōlea (plover) birds as well as the non-native quail. The royal party brought their own rowboats and boat crews, and during their six week stay spent numerous afternoons boating up the Hanalei River and enjoying picnics on the river's banks.

To honor the young Prince Albert and the extended stay of the king and queen in 1860, Wyllie changed the name of his estate to the Princeville Plantation that summer, and made the young Prince Albert the intended heir. Wyllie planned to petition the government of the kingdom for his estate to be officially designated Barony de Princeville, and "suggested the heir bear the title, Baron de Princeville."[41]

He also rechristened his schooner *Prince of Hawaii*, which "plied for many years between Hanalei and Honolulu. The Hawaiian coat-of-arms was painted on her stern, and again in more elaborate colors and with carving on the side of the cabin."[42]

Unfortunately, Prince Albert died in 1862 at the tender age of four. Not long after this tragic loss, the prince's father, King Kamehameha IV, passed away in 1863 at the age of twenty-nine.

Theo H. Davies

Another visitor to the Hanalei region in 1860 was Theophilus Harris Davies[43] who first came to the Islands at age twenty-three from Britain. Davies later became a prominent Honolulu businessman and founder of the "Big Five" firm of Theo H. Davies & Co. He served as the guardian of Princess Ka'iulani when she went to England to attend boarding school. He also accompanied the princess to Washington, D.C. after the overthrow of the Hawaiian monarchy so she could request assistance from President Grover Cleveland in restoring Queen Lili'uokalani to the throne.

During his Hanalei visit, Davies was invited to accompany the royal party to the north shore area of Hā'ena to explore the large caves there and watch the traditional "fireworks" ceremony known as 'ōahi (fire throwing), which involved throwing burning logs of the native hau or pāpala into the seaward winds blowing off the cliffs of Makana.[44] Crowds of people would arrive in canoes from as far away as Niʻihau, and take great delight in watching the lighted wood soar through the air and fall into the sea.

Davies rode to the event with the queen, enjoying "various traditions and legends of places we passed [as they] were narrated to me by the Queen."[45] Other members of the royal party traveled to the event by boat, and a reception met the group at their destination.[46]

Davies recalls,

> Mats were laid on the sand and there we sat, hosts of natives grouped near us—the perpetual pulsation of the ocean in its vesper of praise at our feet—the strange falling flakes of fire afar off in the high air—and over all the clear white light of the moon...whilst our voices blended musically in various part songs. The two young ladies sang soprano, Queen Emma alto, the chronicler tenor, and Henry Dimond bass—and though more than a year has gone, I can almost see the group of white people with our young island Queen in the centre, and hear her sweet melodious notes *Oft in the Stilly Night*...when I saw her next morning sitting on the verandah with her little boy kneeling in her lap, and clasping his hands, whilst she dictated his morning prayer, I thought few sights more beautiful or more holy...
>
> —Theophilus H. Davies, 1862[47]

Carried by the strong winds, the firebrands soared out over the water and "swirled out with bursts of flame and plunged hissing into the sea far below, where at a safe distance the chiefs and people had paddled their canoes out to see the spectacle."[48] People in canoes beneath the cliffs were considered heroic if they were able to catch the burning embers, and would sometimes tattoo themselves with the fiery logs to commemorate the event.[49]

Pulelo ke ahi haʻaheo i na pali
The firebrand soars proudly over the cliffs.
An expression of triumph.
Referring to the firebrand hurling of Kauaʻi,
or to the glow of volcanic fire on Hawaiʻi.[50]

Other Visitors

Aside from Hawaiian royalty, the early missionaries and entrepreneurs entertained many guests. In 1860 Reverend and Mrs. Samuel Chenery Damon and their children arrived from Honolulu. Wyllie rented half of the Kellett house as a summer residence where he dispensed hospitality "in true English style, and when unable to come himself, sent visitors alone to occupy the house."[51] Wyllie's cook, Koka, was in charge of the entertainment. In turn, Reverend Damon baptized the two youngest Wundenberg girls, Gussie and Lina.[52]

While visits to the valley were always beautiful, disputes between families who lived in the area would sometimes become obvious. Theo H. Davies noted,

> I must premise this by saying that of the four white households that hold sway in this lovely district of creation, no two are on friendly terms. From the slumbering sarcastic feuds that obtain in most small places, to the high and mighty eruptions that distract the world's great powers, we may discover their prototypes in this happy valley. Hence my visit to the mission families was made alone. Any attempt to enter into the various causes of feuds and their sometimes amusing exhibitions would overstep my resolution.[53]

In 1861 Robert C. Wyllie brought two guests, Lady Jane Franklin and Miss Sophia Craycroft, to visit his Princeville estate. Lady Jane Franklin was the widow of renowned explorer Sir John Franklin, and her niece was Miss Sophia Craycroft.[54] The sixty-nine-year-old, gray-haired Lady Franklin had just sailed to Alaska searching for information about her husband, who had been lost in the Arctic more than a decade earlier during his fourth expedition there.[55]

Wyllie took them to visit first O'ahu and then the volcanoes of Hawai'i Island. At Hanalei, they were met by Gottfried Wundenberg, who paddled a longboat out to meet Wyllie and his guests. Fulfilling his duty as Princeville Plantation manager, "the burly German rowed the trio upstream to a landing shaded by weeping willow trees below Kellett's hillside house."[56] The guests were greeted at Kikiula by Wundenberg's son and his six daughters.

Lady Sophia Craycroft was not blind to the discord that existed in heavenly Hanalei. When she and her niece attended church at Wai'oli, she writes, "[we] were the innocent cause of renewed strife between high contending parties, the Missionary and wife and the Schoolmaster and wife, whose contentions are fierce and of old standing. It would really have been entertaining—if it had not been rather shocking—to witness the struggle carried on between the two ladies in the church, the instant after the service was over, as to which of two persons (who did not speak to each other if it could be avoided) should succeed in getting my Aunt first to her house. Mr. Wyllie effected a compromise, and we visited both for ten minutes. Here of course is a sad subject of scandal among the natives."[57]

Other embarrassing encounters were witnessed by the guests during the 1861 visit. Davies recalled coming across Wyllie and his guests as he descended into Hanalei Valley with Honolulu businessman Henry Dimond: "My companion not being on as intimate terms with the proprietors, and moreover not wishing to be recognized by the ladies in our rough travelling dress, resolutely refused to take this private road," recalled Davies, "and we descended by another path, half a mile lower down. Just as we reached the river-side, the royal barge containing the two young ladies and Mr. Wyllie passed, and notwithstanding Henry's anxiety to avoid a recontre, we exchanged salutes."[58]

Lady Franklin, firm in her beliefs, did little to quell the existing disputes, and even created discontent among the settlers. Spending much time with the Wundenbergs at Kikiula, she imparted her values on the German household, encouraging a more "proper" upbringing for the children. Josephine Wundenberg King recalled how Lady Franklin "had much to do with making mother [Mrs. Ann Wundenberg] dissatisfied with her life at Hanalei, and told her that she did wrong to bring her family up in such a lonely 'out of the world' sort of place, and urged her to let her have my sister Lina to take to England to educate."[59]

In her own efforts to teach them greater things, Lady Franklin took long walks with the Wundenberg children. It quickly became clear that Lady Franklin herself required lessons in island life, as she "let her skirts get full of 'kukus' which [the children] had to pick out for her while she told [them] stories of the Norman Kings."[60]

It was said that Wyllie was taken by Lady Franklin, an "aristocratic lady, set firm in the belief that English aristocracy and manners were superior to all others. She was intelligent, energetic, adventurous, and most willing to prejudice the Hawaiian monarchy in favor of England."[61] Wyllie apparently intended to make Lady Franklin Hawai'i's first baroness, establishing ties to the monarchies of Europe.[62]

Lady Franklin, however, still grieved for her husband. In his remembrance she visited a mound of earth near Kikiula where William Luxford, quartermaster of the ship that sailed to the Arctic in search of her husband in 1850, had been buried. Luxford's ship had been wintering in Hanalei when the quartermaster died.

She also hiked each day to the top of the hill behind Kikiula to enjoy the expansive view of the sea, which perhaps made her think of her husband who disappeared during his ocean journey. "There she would remain for hours...lost in contemplation of the glorious scene spread out before her, with thoughts wandering often no-doubt to distant icy seas, and scanning mayhap the horizon again and again with eager eyes for the white sail she knew could never come."[63]

Lady Franklin's daily hike to the top of the hill near Kikiula was likely the reason Wyllie gave her that piece of land overlooking the bay. There, she proposed that a high-church Episcopal chapel be built to complement Wyllie's estate. Wyllie believed that Lady Franklin would someday build a castle there,[64] as the two ladies thoroughly enjoyed their stay in Hanalei.

> We passed here twelve delightful days of unbroken repose, free from bustle, interruption, and fatigue—pray don't imagine that this means in indolence; the very reverse is the fact—we read, wrote, drew, sewed, while drinking in the perfume of the flowers such as are cherished in conservatories at home, revelling in beauty which could never satiate, because ever changing.
>
> —Miss Sophia Craycroft, 1861[65]

As delightful as it had been, Wyllie could not convince the two to return. He wrote letters confessing his loneliness in their absence, and attempted to spark memories of the twelve-day Kaua'i tour. In a letter to Lady Franklin, he wrote, "It appears that you and that romantic niece of yours have been roaming about in the interior, examining grizzly bears, big trees, deep mines, gulches and ravines, where I hope neither you nor she will find such a pleasing spot as the 'Crow's Nest,' or as beautiful and healthful a valley as that which it overlooks."[66]

Later, Wyllie was more forward in his requests, writing, "I begin to fortify myself in the belief that your occupancy of the Crow's Nest will become more of a reality than of a romantic speculation."[67] But Wyllie's romantic dreams were to remain unfulfilled.

The Hanalei Sugar Mill

> Mr. Wyllie's sugar mill is expected here in Aug. or Sept. He says he will have a mill so large as to grind all the cane that can be raised in Waioli and Hanalei.
>
> —Abner Wilcox, June 19, 1862[68]

Robert Crichton Wyllie constructed the Hanalei Sugar Mill from 1861 to 1862, with $40,000 worth of machinery purchased from Glasgow, Scotland. The steam-powered mill was built on the east bank of the Hanalei River just down from the Hanalei Bridge, and at the time it was the most modern and productive sugar mill in the Hawaiian Islands. The mill's chimney rose to 110 feet in height, and the mill's rollers were able to express six hundred gallons of cane juice in twenty minutes.

Gottfried Wundenberg oversaw the construction of the new sugar mill as well as the plantation's transition from coffee to sugar.[69] The

The Hanalei Sugar Mill, including a 110-foot smokestack, was built alongside the Hanalei River in 1862. The mill and smokestack can be seen in the middle of this photo, just to the right of the river. On the bottom right of this photo is the Princeville Plantation House. **Bishop Museum**

Hanalei Sugar Mill became the center of a small but busy factory village that included a post office, storage buildings, camphouses, and a butcher shop.[70]

Eleven flat-bottom boats called scows were used to bring sugarcane from the Hanalei Valley fields down the Hanalei River to the mill. A conveyor belt then carried the cane into the mill to be processed. After the juice was extracted, conveyor belts transported the leftover plant material, or bagasse, out of the mill.

Wyllie's first crop of sugar was harvested in 1863. He moved to Honolulu in 1864,[71] and a few months later the management of Princeville Plantation was taken over by H. A. Wiedemann, a friend of Gottfried Wundenberg from their hometown of Hildesheim in Hanover, Germany. Wiedemann managed the Princeville Plantation until the spring of 1865 when John Low arrived.

"Often in the days gone by have we rowed our boat o'er the still waters of that beautiful river," recalled Anna S. Wundenberg Wright, "singing our songs as we passed by the old sugar mill which stood near its bank, and we could see the cane as the mill slowly ground it in its rollers."[72]

From 1860 to 1863 Wyllie continued to expand his land holdings, first purchasing the region above the eastern side of Hanalei Valley as far as Kalihiwai, and then on April 17, 1862, purchasing the ahupua'a of Kalihikai from Keali'iahonui, son of Kaumuali'i, the former ruler of Kaua'i.[73] Wyllie then bought the ahupua'a of Kalihiwai at public auction from J. W. Austin and Charles Kana'ina[74] on October 5, 1862.[75]

His motivations for purchasing more land above his Hanalei Valley coffee plantation were not simply for business purposes, however. His thoughts still often turned to Lady Franklin, who had visited a few years prior and won his heart. Since that time he had dreamed of her return:

"I intend, if I can procure it, acquiring the fine upland plains on the northern side touching the sea, so that your Ladyship may extend your carriage drives and enjoy your sea bathing without trespassing on the domain of our neighbours. Besides, I require the land for the pasture of the oxen, mules, and horses, that I must keep and for the firewood that I shall want of in [operating] my steam machinery."[76]

Despite his failure to draw Lady Franklin back to Kaua'i, Wyllie's large land acquisitions continued. In 1863 he purchased

Wyllie's Broadside
Distributed to Natives of Hanalei

"By apprenticing your sons to carpenters, masons, blacksmiths and coopers, they would in a few years become carpenters, masons, blacksmiths and coopers themselves, and earn much higher wages than 25 cents a day. You know that such mechanics are paid much higher than mere field laborers, porters, boatmen and cart drivers. Why should some of your sons not learn these arts, and by their industry, get as high wages as the foreigners, who now are, with few exceptions, the only men who practice them? If your sons, after learning these arts, work for me as well, and as many hours every day, and as many days in the month as the foreigners, I shall not only pay your sons the same wages as to the foreigners, but prefer your sons to them."

—Robert Crichton Wyllie, 1860s[77]

750 acres of Charles Titcomb's "Emmasville" property in Hanalei Valley for $29,000,[78] extending the Princeville Plantation estate from Kalihiwai to Puʻu Pehu above Hanalei Valley. The Princeville lands now included Poʻokū Heiau, a Hawaiian sacred area, as well as the loko iʻa (fishpond) known as Kamoʻomaikaʻi, located near the mouth of the Hanalei River. A huge grove of the native hala, said to be the largest in the Hawaiian Islands, grew from the heiau area all the way to the current site of the Princeville Hotel, terraced into the oceanfront hillside of Puʻupōā Ridge.

Robert Crichton Wyllie passed away at his Rosebank estate on Oʻahu on October 19, 1865, just two years after he had consolidated the plantation at Princeville. He was buried at Honolulu's Royal Mausoleum at Maunaʻala.

His principal heir was his nephew, Robert Crichton Cockrane, who had arrived on Kauaʻi just three months earlier from Waltham, Illinois, to learn the sugarcane business. As a condition of taking over the Princeville estate, Cockrane was asked to change his name to Wyllie, which he agreed to do.

But Cockrane—or Wyllie, as he is now known—had inherited a plantation plagued with ills. Labor shortages, high costs associated with irrigation and milling equipment, fires, droughts, vandalism, and damage caused by insects called cane borers put the plantation in grave financial condition.

In addition, labor troubles occurred in November of 1865 between groups of workers from two different Chinese provinces, continuing a quarrel that had existed between them before they came to the Islands. Over one hundred men were involved in the wrangle, which continued until fighting among the workers led to a man's death, and plantation manager John Low moved workers from one of the provinces across the Hanalei River.

For the next several years there continued to be a general fear of an uprising among the Chinese laborers at Princeville Plantation. Low placed rows of bayonets in the hallway at Kikiula, which created a hostile atmosphere although the bayonets themselves were never used.[79]

The plantation's misfortunes did not seem to cease. In early 1866, R. C. Wyllie (formerly R. C. Cockrane) was engaged to be married to Ida Von Pfister (daughter of John Von Pfister). On February 4, just eight days before the wedding, several men gathered to listen to a musical performance at the Princeville Plantation House, the home of plantation manager John Low. Wyllie went to get a jug of water to help Low make some limeade, and Low went to pick some limes.

When Wyllie didn't return for some time, Low became concerned, as "[Wyllie] had been off his head for some weeks."[80] Low went to look for Wyllie and discovered him in the outside privy, where he had cut his own throat with a razor and was bleeding profusely from the large gash.

"Dr. Smith, the nearest physician, was summoned from Koloa, and made a record-breaking ride with relays of horses, covering the forty-five miles in three hours," recounted Elsie Wilcox.[81] "An attempt was made to sew up the wound, which Abner Wilcox estimated "was big enough to insert four fingers and a thumb."[82]

For the next several days, Wyllie slipped in and out of consciousness. With assistance, the young Wyllie "prepared a will, giving Princeville, in equal shares, to his mother and his fiance, Ida von Pfister, of Honolulu. Dated *Princeville February 4, 1866*, the bloodstained document carries a wavering signature."[83]

Wyllie struggled to stay alive, writing "I will live" on a piece of paper, and requesting that Wai'oli Church pastor Reverend Johnson be summoned. Doctors also arrived from Honolulu. He endured for several days before dying on Wednesday evening, February 7, 1866. Wyllie, the former R. C. Cockrane, was buried in the Waiʻoli Church cemetery where an iron fence surrounds the unmarked grave.

The financial difficulties of the Princeville estate were said to have been a major cause of Cockrane's despair. Apparently his depression first set in after he examined the plantation's books.

The sale of Princeville Plantation for about $40,000 took place on September 19, 1867. As the original Wyllie had invested about $200,000 in the property, the sale was a large loss. The steam-powered machinery at the sugar mill alone had cost $40,000 when it was imported from Glasgow, Scotland.

> After reading the schedule of the property, the leases and contracts involved in the sale, it was stated that the two mortgages on it with interest amounted to $38,150.00 and that the property would be offered over and above that amount. The bidding was commenced at $50.00 and rose rapidly to $1900.00, at which figure it was knocked down to Mr. E.P. Adams, the real purchaser being his Honor E. H. Allen. The plantation therefore realized $40,050.00, with the prospect of a crop of 500 tons of sugar to come off during the next ten months.
>
> —The *Advertiser*, September 23, 1867[84]

The management of Princeville Plantation changed hands several times before retired American naval officer Captain John Ross took over the position on July 9, 1872. More changes in shares of ownership would ensue during the following years.[85]

New Developments

As land was bought and sold, though the natural beauty of the island did not diminish, the nature of the landscape changed. In his 1875 *Hawaiian Guide Book for Travelers*, Whitney described the Princeville plateau: "Between this valley [Kalihiwai] and Hanalei, the rolling upland is covered with a lauhala forest, reaching to the old silk works of Mr. Titcomb, which were located near the river. Some of these upland tracts, where water can be brought on to them from the neighboring streams, furnish the best of cane land, and will eventually be cultivated with sugarcane or tobacco."[86]

Whitney also described the well-landscaped grounds of Kikiula, the Princeville Plantation House, noting that "its gardens contain the olive, pomegranate, orange and grape, and among roses and shrubbery, the magnificent magnolia grandiflora scatters the exquisite fragrance of its snowy blossoms."[87]

On October 6, 1875, the Princeville Plantation was incorporated. At the time, ownership of the plantation was divided among several parties, including E. H. Allen (five-eighths); Andrew Welsh (one-fourth); and John Ross (one-eighth).[88] In the first years of the 1870s, the one thousand-ton capacity sugar mill was processing a crop that averaged about four hundred tons annually.[89]

In 1877 the Princeville Plantation acquired seven hundred head of sheep to provide manure for the sugarcane fields after the crop was harvested. Within two years the sheep began dying off, and the ranch manager attempted to sell them.

By 1880, Princeville Plantation's sugarcane enterprise employed two hundred laborers to work one hundred acres of sugarcane on the upper slopes and two hundred acres of sugarcane in the valley. The growing ranch also had nine hundred breeding stock, four hundred head working stock, and at least one hundred-fifty steers.[90]

The late 1800s, under the management of Charles Koelling, were years of struggle for Princeville. Koelling installed a diffusion system,[91] not accounting for Hanalei's extremely wet and relatively cool climate or the nature of irrigation. Much of the sugarcane "rotted in the lower fields, the upper fields were, it is said, not plowed deeply enough," wrote Elsie Wilcox, "and at times there was not water enough to flume the cane down to the mill."[92]

In 1890 a bovine anthrax outbreak infected Princeville's cattle, and the herd had to be destroyed.[93] The sugar mill's continual failure to make a profit led to the imminent demise of efforts to grow and mill sugarcane in the Hanalei region. Koelling planted his last crop in 1892 and left Princeville Plantation. The crop was sold by Brewer & Company "to a Chinaman, Wong Fun, who took off the last crop, 497 tons, in 1893."[94] The mill was shut down in 1894.

In 1919 the Hanalei Sugar Mill was demolished. The bricks from the 110-foot smokestack of the mill were sold to the Kīlauea Sugar Company.

> The Princeville plantation brick chimney, for years an outstanding landmark at Hanalei, is a thing of the past. It was demolished on Saturday last by means of dynamite administered at the base, which brought it down with a great crash, that was heard all over the Valley. The bricks are to be sold to Kilauea Sugar Company—

there are about 90,000 of them, and they are a very superior, well made brick, imported 'round the Horn' in the early days when there were not bricks to be had nearer at hand.

—the *Garden Island*, September 23, 1919[95]

Princeville's next owner was Albert Spencer Wilcox, who had bought an interest in the Princeville Plantation in 1892. By 1895 Wilcox controlled all but one-eighth of the estate.[96] The upper plateau lands from Kalihiwai to Hanalei were planted with imported grasses and used for cattle ranching, and the lower lands in Hanalei Valley were rented to Chinese rice farmers. By May of 1899, Wilcox had secured complete ownership of the Princeville estate, and continued converting the property from sugar fields to ranchlands.

In June of 1916 Wilcox sold his Princeville lands to the Līhu'e Plantation but maintained ownership of his Hanalei beach house as well as the Wai'oli Mission House "and some kuleanas along the beach."[97]

The Līhu'e Plantation was particularly interested in obtaining rights to divert water from the Hanalei River. In 1915 J. M. Lydgate wrote a report to Princeville Plantation's manager, Walter Foss Sanborn, regarding the diversion of water in the Hanalei River to the south side of the island, "where it could be disposed of at lucrative rates,"[98] to satisfy the needs of the thirsty sugarcane plantations.

A second outbreak of bovine anthrax occurred in 1917 at the Princeville Ranch, which initiated a program of serum and vaccine administration.[99] Silver oak trees were planted over the cattle burial sites from both the 1890 and 1917 outbreaks.

Princeville Ranch House

Walter Foss Sanborn came to Kaua'i in 1901, serving as the U.S. District Commissioner for Kaua'i and Federal Court Representative. There he met Lena Deverill, daughter of Alfred Palmer Deverill. Alfred had come to the Islands as part of a contingent to present a christening gift to the Crown Prince Albert from his godmother, Queen Victoria.[100]

Walter and Lena married in September of 1906, and moved into the Princeville Ranch House. A year later Lena gave birth to a daughter, Helen, and in the years that followed, the couple had three sons: Walter F. Jr., Percy, and John (Jack).

At the ranch house, the Sanborn children "rode with the cowboys, drove cattle, and watched the roping and branding." [101] They were taught by Hawaiians how to fish for mullet[102] on the Hanalei River at the first rapids. They also delighted in going to movies at Waiʻoli Mission Hall (the old Waiʻoli Church), where a Packard car parked outside the church building provided electricity to run the movie projector, "which continually broke down or had to be stopped to rewind the old reel before going on with the next." [103]

The ranch house served as center of operations for the entire Princeville Ranch. A downstairs storeroom of the house held flour and other supplies that were sold to cowboys working on the ranch, and a nearby building housed the ranch office. The ranch's branding corral, blacksmith shop, and a home for the blacksmith were located near what is now the intersection of Kūhiō Highway and Ka Haku Road.

Other ranch operations buildings were also located in this area, including milking pens and a stable with corrals.[104] Homes for the cowboys, who were mostly Hawaiian, were built on both sides of the highway near the current site of the Princeville Shopping Center.[105] A wagon path lined with plum trees led from the Princeville plateau

The house that was known as Kikiula when it was the residence of Godfrey Rhodes was later called Princeville Plantation House and then Princeville Ranch House. **Hawaiʻi State Archives**

down to the shore,[106] the route by which the ranch's mules and horses were taken down to the shore at 'Anini once a week to be bathed.[107]

The Sanborns, like previous families that had lived at the ranch house, sought to modernize the home with additions, including "outbuildings for Walter's office, the servant's quarters, a warehouse, chicken coops, pig-pens, and a building for small-animal supplies,"[108] as well as a laundry room fashioned out of corrugated iron, and stables. They planted flower and vegetable gardens, and fruit trees.

The gardens tended to attract bees, however, which nested in the home's walls at night. Unable to eradicate the bees, Walter was said to have told his children, "Sit still and they won't sting."[109] The bee infestation grew worse, until the walls of the ranch house dripped with honey. Finally the structure had to be abandoned.[110] The old home, which was originally known as Kikiula when it was built by Godfrey Rhodes in 1845, was torn down in the fall of 1918. The Sanborn family moved to their beach home in Hanalei.

Though the ranch house had been destroyed, activity at the ranch continued. Sanborn also became involved in the building and operating of a poi mill in Hanalei, and served as the north shore's tax assessor and collector.[111] Sanborn retired from his duties as ranch manager in 1927.

Fred Conant replaced Walter Foss Sanborn as Princeville Ranch manager, and built a ranch office just to the east of the current entrance to Princeville, "near the pink plumeria tree which was the inspiration for the Princeville Resort logo."[112] An area of the upper slopes was planted with pineapples, though the lands of the Princeville Ranch continued to be used primarily for cattle ranching through the 1930s.

To facilitate the shipping of cattle to Honolulu, Conant built a corral near the Hanalei Pier. Nearshore waters were shallow, so the cattle had to be "roped, dragged into the water and swum out to whaling boats."[113]

Up to five cattle were tied to each side of the long and narrow whaleboats, and a cable was rigged to pull the whaleboat out to the freighter. Straps were then slung beneath the belly of each animal, and one by one the cattle were hoisted aboard the freighter.[114]

Conant built his new home near the current Hanalei Valley Lookout. From there he could gaze down, as Whitney did decades before, upon the valley in its splendor:

Hanalei is one of the most tropical districts on the island, because of the many mountain streams which traverse it. The view from the plateau is unsurpassed. The wide Hanalei valley, with its beautiful river of the same name, can scarcely be equated for loveliness. The mountains in the distance noted not so much for their height as for their peculiar formation, and their distinctive, broken, curved and jagged peaks, throw their weird shadows over a vale luxurious with forest growths.

—Whitney, 1890[116]

Hanalei's First Catholic Chapel

Catholic presence in the northern Kaua'i region was initially most prominent to the east of Hanalei in the nearby community of Moloa'a. "Hanalei was never much of a Catholic mission center," wrote Damon, "but at Moloaa, the meandering valley some twelve miles to the east of Hanalei, a school was conducted where the Hawaiian children were taught to spin while reciting their lessons."[117] In 1854, a sixty-two-foot by twenty-one-foot stone church named St. Stephen's was completed.

Ten years later, Hanalei's first Catholic chapel was built on the western bank of the Hanalei River near the river mouth. The chapel was built on land purchased from King Kamehameha III in 1849 by Frenchman John Brosseau. Upon Brosseau's death, the land was bought by Henry Rhodes, who then willed it to his brother, sea captain Godfrey Rhodes. Godfrey and his wife, Anna Louisa, both Catholic, then deeded the Hanalei land to Father Maudet in 1860 for the Catholic chapel.

The chapel was blessed on the site near the Hanalei River on October 3, 1864, and dedicated to Saint Maxime, patron saint of a friend of the Rhodes family. The chapel and a rectory, a small house for the priest, were built by Brother Arsene Bernat and blessed by Father Maudet.

A tall and slender wooden church belfry was built on the Hanalei Catholic chapel site around 1900 by Father Sylvester, who had long served the Hanalei area. The belfry was added because Father Matthias "declared that the rectory stood out rather more than the church itself."[118] Eventually the Catholic chapel was outlasted by the rectory, which was used to hold mass after the church was gone.

The Roman Catholic Parsonage was located next to the Chapel, which was built in 1864 near the Hanalei rivermouth. **G. Bertram, Bishop Museum**

Royalty Visits Hanalei

In anticipation of the visit of King Kalākaua, large logs of ʻōhiʻa lehua were bored out and packed with gunpowder. These improvised cannons were set up on a hillside near where his boat would drop anchor. Upon his arrival, the log cannons were fired one after another, greeting the king with a royal 21-"gun" salute.

Masses of people awaited the king as he rowed to the wharf at Hanalei. As he walked beneath an arch that read "God Save the King," upon a path lined with yellow and red ʻōhiʻa lehua blossoms, the national anthem was played by the Royal Band, and children scattered flowers in the king's path. King Kalākaua was then led to a nearby area thatched with ferns and fragrant native maile, and a grand lūʻau (Hawaiian feast) commenced.

King Kalākaua's party later journeyed up the Hanalei River, some riding horseback while others rowed up the river in boats. Kalākaua stayed the night at the home of Kaukaha, and in the morning the royal party left Hanalei Bay and sailed around the Nā Pali Coast to Waimea.[119] Hanalei was the first stop on the newly elected monarch's royal tour of the Hawaiian Kingdom.

The bell from the 1864 Catholic chapel was moved to St. Williams Church in Hanalei town where it remains today. **Bob Waid**

Just over a decade later, during Kalākaua's world tour, Princess Regent Lili'uokalani arrived in Hanalei Bay. She traveled to Kīlauea, where she had been invited by one of the Kīlauea Sugar Plantation's owners, R. A. Macfie Jr., to commemorate the Kīlauea Sugar Corporation's purchase of a railroad engine as well as three miles of track and twenty-four railroad cars to carry the sugarcane. Lili'uokalani drove in the first ceremonial spike.[120]

As Queen Lili'uokalani she visited Hanalei again, arriving at Nāwiliwili Bay in the pre-dawn hours of July 8, 1891. She was accompanied by Prince Jonah Kūhiō Kalaniana'ole, grandson of Kaua'i's former ruler, Kaumuali'i; nephew and adopted son of Queen Kapi'olani and Kalākaua; and heir presumptive to the throne, as named by Lili'uokalani.

She was taken by carriage to Hale Nani, the home of William Hyde Rice, where hundreds of children greeted her. Ho'okupu (gift-giving ceremonies) took place, and the Royal Band performed under the direction of conductor Heinrich "Henry" Berger.[121]

Two days later, after a visit to the Makee Plantation in Keālia, Queen Lili'uokalani and her party rode by carriage to Hanalei where more receptions were held. After returning to Kaua'i from a side-jaunt to Niʻihau, the queen's party was welcomed at Waimea by a salute fired from the fort. Following a visit to Kōloa, the queen was honored with a traditional lūʻau attended by about two thousand people in Kalapakī at the home of the Rice family.

The Deverill House—Hanalei Hotel

In 1838 a Western-style, timber-framed home was constructed near the Waiʻoli Mission House for Protestant teachers Mr. and Mrs. Edward and Lois H. Johnson. The Johnsons arrived at the Waiʻoli mission station in 1837 and lived in the home until 1867 at its original site.

Around 1890, the former Johnson home was rolled on logs of ʻōhiʻa lehua to a site closer to the beach and to the east, where it became the home of William and Sarah Deverill. Sarah had lived in the home as a child when she was a ward of the Johnson family.[122]

William Edward Herbert Deverill (1848–1904) had come to the Islands from Lancashire, England, arriving at age eighteen with his brother Alfred Palmer Deverill. William Deverill had studied in France, and when first arriving on Hawaiʻi Island he worked at Kohala Ranch. He also worked in Hilo and later in Honolulu, where he was hired by Chase and Dickson photographic galleries. Deverill

Deverills on porch. **Bishop Museum**

served as deputy sheriff under Samuel Wilcox in Līhu'e before moving to Hanalei in 1875.

There he met and married Sarah Benson Fredenberg, a part-Hawaiian who had grown up in Hanalei. Sarah was the granddaughter of Captain Kellett, Hanalei's former pilot of the port.[123]

The Deverills traveled to O'ahu in 1887, where William ran the Lunalilo Home, which was created by the terms of King Lunalilo's will to benefit sick and poor Hawaiians (particularly older Hawaiians). The Deverills returned to Hanalei in 1890.

The Deverills often opened up their home for guests to rest the night after long journeys to Hanalei Bay. Originally, the home had two stories, with five upstairs bedrooms and verandas on both levels facing Hanalei Bay. Extending out from the back of this part of the home was a structure containing the kitchen and pantry as well as the dining room.

When guests arrived, the Deverills and their six children would prepare the main portion of their home for enjoyment, and sleep in rooms on the western side of the house. After phone service was installed in 1891, a phone call from Līhu'e would alert the Deverills of arriving guests so they could begin making preparations.

Extensive remodeling made the home site a community center, with a lānai walkway that connected the main building to a separate structure that housed a Hawaiian Kingdom post office

The Deverill House was built in 1838 near the Wai'oli Mission as the home of Reverend Edward and Lois Johnson. In 1890 the home was moved on 'ōhi'a lehua log rollers to the other side of Hanalei town and became known as the Hanalei Hotel. **Deverill, Bishop Museum**

and a tax office.[124] A separate building near the Hanalei Hotel housed a dispensary where a medical clinic was offered twice a week by a Kīlauea doctor. The dispensary building also had an ironing room, and for many years was the quarters of the head helper, cook, and baker.

The back side of the Deverill House had tanks to catch rainwater, and a hale liʻiliʻi (outhouse). Further, there was a chicken house and a barn, a vegetable garden, and rice paddies. Beyond the rice paddies sat the Deverills' boat house, on the banks of the Hanalei River.

The Deverill children sometimes escorted guests to local scenic spots, inspiring prominent artists like Otto Wix, Robert Barnfield, and D. Howard Hitchcock to paint Hanalei landscapes.

Sarah Deverill's many roles included serving as manager of the Hanalei Hotel, where she charged guests $3.00 a day for room and board. Sarah was also a midwife, and she was known as a gracious and dependable hard worker. In the early 1890s Sarah operated a butcher shop, slaughtering animals and selling beef.

William Deverill had a multitude of jobs, serving as district sheriff, tax assessor, road supervisor, and property manager for Albert Spencer Wilcox. As an agent for the Inter-Island Steam Navigation Company, he was also in charge of all steam freight arriving or being sent from Hanalei Bay.[125] In time, he started a coffee plantation on leased land in Hanakāpīʻai Valley on Kauaʻi's Nā Pali coast.

Deverill was an avid photographer and used his darkroom at the Hanalei Hotel to develop his own pictures as well as those of his guests. Japanese residents often referred to William as "Deverill Man," and many Hawaiians called him "Kepolō" (Devilish).[126] William Deverill died in 1904, and his grave site may still be seen alongside Waiʻoli Mission Hall (the former Waiʻoli Church) in Hanalei.[127]

After William's death, Sarah assumed many of his former duties, including serving as the region's tax assessor and postmistress. The Hanalei Hotel remained in operation until 1920 when the automobile became popular and road improvements allowed faster access to Hanalei from Līhuʻe. With these improvements, visitors no longer needed to stay the night in Hanalei.

Sarah Deverill passed away in Honolulu in the 1930s.

Chapter 4

The Rice Era and the Beach Houses of Hanalei
1900–1950

Roads and Bridges

The large waves that buffet Kaua'i's north shore during the winter months made sea travel difficult and gave added importance to area roads that were used to bring people and goods to and from the region. As the amount of travel being done increased, gradual improvements were made to Kaua'i's road system.

An 1851 report by Godfrey Rhodes, vice president of the Royal Hawaiian Agricultural Society, stated: "The condition of the roads under the superintendence of foreigners is wonderfully improved, and the amount appropriated by government for their further improvement will render them tolerably good and easy for traveling on horseback. It is hoped that in the course of a very few years the whole of the distance between Hanalei and Waimea will be traversed by a good carriage road."[1]

The original road down into Hanalei Valley passed the home known as Kikiula—later renamed Princeville Plantation House and then Princeville Ranch House—and reached the valley floor just upriver from the current site of the Hanalei Bridge (built in 1912).[2] Around 1885, the main route into the valley was realigned, becoming a steep, winding route with three switchbacking S-curves down to the shoreline.

There, travelers would catch a hand-pulled ferry which was "supported by government and the Princeville Plantation jointly."[3] It was the only means by which travelers from Hanalei could cross the numerous rivers.

In the mid-1800s, Josephine Wundenberg King recalled, "there were no bridges in Wainiha, [and] although there were ferry scows

Before the Hanalei Bridge was built, horses and passengers crossed the river on a hand-pulled ferry. **Kaua'i Museum**

at Lumahai and at Hanalei and Kalihiwai, I never liked crossing on them, for I was pushed off one at Princeville once by a kicking horse and never got over the fright. Most horses were nervous on them, and they were often leaky and tipped too much for comfort, mentally and otherwise. In the very old times natives paddled people over the rivers in canoes and swam our horses over for us, which was the safest if not the most convenient method."[4]

Times continued to change. In 1895 an iron-truss bridge was erected over the Hanalei River, and in 1904 wooden timber bridges were constructed over the streams flowing from the valleys of Waipā, Waikoko, Wainiha, and Lumaha'i. The road down into Hanalei Valley (Route 560) came into use around 1900, replacing the steep, switchback trail with a gentler route.

By 1912 the government had replaced the rusted iron bridge with steel, making travel safer and easier for visitors to the Hanalei region. The Carnegie Steel truss pieces were prefabricated in New York City by the firm of Hamilton & Chambers for the Territory of Hawai'i, and the connections were riveted at the bridge site. The bridge spanned 113 feet over the river. It is Hawai'i's oldest American-made, steel, through-truss bridge.[5]

Work in 1934 strengthened the structure, increasing its twelve-ton load limit. In 1957 the Hanalei Bridge was damaged by a tsunami (tidal wave); reinforcements were added in 1959. Warren trusses were added in 1967. (See *Chapter 5*.)

The collapse of three of the region's wooden bridges in the summer of 1912, caused by heavily loaded wagons being used to move large amounts of crushed rock for road construction, gave impetus for the construction of new bridges on Kaua'i's north shore.

> Three bridges in the Hanalei District which are to be replaced with new ones, had collapsed. One bridge had been but fairly cleared by a loaded wagon, when it fell and crashed into the stream, while a second bridge went down carrying a part of the wagon with it. Fortunately, the team had secured sound footing and were able to withstand the strain. A third bridge collapsed with no great loss, as the timbers were useless.
>
> —the *Garden Island*, 1912[6]

During the next two years, concrete bridges were erected at Wai'oli, Waipā, and Waikoko[7] by County Engineer Joseph Hughes Moragne (and later R. L. Garlinghouse), who undertook an extensive bridge building program.

The larger vision of these engineers was to link the north and west shores of Kaua'i with a series of new bridges and a paved, improved road, making Kaua'i's modern road system the envy of the

Hanalei Bridge was built over the Hanalei River in 1912. In the background is the Hanalei Sugar Mill. **Kaua'i Museum**

Islands.[8] In the first issue of 1913, the *Garden Island* newspaper reported "new concrete bridges now under construction are assuming a finished appearance. A new steel bridge has also replaced the old structure across the Hanalei River."[9]

The Waiʻoli Bridge was a concrete, cast-in-place, multi-span structure with pointed cap railings. Waipā Bridge was a double span, cast-in-place bridge, with pointed cap railings and beveled trim. An additional span was added in 1946, lengthening the bridge to accommodate the new course of Waipā Stream after it was altered by the 1946 tsunami.

Waikoko Bridge, originally a concrete, cast-in-place structure built in 1912, partially collapsed during the 1946 tsunami. To make the bridge passable after the tidal wave, rocks were stacked atop the fallen structure. This repaired bridge remains in use to the present day, with low rock walls along the sides of the bridge serving as railings.

The Kauaʻi "Belt Road" was completed by about 1920 and extended from Mānā to Hāʻena. Around the same time, rock was quarried from the eastern side of the Hanalei rivermouth to pave Weke Road. Mules brought the rock over a floating bridge constructed

The Waikoko Bridge, knocked down by the 1946 tsunami, was hastily rebuilt and remains in use today. **Bob Waid**

across the Hanalei River. The rock was crushed near the pier and then used to pave the road.

Mahi Mahi Road, located about half a mile from Hanalei Pier, was also paved around that time. Mahi Mahi Road provides access from Route 560 (formerly known as the Government Road) to Weke Road and the beaches of Hanalei.

Wai'oli Mission in the Twentieth Century

As Hanalei moved into the twentieth century, the descendants of pioneering Wai'oli missionaries Abner and Lucy Wilcox restored the old mission buildings and also built a new church building. In 1912, a new church was built by Sam, George, and Albert Wilcox in honor of their parents. The church, just east of the original 1841 Wai'oli Church, became known as Wai'oli Hui'ia Church Sanctuary.

The church was designed in the American Gothic style and included a front gable "with an immense stained glass window with a pointed arch."[10] The Wilcoxes also built a bell tower. Here they placed the bell from the Wai'oli belfry, which had sounded its tones to the congregation since 1843.

The green, spired building cost $10,500 to build, and was dedicated with much celebration. On October 22, 1912, the *Garden Island* newspaper reported, "Reverend W. B. Oleson gave a brief resume of the history of the church. A hermetically sealed copper box containing the current newspapers of the day, including the *Garden Island*, was placed in a recess in the corner stone and cemented in by Mrs. S. W. Wilcox...a generous luau hot from the imu followed the dedication service."[11]

More good press was received a week later, stating, "The New Church Building just dedicated at Hanalei is one of the most artistic and graceful churches on the Islands. But even more important, perhaps, it is an exceedingly well-built church...acoustically the best type of building with a charming gothic finish of steep roof and pointed windows."[12] The structure's fine stained glass windows were said to be "works of art upon which the eyes ever delight to feast."[13] The windows were said to reflect "all the colors of the rainbow intensified."[14]

The Wai'oli Hui'ia Church remains one of the most photographed buildings in Hanalei today.

A gathering of missionary children, descendants, and friends in front of Waiʻoli Mission Hall during the dedication of the New Waiʻoli Huiʻia Church on November 21, 1921. **Kauaʻi Historical Society**

Albert Spencer Wilcox, who had spearheaded much of the Waiʻoli Huiʻia Church's construction, considered the Mission House at Waiʻoli to be in hopeless disrepair and had contemplated burning the structure down. Nothing was done, however, and when he passed away in 1919 the Waiʻoli Mission House, as well as the adjoining mission lands, were sold to the children of Samuel and Emma Wilcox: Elsie Wilcox, Mabel Wilcox, and Lucy Etta Wilcox Sloggett. The three sisters undertook an extensive restoration of the Waiʻoli Mission House and Waiʻoli Mission Hall (the former Waiʻoli Church).

Prominent Honolulu architect Hart Wood was chosen to oversee the restoration project, and his plan encompassed the whole of the twenty-acre site, including landscaping, fencing, and "draining and leveling of the common for the park."[15] "I hope to restore everything to its former condition," wrote Wood, "and to retain the simplicity and unpretentiousness of the original."[16]

Wood took great care to retain the original features of the house, including the uneven widths of the original floorboards, and the lath and plaster of the interior walls.[17] He even salvaged some of the home's original furnishings such as Abner's upholstered rocking chair as well as "a whale oil metal lamp, candlestick, the bookcase, many of Abner and Lucy Wilcox's books and—remarkably—all the letters of Abner and Lucy Wilcox."[18]

Once the Wai'oli Mission House restoration was completed, the Wilcox sisters brought many of their grandparents' keepsakes back to the house, including furniture, bedspreads, and shells that had been handed down through two generations. "Pitchers, a mantel clock, inkwells, Shaker boxes, the Chinese work basket and ceramics were returned to Waioli. George Wilcox brought back his mother's Connecticut album quilt, and Lucy Etta Sloggett brought back her grandparent's center table."[19]

In 1921 a rosewood table was returned "to its place in the beautiful front room at Waioli," recalled Ethel Damon, "and as, for the first time in many years, the feet of guests again trooped over the low moss-green sandstone steps and through the broad, window-paneled front door, Etta Sloggett welcomed us all to the old house. That was a beautiful November day."[20]

The restoration was also celebrated with a church service that "reconsecrated its stately walls to the service of the community."[21] Samuel Whitney Wilcox spoke to the gathering, and "told in flowing, beautiful Hawaiian of boyhood days at Waioli. His grandson and namesake gave over the old church keys to the Hawaiian leaders of

Wai'oli Hui'ia Church was built in 1921 by the Wilcox brothers in honor of their missionary parents, Abner and Lucy Wilcox. On the right is the original Wai'oli Church, built in 1841. **Bishop Museum**

Hanalei Valley & River, 1929. **Hawai'i State Archives**

the community. And afterward a great feast, a true paina luau, was there spread out for the visiting multitude."[22]

In 1922 Elsie and Mabel Wilcox, along with Ethel Damon, visited the East Coast of the United States to purchase objects for the restored Mission House, including a chest of drawers that had been used by Abner Wilcox's parents at their home in Harwinton, Connecticut.[23]

The Mission House at Wai'oli was the residence of the Alexanders from 1836 to 1843, then home to Mr. and Mrs. George B. and Malvina Rowell until 1846. The Wilcoxes lived in the Wai'oli Mission House from 1846 to 1869.

The 1841 Wai'oli Church served the congregation until 1912 when the new Wai'oli Hui'ia Church was built. In 1921 the old church building was restored, and is now known as Wai'oli Mission Hall, or Church Hall.

In 1934, a century after the arrival of the Alexanders at Wai'oli, a lū'au feast was held to celebrate the Wai'oli Mission Centennial, the hundredth year since the founding of the Wai'oli mission station by pioneering missionaries William Patterson Alexander and his wife, Mary Ann.

About one thousand people, including many Alexander descendants, attended the Centennial along with seven different choir groups from Kauaʻi churches. A memorial address was given by Mary Alexander, the granddaughter of William and Mary Ann Alexander. The church choirs sang classics including "Hawaii Aloha and Na Molokama," which "brought back the old days."[24]

Also in 1934, to commemorate the Mission Centennial, a wing was added to Waiʻoli Mission Hall to house a kitchen. By 1945, Waiʻoli Church, Hāʻena Church, and ʻAnini Church had joined to form the Waiʻoli Huiʻia Church, which was a Congregational Church until 1957 when it became a United Church of Christ.

The Waiʻoli Mission House was incorporated as a museum in 1952, and Elsie and Mabel Wilcox, along with Lucy Etta Wilcox Sloggett, established an endowment to guarantee the continued preservation of the historic home, which was opened to the public free of charge.

In the 1950s, Waiʻoli Park was leased to the community and became a public park.[25] The Waiʻoli Church parsonage was built in 1966. (See *Chapter 5*.)

The Hanalei River

Hanalei Valley's agricultural productivity is largely due to the plentiful water supply provided by the Hanalei River. The watercourse flows some sixteen miles through Hanalei Valley and drains a watershed of about nineteen square miles.

Flow rates on the Hanalei River range from twenty million gallons per day to more than six billion gallons per day.[26] The Hanalei River is one of the five largest rivers in the Islands, and drains into one of the state's largest bays, Hanalei Bay.

> The landing is within the mouth of a small river, which carries, for a considerable distance up, from one to three quarters of a fathom, into fresh water, and is further navigable for boats or canoes (drawing three feet) several miles...The scenery is beautiful, and my surprise is that such a favourable situation should so long have been overlooked.[27]
>
> —Captain Edward Belcher, 1843[28]

As the Hanalei River winds its way across the coastal plain, some of its water is diverted into the taro patches of Hanalei Valley. This water is channeled to and from the fields through a series of canals and ditches that eventually return the water to the river.

Water diversions from the Hanalei River were being considered as early as 1915. While attempts to grow sugarcane in the Hanalei region had been unsuccessful, the crop continued to thrive on the rest of Kaua'i; the increasing size of the sugarcane plantations led to the need for more water, and the Hanalei River could provide it.

Large-scale water diversions of the Hanalei River for use on distant sugarcane plantations began in the early 1900s, in part due to the work of Joseph Hughes Moragne, who was an engineer for the Līhu'e Plantation from 1919 to 1937. Moragne supervised "the development of a complex water collection and transfer system, one that spanned and connected several watersheds from Hanalei to Koloa."[29] In 1925 the Ka'āpoko Tunnel was constructed to bring water from the Hanalei River to Wailua.

In 1926, Moragne engineered and built the 6,028-foot Hanalei Tunnel at a cost of $294,261 to divert water from the Hanalei River to Līhu'e. Beginning at the 1,250-foot elevation of the Hanalei River basin, the Hanalei Tunnel carried water through to the Wailua River basin and down into the Maheo Stream, which flows into the north fork of the Wailua River at an elevation of about 700 feet.[30]

From the Maheo Stream the Stable Storm Ditch carried the water west to a south fork tributary, and then finally to the sugarcane fields of Līhu'e.[31] In 1928 a 3,558-foot tunnel was built at a cost of $150,000 to divert water into the Hanalei Tunnel from the Ka'āpoko tributary of the Hanalei River.[32]

> Hanalei river is lined with luxuriant foliage, and a boat ride on its smooth bosom, in a bright moonlight, rivals the Arabian Nights enchantment.
>
> —Whitney, 1875[33]

The Rice Era

The rice era followed various failed agricultural attempts in the valley, including crops of mulberry for silkworms, coffee, tobacco, and sugarcane, as well as attempts to raise cattle. By 1870 rice had become a significant agricultural product throughout the Islands and would soon dominate the Hanalei landscape. In 1879, five Chinese farmers leased forty-two acres of Hanalei Valley land for $15 per acre per year from the Princeville Plantation.[34]

In 1880 an established Chinese rice factoring company, the Chulan Company, attempted to lease seven hundred acres, but Princeville Plantation manager Charles Koelling was concerned that Princeville's upper plateau lands might be less fertile than the lower valley lands, and so he would not grant such a large lease.[35] The Chulan Company settled for three hundred acres, paying $20 per acre per year.

By 1882 sugarcane had all but disappeared in Hanalei's lower valley in favor of rice. Other nearby valleys, and virtually all suitable land along Hanalei's coastal plain, had also been planted with the crop.

A decade later, about 750 of the 7,321 acres of rice grown in Hawai'i were in Hanalei and Wai'oli valleys. Mokulē'ia in O'ahu was the second-largest rice-producing area in the Islands, with 738 acres in cultivation, followed by Waikīkī, which had 542 acres planted in rice.[36] Ninety percent of Hawai'i's rice came from Kaua'i and O'ahu. Hanalei was the top rice-producing region by 1920.[37]

Chinese were the predominant ethnic group working in Hawai'i's rice industry during its early years. In 1884 the Chinese population of Hanalei was 459, increasing to 689 by 1896.[38] In 1895 Eric

Hanalei Valley Rice Fields & Bay. March 1920. **Kaua'i Museum**

Knudsen wrote in his journal: "Rice field and taro patches covered the flat bottom lands as far as the eye could see...many Chinamen were working in the fields."[39]

In the early 1900s the Japanese population increased by about 30% as the Chinese population steadily decreased, and by the 1920s there were about equal numbers of Chinese and Japanese rice growers and millers.[40]

As the Japanese population increased, they soon became the Islands' principal rice consumers and began to plant accordingly. The Hanalei landscape was soon covered with shorter grained varieties of rice, which were softer, more glutinous, and more flavorful than the Chinese varieties.[41] Rice imports from Japan also increased, rising from about nine and a half million pounds in 1905 to nearly thirty million pounds in 1910.[42]

Growing and Milling Rice

Hanalei's wet climate allowed just one rice crop per year, planted in May and harvested in September. Drier areas on Kaua'i, such as Hanapēpē, could produce two crops a year.[43] The rice farmers of Hanalei were kept busy year-round, however, by all of the other tasks involved in rice farming, including milling, equipment repair, field preparation, ditch clearing, ditch maintenance, and growing food to eat.[44]

Farmers would begin the season by soaking the seeds in a stream for two days. They would then germinate the seeds on a threshing floor by covering them with wet bags that were lifted and replaced several times daily to provide aeration.[45]

The rice seeds were then planted in beds that were immersed in about two inches of water. When the plants reached a height of about two inches, peanut meal or sodium nitrate was added. After about three weeks the seedlings were tied into bundles. This was generally done in the evening and into the night, and then the next day the seedlings were transplanted into the rice paddies.

In the early years of Hanalei's rice era, oxen and water buffalo were used to plow the fields. Small farmers helped each other plant the seedlings, while large plantations hired extra workers known as "planting gangs." Planters usually walked backward while holding a bundle in one hand, using the other hand to poke the plants into the ground, planting up to six rows at once.

About one week after a field was planted it was flooded around four inches deep, then harrowed to root up weeds and level the ground. About every three weeks the paddies were drained and weeded.

After the second weeding, fertilizer was applied to the dry ground, and after about two weeks the ground would start to crack. Then the fields were flooded again, the grain began to form, and the plants' green husks filled with a sweet, milky fluid that gradually solidified as the grain turned a golden color. Within a few weeks the fields were drained and the rice was harvested.

The major pests in rice production were human-introduced Chinese sparrows known as nutmeg mannikins (also called rice birds[46]), which drank the milky rice as it matured and also ate the kernels. To deter the birds from damaging the rice crop, poles were set up throughout the fields to hold a system of rock-filled cans and other noise-making devices. These noise makers were all linked together by a cord that was repeatedly pulled to scatter the birds.

Some farmers shot the birds with "old muskets…filled with powder and stuffed with rags or paper."[47] "In the early Twenties," recalled Frank Kurihara, "you could buy gunpowder, B-B shot, sticks of dynamite in the stores. Even the rice bird guns that looked like a Daniel Boone musket, which we used to chase the rice birds away."[48]

"If left alone," recalled Kurihara, "[the birds would] wipe out a patch in no time. To chase them away, we'd fire our rice bird guns, or rattle tin cans, strung all over the fields. We also ordered silk nets from Japan, which were about ten by thirty feet in area, and strung them all over the fields, like a volleyball net, wherever those pesky birds congregated."[49]

When the rice was ready to harvest, the stalks were cut with a serrated sickle and allowed to dry before being bundled with cord made from the native hau tree.[50] The bundles of stalks were brought to the threshing floor and laid out in concentric circles in three layers totaling up to five hundred bundles.

Threshing took up to five days, and was done by horses attached to ropes tied to a pole at the center of the threshing floor. The horses walked around and around, trampling the grain to separate the seed from the stalks, which were raked away as each successive layer was threshed. The horses were eventually replaced by tractors.[51]

Winnowing separated the chaff and dust from the grain. The rice was raked into rows aligned with the wind and repeatedly sieved and sifted, and then dried by repeated spreading and raking. Finally, the rice was placed in hundred pound sacks that were sewn closed and stored in a granary. The end of the harvest was celebrated with elaborate banquets held by the rice plantations.[52]

By 1893 there were at least five rice mills in the Hanalei region, including one near the Hanalei River about midway between the Hanalei Bridge and Hanalei town. The earliest rice mills usually consisted of two large mill stones that raised a pestle-shaped stone and dropped it into a stone bowl.[53]

One of these old-style mills was the See Tai Wai Rice Mill, located in Hanalei town near the Say Dock House. Other early rice mills were located at Wai'oli, Waikoko, and Wainiha.

Rice mills operated for up to three months after harvest, and the smaller rice farms brought their rice to the mills run by the larger plantations, such as Shing Kon Sung (Soy Sung Wai), located in the bend in the Hanalei River near the rivermouth.[54] Chinjiro Tasaka farmed rice on the east side of Hanalei Bay at Pu'upōā Marsh (Kamo'omaika'i Fishpond) and took his rice by horse to the Hanalei River where it was carried across by boat and then hauled in Chock Chin's wagon to the Chock Chin Rice Mill at Waikoko.[55]

Rice milling was done to clean and shell the threshed rice, removing the hulls and bran. The mills' wheels were usually powered by water, so the rice mills were usually located near a river or other water source.[56] The rice was husked and polished, then graded and bagged for shipment to market. An adjacent granary held paddy rice and bran rice middling used for animal feed.

The waters of the Hanalei River were an integral component of rice growing and milling, powering the mill's machinery and driving the network of belts and conveyor systems. Runoff also provided hot baths that soothed the sore muscles of the rice workers. At the Haraguchi Rice Mill on the Hanalei River, workers were "treated to a traditional Japanese furo bath following their workday."[57]

In 1910, 503 farms in the Hawaiian Islands grew rice on 9,435 acres of land, only increasing in production until 1917. Total acres farmed in rice began to decrease rapidly when rice acreage climbed from 1,400 to 80,000 acres in California.

By 1919 there were 546 rice farms in the Hawaiian Islands, but total acreage had dropped to 5,801 acres. California rice producers continued to dominate the rice industry in the early 1920s, when hired hands on Hanalei's rice farms were paid about a dollar a day and worked six days per week.[58] By 1930, total acreage being farmed in rice in the Hawaiian Islands was 2,045 acres, on a total of 227 rice farms. Just three years later, only 825 acres were still being farmed in rice.[59]

Diesel engines eventually replaced the region's water-powered rice mills. The leather-type wheels of the new hullers caused less breakage of the rice than the stone rollers of the earlier Chinese mills. In the 1930s, the Haraguchis ordered a Japanese-made huller as well as hulling equipment from New York's Englebert Huller Company.[60]

Hanalei Pier

Today one of the most scenic views anywhere is from the end of the Hanalei Pier, bound by the turquoise waters of Hanalei Bay and the waterfall-lined mountains wrapping around the crescent-shaped shoreline. The pier extends from Black Pot Beach Park, the site of many local gatherings.[61] People of all ages surf the waves that break alongside the pier and down the beach. Hanalei Pier is also a favorite place for local kids to play.[62]

> Its mouth, where [Hanalei Bay] opens on the Pacific, is from two to three miles wide, but the boundary mountains gradually approach each other, so that five miles from the sea a narrow gorge of wonderful beauty alone remains.
>
> —Isabella Bird Bishop, 1873[63]

The first Hanalei Pier, built primarily for use by rice farmers needing to load their cargo, was constructed of wood in 1892 near the mouth of the Hanalei River. In 1911, when the rice industry in Hanalei was thriving, construction began on a longer, more substantial pier at the same location. The new Hanalei Pier was completed in 1912, using the relatively new technique of reinforced concrete. The architectural design was provided by the firm of Conney and Morris, and the pier had a wooden deck.

The milled rice was brought down the Hanalei River on small, flat-bottomed boats. After being transported downriver, the rice was offloaded at a landing near the river mouth. Small whale boats known as "lighters" carried rice to the steamers anchored out in Hanalei Bay.[64]

Cargo including farm supplies and canned food were brought in the same way, using small boats to row to and from the pier as the large interisland steamers docked in the deeper waters of the bay. At the foot of Hanalei Pier was a freight storage warehouse connected to the pier by railroad tracks.[65]

Walter Foss Sanborn, manager of the Princeville Plantation, also supervised the loading and unloading of vessels at Hanalei Pier, checking freight. Eventually a derrick was installed at the end of the pier to load and unload cargo going out to, or coming in from, the freighters. Once each month these freighters would travel north, stopping at Ahukini, Anahola, Kīlauea, and Hanalei.[66]

Community members would gather at the pier when ships arrived in Hanalei Bay with cargo. On these "boat days" local children sometimes swam out to the ships and "merchants from all the stores arrived to sort out their goods, farmers loaded theirs, and individuals came to pick up special orders...Arriving provisions included huge redwood boxes with ice packed in rice husks."[67] The arrival of goods was a huge event, and the Hanalei pier remained central in all the activity.

The wooden deck of Hanalei Pier was replaced with reinforced concrete in 1921, and the pier was extended. Princeville Ranch soon

Bags of rice being taken out to a ship waiting off of Hanalei Pier. Initially built in 1892, the pier was rebuilt in 1918, with a concrete deck and extension added in 1921. The shed at the end of the pier was built in the 1940s, and the pier was also rebuilt after damage by Hurricane ʻIniki in 1992. Hanalei Pier is listed on both the Hawaiʻi and National Registers of Historic Places. **Kauaʻi Museum**

Rice boats coming up the river. **Hawai'i State Archives**

began shipping cattle from Hanalei Bay, and in 1927 a temporary corral was built on the beach near Hanalei Pier.[68]

In the early 1930s, however, a breakwater was built in southeastern Kaua'i at Nāwiliwili Bay, which then became the island's preferred loading and unloading point for freight. The rice industry, which had thrived in the valleys of Hanalei and Wai'oli since the late 1800s, was in decline. Rice exports from Hanalei fell off sharply, as did the commercial use of Hanalei Pier.

Hanalei Pier has been seen in many Hollywood movies, often as a backdrop. Scenes from *Bird of Paradise* were filmed on Hanalei Bay in 1950, and *South Pacific* was filmed there in 1957. During the 1960 filming of *The Wackiest Ship in the Army*, starring Jack Lemmon, the filming barge at Hanalei came loose twice, causing damage to Hanalei Pier. Repairs to the pier were later financed by the film studio and the barge company.

Hanalei in the Early 1900s—
A Journey through Old Hanalei

The Hanalei region was particularly prosperous from about 1890 to 1925 due to the rice industry. This wealth led to the opening of numerous stores and mills that dotted the landscape from Hanalei Bridge to Hanalei town and beyond.[69] Also constructed during this period were places of worship, including Christian churches and Buddhist temples, and Japanese and Chinese language schools.

Local stores were central to the rice farming community's social life, particularly on Sundays when residents gathered to exchange news and make business deals. Stores provided items for sale that could not be grown or produced locally, including "canned goods, staples like flour and sugar, butchered meat, baked goods, kerosene, and later gasoline, yardage and sewing supplies, hats, clothing, watches, and some farm supplies."[70]

The 1914 *Polk-Husted Directory of Honolulu and the Territory of Hawaii* listed eight general merchandising stores (seven Chinese-owned) and twelve Chinese rice-planting companies in the Hanalei region.[71]

Some Chinese-owned stores in Hanalei in the early 1900s were Ah Hoy Store (later called Ching Ma Leong Store); Chong Hing Store; T. S. See Wo Store; Ching Young Store; and Chock Chin Store (later called C. Akeoni Store, Lau Store, and Hanalei Store[72]). There was also "a Chinese store about half-way up the valley,"[73] and the Japanese-owned Hamamura Store.

Ah Hoy Store, located just above Hanalei Bridge on the Hanalei side of the road, was a general merchandise store and auto livery. Ah Hoy was later renamed Ching Ma Leong Store and relocated to the Trader Building (which was rebuilt after Hurricane 'Iniki, and is now the site of the Dolphin Building) on the banks of the Hanalei River just before Hanalei town.[74] Across the road from Ma Leong was the Takahashi rice farm.

On the river road, now 'Ōhiki Road, were the rice farms of the Haraguchi family and the Atuck Wong family. Also on the river road was the Haraguchi Rice Mill,[75] built in 1930 to replace the Chinese-owned Man Sing Rice Mill,[76] which had burned down earlier that year.

The Haraguchis—A Tradition of Farming

Tomijiro and Ine Haraguchi immigrated to Hawaiʻi from Fukuoka Prefecture, Japan, in the early 1900s. Tomijiro and Ine had four sons: Kahyohei (Kahei), Sueji, Fujio, and Fusao.

Along with farming rice, the family fished commercially in the waters of Hanalei Bay, using a sampan built at Kukuiʻula. The boat was named *Asa Kura Maru* after the Haraguchi's home village in Japan.[77]

The eldest son, Kahyohei—whose name was "shortened to Kahei because people had difficulty pronouncing his full name"[78] —worked as a contract laborer for the Gay & Robinson sugar plantation and then worked in the pineapple industry in Kapaʻa while maintaining a rice farm in Hāʻena near the current site of the Hanalei Colony Resort.[79] His eldest son, William, worked for many years at the Haraguchi Rice Mill, milling rice for farms as far away as Kapaʻa.

The Haraguchi family continued their Hanalei rice farming operation during a time when many other farms and rice mills throughout the Islands were forced to shut down. In the 1930s the Haraguchis still farmed about seventy-five acres of rice. In 1949 they modified a gasoline-powered, three-fourth-horse, clipper tractor and later purchased a combine.[80]

The Haraguchi Rice Mill finally shut down in 1960, the last rice mill operating in the Hanalei region. Like many other rice farms throughout the Hawaiian Islands, it succumbed to mainland competition, and damage to the crops by rice birds[81] made it difficult to maintain a profit. The rice farms were then used for other crops, and the Haraguchi Rice Mill was later used to mill taro.

The Haraguchi family's tradition of farming in Hanalei Valley is now on its fifth generation and counting. Today the Haraguchis continue to farm large expanses of taro in Hanalei Valley (see *Chapter 5*).

Just upriver from the Haraguchi Rice Mill, on the west bank of the river across from the Man Sung Wai Rice Mill,[82] the rice farmers of a Chinese fraternal society built a Chinese Temple as well as a clubhouse and social hall known as the Yee Hing Society Community Home.[83]

The Yee Hing served various functions for the charitable association called Yee Hing Hui, and was a place where "bachelor Chinese men and travelers found a ready welcome to live there or spend a few days gossiping or gambling, playing ma jong or rolling dice."[84]

A large room on the upper floor of the Yee Hing was used for dinners and banquets. Rooms on the lower floor were rented to older Chinese workers,[85] and "vegetables, pigs, chickens and ducks were grown and raised."[86] The Yee Hing also served as a Chinese language school for children.

Sundays in particular drew large crowds at Yee Hing, which for a time was also the home of Chinese school teacher Wong Lee Yau.[87] After the decline of the Chinese population in the Hanalei region, Princeville Ranch manager Fred Conant had the Yee Hing building torn down.[88]

Just east of the Wai'oli Bridge once stood the Nakatsuji Rice Mill (formerly Hop Chong Wai Rice Mill), managed by Ah Hoy. Across from the mill lived retired Kealia Plantation manager Charlie McKee.[89] The Wong, Hashimoto, Kobayashi, Hiramoto, Koga, Morimoto, and Zaima families, as well as the Azeka and Matsuda farms, were also in the area.[90]

Another rice mill of the Hanalei region in the early 1900s was the Hiramoto Rice Mill (formerly Hee Fat Rice Mill), located at Waipā. Chinese rice farmer Hee Fat was among the largest of Kaua'i's rice farmers, cultivating about six hundred acres of rice in Hanalei and Kapa'a.[91] At the far end of the coastal plain in the ahupua'a of Waikoko was the Chock Chin Rice Mill.

Another rice era structure located along 'Ōhiki Road was a Japanese Hongwanji used by Japanese Buddhists of the rice farming community. Altar shrines from the Hongwanji were later relocated to a newly built Hongwanji in Kapa'a.[92]

On the lower western slopes of Hanalei Valley is the Hanalei Chinese Cemetery, also known as Ah Goong San (Grandfathers' Mountain) and often referred to as the Community Cemetery.[93] The Chinese Cemetery covers a piece of land about 525 feet north to south, and about 200 feet from east to west, with at least seventy-five tombstones.

A semi-circular cement altar at the cemetery serves as a "mass grave monument for single Chinese men,"[94] and was erected in 1906 by the Chinese fraternal society known as Yee Hop Tong. After ten years of burial at the Chinese Cemetery, according to tradition, "the body is exhumed and the bones are carefully collected, cleaned, arranged in certain order, and reburied in a large urn in the reserved section."[95]

Chinese Society members met at the cemetery the day before Ching Ming Day (Decoration Day) every April to clean up the gravesites and maintain the general area. On Ching Ming Day, food was placed at the center of the altar for the departed souls.

Typical offerings included "five bowls of rice, five cups of whiskey, a platter of cooked chicken (male), cooked pork, cooked bean curd, cooked tofu, a platter of Chinese pastries, five oranges and five tangerines and a Chinese roast pig."[96] Firecrackers were set off, and incense was burned as well as candle punks. After the ceremony everyone went to the Yee Hing where the food items were consumed.

Gravesites in the Chinese Cemetery date to at least the 1930s. The site is shown in an 1848 Land Court Awards map created before significant Chinese immigration to Hawai'i took place, and thus was likely used by Hawaiians previously.

Most of the tombstones at the Chinese Cemetery are inscribed with Chinese characters. Past advisors and caretakers of the Chinese Cemetery included Mr. Chong Hing, Mr. Wong Wo Tuck, Mr. Say Dock, Mr. Sam Kent Ho, Mr. Larry Ching, Mr. Ma Leong, and Mr. Harry Ho.[97]

Further up the river road (now 'Ōhiki Road) past the Chinese Cemetery was the home of a Spanish family named Pisante. In this general area upriver from Hanalei Bridge on both sides of the river, some rice era buildings are still standing, including the Mal Quick House (1925); the Wong House (on a 1910 rice mill site); the Haraguchi House (1930s); the Mike Fitzgerald House (1925); and the Jed Mamaril House (1930s).[98]

Back on the Government Road (Route 560) and proceeding toward Hanalei town there were a series of rice farms and rice era stores. About a quarter mile from Hanalei Bridge on the mountain side of the road was Chong Hing Store, a general merchandise and grocery store owned by the grandfather of Kaua'i County Council member Kaipo Asing.

Past Chong Hing were the rice farms of the Ueda, Takenaka, Liu, and Miiki families, and further in toward the mountains was the Lum farm.[99] Makai of the main road between Chong Hing and the Trader Building[100] was the Japanese-owned Hamamura Store.[101]

Hanalei Museum, 1967. **Bishop Museum**

The land on the other side of the Government Road is enclosed within the great bend in the Hanalei River. In ancient times this land was called Pāʻele, which means "Black" or "Dark."[102] During the rice era this area between the Hanalei Bridge and the Hanalei river mouth was the site of the Shing Kon Sung Rice Plantation (formerly Soy Sung Wai). Today on this land is the Hanalei Gardens Farm and Bison Ranch.[103]

On the seaward side of the road at the eastern end of Hanalei town was the Trader Building (the site of Ching Ma Leong—formerly Ah Hoy—Store), and Mrs. Shiraishi's Barber Shop. Just west of the barber shop was I. Nakatsuka General Store,[104] which operated from about 1900 until the 1950s. The Nakatsuka family lived behind the store, which later became part of the Tahiti Nui building (see *Chapter 5*).

Near the eastern end of Hanalei town lived the Shak, Tasaka, and Hoe families as well as the renowned Hawaiian composer and singer Alfred ʻAlohikea. On the mountain side of the road was the home of the Ho Pak Yet family. During the second half of the 1900s this was the residence of Harry Ho, a school teacher and principal on Kaua'i's north shore at Hanalei School and Hā'ena School.[105]

Harry Ho was a respected local historian, and in the 1960s the Ho residence was known as the Hanalei Museum and Snack Shop. Harry Ho passed away in 1989 at the age of 83.[106] The museum was destroyed by Hurricane 'Iniki in 1992.[107]

The Ching Youngs

One of the most prominent and successful early rice farming families living in the Hanalei region was the Ching Young family. Descendants of the original Ching Youngs continue to play influential roles in the Hanalei community today.

Around 1900, Ching Yuk Hom (Ching Young) came to Hawai'i from China's Chung San District. Ching Young initially settled in Kapa'a on Kaua'i's east side, where he ran a chop suey house and mercantile store called Kwong Chong Kee with his brother and his business partners, the Tam family.[108]

Ching Young and one of his brothers later leased a piece of land in Hanalei from the Wilcox family[109] and opened a rice mill and store. The store building was constructed in 1906 and "may have been operated by a Mr. Chu (or Chew) before the Ching family took over in 1907."[110]

Ching Young married Dang Ha Ching, who was born in Hanapēpē, Kaua'i. Their marriage had been arranged by a traditional Chinese matchmaker.[111] The newlyweds lived in Kapa'a where they gave birth to Florence and Ellen, the first two of their eight children.[112]

The Ching Young family moved to Hanalei in 1911 to work full time at Ching Young Store and Ching Young Rice Mill. In 1914 the Ching Youngs became the sole owners of the enterprise when they bought out co-owner Tam Kee of Kapa'a. Supplies such as dry goods and denim that were needed to stock the Ching Young Store were brought by the steamships that came to Hanalei to transport the valley's rice.[113]

While living in Hanalei, Mr. and Mrs. Ching Young gave birth to six more children: Dora, Laura, Lawrence, Douglas, Calvin, and Janet. The Great Depression of 1929 caused financial hardship for the Ching Youngs, and in the early 1930s Mr. Ching Young was debilitated by a major stroke. He passed away in October of 1933 when his youngest child was just four years of age.

After the death of Mr. Ching Young, Mrs. Ching Young continued to run the store and rice mill and raise her eight children. A deeply religious person, Mrs. Ching Young maintained a Taoist altar in her home and faithfully practiced her Chinese traditions.

In the 1930s the decline in Hawaiʻi's rice market brought continued hardships for the store and rice mill. When supplies to the Islands were cut off in 1936 by a West Coast shipping strike, however, five thousand bags of rice helped supply the entire island chain.

The Ching Young Rice Mill closed in the mid-1940s, but the store remained in business. After the 1941 bombing of Pearl Harbor, the demand for products helped ensure the survival of the Ching Young Store, which once again supplied rice to the Hawaiian Islands.

Ching Young Store was built in 1906 and was later the location of the Hanalei Post Office. The building remains in use today, housing various art and gift shops. **Hawaiʻi State Archives**

Mrs. Ching retired in 1950 but remained active in the Kauaʻi community. Her eldest son, Lawrence L. T. "Larry" Ching and his wife, Jeanie, took over the family business, which prospered throughout the 1950s and 1960s when sugarcane regained status as a major cash crop. A post office was opened at the Ching Young Store in the 1950s.

Mrs. Ching passed away in 1967 at the age of eighty. Larry Ching continued the operation of the store as tourism became an integral part of Kauaʻi's economy. In the next decade, Larry began to develop the Ching Young Village Shopping Center. In 1975 a new Hanalei Post Office was built on the land next to Ching Young Store, which was owned by Mrs. Clorinda Nakashima.

The Ching Young Store was sold to the locally owned Big Save family of markets, and the Chings continued to develop the Center's many shops and businesses. Larry Ching passed away on September 7, 1997.[114]

Today the Ching Young Center continues to be run by the Ching family. The original Ching Young Store building is located on the eastern side of the expanded Ching Young Village Shopping Center. The old store building is now occupied by two art and gift stores called "Evolve Love" and "On the Road to Hanalei." The Kodama Barber Shop was located just west of Ching Young Store in the area between the current Hanalei Post Office and Big Save Market.

A Chinese Christian (Congregational) church was located across the road from Ching Young Store, in the area where the Hanalei Center (Wailele Building) is now located. Frank Kurihara referred to the Chinese church building as "Mr. Low's Chinese School and Temple."[115] Reverend Tsui Hin Wong was the church minister in 1930.[116] Next to the church was a parsonage, which later became the office of Ironwood Realty before the building was destroyed by Hurricane ʻIniki in 1992.[117]

The Say Dock House is located just west of where the Chinese church and parsonage were located, and is today one of the few remaining rice farmer homes still standing in the Islands. A concrete threshing floor, though quite aged and broken, still remains in front of the Say Dock House. Two other rice farmer homes in Hanalei had concrete threshing floors, but neither remains standing.

Located near the Say Dock House was one of Hanalei's earliest rice mills, the See Tai Wai Rice Mill. See Tai Wai was an old-style

Kenichi Tasaka

Kenichi Tasaka was born in 1896, the second of eight children of Chinjiro and Kiyo Tasaka. Chinjiro worked at Kīlauea Sugar Plantation before leasing land near Puʻupōā Marsh (Kamoʻomaikaʻi Fishpond), where he farmed rice for nearly two decades.

As a child Kenichi helped his father on the rice farm, worked for the Birkmyres, Deverills, and Sanborns, painted cars in Honolulu, worked as a mechanic for the Kīlauea Sugar Plantation, painted houses, and worked for the County of Kauaʻi Water Works Division.[118]

In 1927 Kenichi married Asayo Kodama and they would have four children. Around 1940, the Tasakas built a home next to Waiʻoli Park and began farming rice nearby. Kenichi eventually took over his father's rice farm at Waiʻoli, and then later farmed taro, as did his brother Bobby Tasaka. During World War II the two front rooms of Kenichi and Asayo Tasaka's home were used as a store and saimin stand.[119]

"Kenichi Tasaka became a well-known grass slipper maker in his later years. He made them from rushes growing in the swamps. He lived to a ripe old age of one hundred."

—Frank Kurihara[120]

mill that used large stone weights to lift a pestle-shaped stone that was dropped into a stone bowl.[121]

The T. S. See Wo Store was located just west of the Say Dock House and across the road, at the current site of the Church of Latter Day Saints.[122] Also on the makai side of the main road in this area were Katayama Store and Takenaka Auto Repair [Takahashi's Garage and Repair Shop]. West of the auto repair shop was Nagaoaka Restaurant and Bakery, considered by some to be "the best eatery in town."[123] Just past the restaurant was a gas station.

The 1914 *Polk-Husted Directory* listed other rice plantations and stores in the Hanalei region, including Ah San, Ah Ching, Chock Lung, Chong Sing, Chong Wai, Hop Sing, Man Sing Co., Sing Fat Wai Co., Sing Yick Co., Soy Sung Wai Co., Tai Kan, Tai Sing Wai, and Sing Wai Co.[124]

Churches

Located at Mālolo Road and Route 560 was the Hanalei Shingon, a Japanese Shingon temple that began operating as early as 1903. Next to the Shingon was a Japanese language school[125] built in 1934. The Shingon temple became a popular gathering place that served as the site for various local functions and celebrations, including weddings and funerals as well as the Obon Dori celebration held each July as part of a Japanese Buddhist holiday honoring the departed spirits of ancestors.[126]

The north shore community looked forward to the traditional Bon Dance, which included a carnival with food and games. Eventually the event became so popular it had to be held across the street at a larger site in Waiʻoli Park.[127]

After the Japanese attack on Pearl Harbor on December 7, 1941, things changed quickly. Many of the most influential Japanese and Japanese Americans,[128] including community leaders, ministers, Buddhist priests, and principals of Japanese schools, were detained and sent to internment camps.[129]

The forced internment of the Japanese teachers and ministers of the Hanalei Shingon brought an end to the use of the temple for religious purposes, though it would later be moved across the main road to a site behind the Lily Pond House, where it was used as a clubhouse for the community's young Japanese men.[130]

Despite the harsh and often racist treatment Japanese residents received after the Pearl Harbor attack, many Japanese throughout the Hawaiian Islands volunteered for the war effort.[131] They formed the 100th Infantry Battalion and 442nd Infantry Regimental Combat Team,[132] which together became the most decorated units in U.S. history, earning more than eighteen thousand total awards for their valorous fighting in Italy, Germany, and France.[133]

In 1955 St. Williams Catholic Church was built on the original site of the Shingon temple and language school.[134] The former Japanese language school building was moved to a lot on the shoreline of Hanalei Bay where the former Sloggett Beach House once stood.[135]

The church bell now suspended between two poles in front of St. Williams is the bell from the former Catholic chapel that was built near the Hanalei river mouth in 1864 (see *Chapter 3*).

Chock Chin

Chock Chin was a prominent Chinese rice farmer and store owner in Hanalei. The father of twelve children from three different wives, Chock Chin built a home on leased land on the mountain side of the Government Road (Route 560) near the current site of Waiʻoli Park.[136]

Across the street from his home he established the Chock Chin Store in 1901.[137] The site included a bakery, restaurant, butcher shop, tailor, blacksmith, and saloon, as well as a general store.

The entire family worked at the business; Mr. Chock Chin managed the store and was the baker; his wife, Chun Shee, was the cook; the children worked the register and delivered bills; and one of the sons drove a "freight wagon pulled by two white mules."[138]

Chock Chin's bakery sold bread with guava jelly for ten cents a loaf, and it was a favorite lunch item of local children who walked to the store from nearby Hanalei School. Chock Chin also raised "papayas, mango, avocado and loquat, mulberry, bananas, cows, chickens and pigs...sweet potato, corn, sugarcane and string beans and also a grove of bamboo."[139] He also engaged in various other entrepreneurial activities, including selling small dishes of ice cream at the Kīlauea ballpark.

The Chock Chin Store was later changed to C. Akeoni, Lau Store and then Hanalei Store in 1931 after Chock Chin died and Mrs. Chock Chin sold the store to Charles Lau, a rice and taro farmer. The Hanalei Store remained open as a restaurant, meat market, and general store until 1941.[140]

Still remaining from Chock Chin's era is the lotus pond (now called The Lily Pond) he dug alongside the main road in Hanalei town. A freshwater spring fed the pond, which Chock Chin stocked with edible lotus roots and fish.[141] The lotus plants failed to grow, and later Mrs. Chock Chin planted water lilies in the pond.

The Tasakas would replant lilies and stock the pond with carp. Unfortunately the fish were washed away by the 1946 tsunami.[142]

The Lily Pond House is a small, two-story structure that was originally located on the shoreline of Hanalei Bay,[143] where it was used as a caretaker's quarters for the manager of Kauaʻi Electric.[144] The house was later moved on coconut palm rollers to its current site next to Waiʻoli Park.[145]

The Lily Pond House was built in 1933 near the shoreline of Hanalei Bay. It was later moved on coconut palm rollers to its current site near Wai'oli Park. Private residence—please do not trespass. **Bob Waid**

The Hanalei Post Office

The Hanalei Post Office was described as a "peripatetic institution, its changing location primarily determined by who ran the post office."[146] Serving as postmaster from 1846 to 1856 was Captain John Kellett, who was also Hanalei's pilot of the port and customs collector. Succeeding Kellett as postmaster was Wai'oli missionary Abner Wilcox, who served at the post until 1863.[147]

In the late 1800s a succession of Princeville Plantation managers served as postmasters.[148] The Hanalei Post Office was located along the old switchback road down into Hanalei Valley. Eventually it was moved down the hill to the small, busy factory village that was erected on the east bank of the Hanalei River, near the Hanalei Sugar Mill.[149]

Mail came to Hanalei by schooner from Honolulu, and irregular weekly steamer service and overland mail were also provided. From the Hanalei Post Office, carriers brought mail to Lumaha'i, Wainiha,

The old Hanalei Post Office boxes (c. 1950) may still be seen today on the ocean side of Kūhiō Highway across from Wai'oli Park. **Hawai'i State Archives**

Hāʻena, and Kalalau. The Kalalau carrier "wrapped mail in banana leaves to keep it from getting soaked."[150]

Around the turn of the century, the Hanalei Post Office was run by Sarah Deverill, who moved the office to her home, which was also the Hanalei Hotel. In 1915 the Hanalei Post Office was located on the land of Sheriff James K. Lota[151] on Weke Road, and in the 1920s the post office was located on the mountain side (mauka) of the Government Road at Mahi Mahi Road.

Sometime around World War II, when the postmistress was Julia Lota (Sheriff James Lota's sister, who later became Julia Rodrigues), the post office was moved to a location near the current Aloha School, on the seaward side of the Government Road (Route 560),[152] where the old post office boxes may still be seen today.

In the 1950s the Hanalei Post Office was relocated to Ching Young Store. In 1975 the current Hanalei Post Office was built next to the Ching Young Village Shopping Center on the land of postmistress Clorinda Nakashima.

Hanalei School

Hanalei School, which originated as part of the missionary station founded at Waiʻoli in 1834 to prepare native children to become teachers in Kauaʻi's common schools (see *Chapter 2*), sits on the western end of town. Nearby is the mission complex, comprised of the 1841 Waiʻoli Church, the 1912 Waiʻoli Huiʻia Church, and the old Waiʻoli Mission House (see *Chapter 2*).

Hawaiians were initially taught in their native language with the goal of helping Hawaiians to read a translated version of the Bible.[153] The school also offered vocational training and training for teachers who taught on Kauaʻi and Niʻihau.[154]

In 1862 Hanalei's first English school was established by Louise Johnson with financial support provided by the Hawaiian government. In 1881 the Hanalei English School formally became a government school (public school).

By the turn of the century, enrollment had increased to forty-eight boys and forty-eight girls. Two teachers, Florence and Lena Deverill, educated the children.[155] A new school building was constructed by the Territory of Hawaiʻi in 1926 to accommodate the growing need, and the Old Hanalei School building was moved to the center of Hanalei town near the Aku Road intersection with Route 560. The restored schoolhouse building is now home to several businesses, including the Hanalei Surf Company, Gourmet Restaurant, and some small art and clothing shops. A new Hanalei School was built very near its former location.

Enrollment at Hanalei School in the 1900s ranged between about 50 and 120 students. Today enrollment is about 300 students.[156]

Black Pot Beach Park and the Hukilau

Black Pot Beach Park is located between Hanalei Pier and the Hanalei river mouth. The name of the park hearkens to the big black pot that was used to boil the day's catch of fish, which was shared among everyone. The tradition of the hukilau involved a group of people working together to entrap fish using a seine net.[157]

During the mid-1900s the tradition of the hukilau was still commonly practiced in Hanalei Bay. A kilo, or spotter, stood atop a high spot overlooking the bay waters and used hand signals to tell the konohiki, or local leader, where the school of fish was located. Fishermen in the water then surrounded the school of fish with a net, and pulled the catch toward shore. The co-operative effort of spotting, netting, and gathering the fish brought the community together, and they all shared in the catch.

One konohiki was Alfred ʻAlohikea, the Hawaiian composer of "Hanohano Hanalei"[158] and many other popular local songs.

Lumahaʻi Hula[159]
Grand is Hanalei in the pouring rain,
Slippery is the limu of Manuʻakepa.
Swim in the waters of Lumahaʻi,
The misty-faced lehua of Luluʻupali.
Heated is Hāʻena in the sea spray,
What does Lohiʻau, the lover do?
The story is told,
Slippery is the limu of Manuʻakepa.[160]
> —From a chant to Queen Kapiʻolani entitled "Hanohano Hanalei."
> Alfred ʻAlohikea wrote the melody.[161]

Two frequently caught species during the hukilau were akule (bigeye scad) and ʻopelu (mackerel scad). "In akule, or halalu,[162] or 'opelu season," recalled Frank Kurihara, "the fish came into the bays by the hordes to spawn."[163]

Many Hawaiian fishermen observed certain rituals and practices, offering banana and kava root to fish gods, and keeping stone fish

This 1890 Hanalei School photo was taken in front of the old school building. A new school building was constructed in 1926 and was later moved to the center of Hanalei town for commercial use. **Deverill, Bishop Museum**

Hanalei School May Day celebration. **Kauaʻi Museum**

Hukilau. **Hawai'i State Archives**

god images, known as kū'ula, which were used to attract a good catch. A Japanese fishing temple was located along the riverbank below the "pine tree road" that led up to the Birkmyre home, and another was located on the opposite side of the Hanalei River just up from the former site of the Catholic Church. Local fishermen often visited the shrines and held annual celebrations attended by friends and family.[164]

The renowned host at Black Pot Park in the 1950s and 1960s was local fisherman Kalani Tai Hook.[165] Today his daughter, Catherine Ham Young, along with the whole Ham Young 'ohana, are prominent and beloved local residents of the Hanalei region, and gracious hosts at the annual Tai Hook Regatta outrigger canoe paddling race held

"During summer months, to this day, the kilo [spotter] watches the sea from a height, and catching sight of ripples and shadows betokening a school of fish, hastens word to waiting fishermen on the beach who row out beyond the speeding fish and drop their long net around them, then, often up to their necks in the sea, and strung out along both sides of the net back to the shore, all stand ready for the hukilau, the hauling in of loaded net, sparkling with the silver flash of leaping fish."

—Ethel Damon, 1950.[166] **Hawai'i State Archives**

in her father's honor. She is also known to go to great lengths to welcome and feed the crew of the *Hōkūle'a* voyaging canoe when they sail into Hanalei Bay.

Beach Houses

As the Hanalei region moved into the twentieth century, prominent individuals and families—including the Sanborn, Fayé, and Wilcox families—constructed second homes along Weke Road on the shoreline of Hanalei Bay. Several of these beach homes still stand today as reminders of Hanalei's storied past. Some of these historic structures are detailed below, beginning at the eastern end of Weke Road.

Albert Spencer Wilcox, son of pioneering missionaries Abner and Lucy Wilcox, purchased an interest in the Princeville Plantation in 1892. In 1899, when he secured complete ownership of the land, he built the main house of his estate on Hanalei Bay. Albert lived in the house with his wife, Emma Kauikeōlani Napoleon Mahelona, widow of Samuel Mahelona.

Albert and Emma named their Hanalei home after Emma's namesake, Kauikeōlani, translated as "beautiful vision in the morning mist,"[167] and "place in the skies [of] heaven."[168] It originally had three bedrooms and a twelve-foot-wide wrap-around veranda.[169] The outside of the historic beach home was covered with sand, a technique used at the time to provide termite protection.

Kauikeōlani Estate is currently owned by Patsy Wilcox Sheehan [Alice Patricia Kuaihelani Wilcox Sheehan], the great-great-granddaughter of Abner and Lucy Wilcox. Today the central parlor portion of Kauikeōlani remains somewhat of a living museum.

Historic Kanoa Pond is located on the western side of Hanalei River near the river mouth, on the property of the Albert Spencer Wilcox House. The pond once covered ten acres, and in the mid-1800s was owned by agricultural entrepreneur Charles Titcomb. Titcomb sold it to Princeville Plantation owner R. C. Wyllie in 1863.[170]

Helen Sanborn Davis, who grew up in Hanalei in the early 1900s, recalled that the pond "was stocked with fish and Samoan crabs for the dining table."[171] Kanoa Pond was also a lily pond where locals caught bass and blue gill.

Kamoʻomaikaʻi Fishpond, also known as Puʻupōā Marsh, was located on the east side of the Hanalei River near the river mouth, near where the Princeville Hotel is now located. The ancient fishpond was placed on the National and State Registers of Historic Places in 1982.

The Sanborn Beach House was erected in 1910 on the shoreline of Hanalei Bay. Built in the plantation style, the Sanborn home features a hip roof and wide window frames, single-wall, board-and-batten architecture, and trim balustrade posts. Thatched homes of native Hawaiians had been located along Hanalei Bay for many centuries before Western contact, but the Sanborn House was the first shoreline home built using Western-style materials; thus it is often referred to as Hanalei's first "beach house." Numerous other Western-style homes were built along Hanalei Bay in the early 1900s, but most were later damaged by tsunamis, hurricanes, and salt air. The Sanborn Beach House remains one of the last of the old beach homes of Hanalei still standing.

While the Sanborns lived primarily at the Princeville Ranch House, center of operations for the large Princeville cattle ranch, they kept their property on the beach. When a tsunami struck Kaua'i's north shore in 1957, it moved the ocean home ten feet off its foundation.[172] Walter and Lena's daughter Helen (later Helen Sanborn Davis Hibbard) credited an avocado tree for halting the movement of the house, which suffered only minor structural damage and was simply re-posted in its new location.[173]

In 1970 Jack Sanborn, son of Walter Sanborn, died, and his sons Pete, Alan, and Bill each received one acre of property. At this time a wing of the house (a master bedroom) on the western side off the kitchen was removed and relocated across Weke Road for use as a two-bedroom house. This small structure would become known as the Reed House,[174] and would be used as part of the Sanborn Poi Mill. The poi mill operated until the mid 1950s[175] when it was taken over by new owners who eventually abandoned their efforts.[176]

> The Hanalei District of Kauai is not going to be the same without Walter Foss Sanborn. His tall, active figure, still erect in his late seventies, his shock of unruly hair, now snowy, his twinkling eyes and an assumption of gruffness that they belied, had been familiar to the district since he came there some 55 years ago to manage the late Albert S. Wilcox's plantation. Now in retirement, he made his home in a rambling shoreside dwelling, surrounded by broad, carefully tended lawns and gardens, within reach of the village social center. Outspoken always, Walter Sanborn sometimes antagonized associates who could not believe that anyone could pull so many facts out of his mind without grievous error. Yet that was what he did, and differences of opinion were swept away before an avalanche of

facts. Behind his gruff exterior was a soft heart, as every child knew instinctively. He was a sucker for kids.

—*Honolulu Advertiser* editorial, 1950[177]

Just west of the Sanborn House is the Fayé Beach House, built in 1915 by Hans Peter Fayé, nephew of sugar planter Valdemar "Kanuka" Knudsen. The two-story, wood-framed structure was built by Fayé as a vacation home. The structure was damaged by the 1957 tsunami and required repairs.

Fayé was born in Norway and moved to Hawai'i in 1880. He later developed sugar plantations on western Kaua'i, harvesting his first crop in 1886 with the help of Chinese laborers provided by Leong Pah On, who was known as Kaua'i's "Rice King."[178]

In 1893 H. P. Fayé married Margaret Lindsey at Moloa'a, and they would have eight children. Fayé's Mana Sugar Company merged with Kekaha Sugar Company in 1898, and Fayé managed the operation for the next three decades. H. P. Fayé's son Lindsay later managed Kekaha Sugar Company. Another son, Alan Fayé, managed the Waimea Sugar Company, a plantation that was run by the Fayé family. Remnants of the sugar mill can be seen today in Waimea town.

Just up from the Fayé Beach House on the opposite side of Weke Road is the former Princeville Ranch Manager's House. The home was built under the direction of Fred Conant, who became manager of the Princeville Plantation in 1927. Later the home became the residence of Larry and Jeanie Ching. The home is a private residence—please do not go on the property.

In 1914 Charles, Elsie, and Mabel Wilcox and their parents, Samuel and Emma Wilcox, along with Ethel Damon, bought five adjoining beachfront lots in Hanalei at an auction. Mabel Wilcox and her brother then planned the house named Mahamoku, or "island of peace,"[179] and commissioned Sam Itchioka, a Japanese carpenter, to build their dream home. During construction, Samuel Wilcox and three of his children, Charles, Elsie, and Mabel, frequently visited the site and occasionally suggested changes to the house plans.

Mahamoku is a one-and-a-half-story, L-shaped, wood-framed house with vertical redwood boards in double-wall construction and a high-pitched gable roof.[180] The home's interior is described as

Mahamoku, "Island of peace," was built on the Hanalei Bay shoreline in 1914 by Mabel and Charles Wilcox. Private residence—please do not go on property. **Kauaʻi Museum**

"barn-like" with "darkness contributing to the atmosphere of rest and comfort at the edge of the ocean and with bright, breathtaking scenic views of Hanalei on all sides."[181]

Cantilevered loft balconies extend from each end of the home and are covered by overhanging eaves. A series of windows in the central living area allows tradewind breezes to cool the house. Itchioka added a three-window dormer on the ocean side of Mahamoku, which was strongly disapproved of by Mabel Wilcox, though it was left in place.

Chapter 5

Hanalei Today:
Art and Nature
1950–2006

Hurricanes and Tsunamis

Life on a tropical island in the middle of the Pacific Ocean includes the possibility of various natural disasters—landslides, volcanic eruptions, earthquakes, floods. Historically, the most destructive events in the Hawaiian Islands have been hurricanes and tsunamis, both of which have unleashed their power primarily on Kaua'i.

In recent history, the two hurricanes that devastated the northernmost island were Hurricane 'Iwa and Hurricane 'Iniki. 'Iwa, which is also the Hawaiian name of the great frigatebird, struck Kaua'i on November 3, 1982, bringing gusts of wind with speeds of more than one hundred miles per hour and causing damage totaling more than $230 million, including many structures in the Hanalei region. 'Iniki, which means "sharp and piercing, as wind or pangs of love,"[1] made a direct hit on Kaua'i on September 11, 1992. The hurricane began brewing southeast of the island, slowly moving north-northwest at about twenty miles per hour. Winds within the storm, however, had grown to more than one hundred miles per hour before the hurricane's path turned due north and it made a direct hit on Kaua'i.

For well over an hour Kaua'i's residents endured ferocious winds. Roofs detached from their houses, breaking up in the vortex of wind; debris flying at rapid speeds smashed windows and crashed violently into buildings. Homes were blown off their foundations.

Then the wind stopped. People ventured outside to glimpse the destruction. The air was still, the sky cloudy along the horizon but pure blue overhead. Kaua'i was in the eye of the hurricane.

Within minutes the other side of the eye struck, with winds blowing in the opposite direction, this time all at once in a rush of wind. As 'Iniki proceeded over the island of Kaua'i, the Navy's Mākaha Ridge radar station clocked the wind at 227 miles per hour, the last measurement taken before the wind gauging equipment was blown off the mountain.

Hurricane 'Iniki caused more than $3 billion in property damage on Kaua'i. 90% of the 8,200 hotel, condo, and bed and breakfast rooms on Kaua'i were shut down by 'Iniki; 14,000 homes and apartments were damaged, 1,421 completely destroyed. The community of Princeville sustained the most damage, with 279 homes destroyed. The Princeville Hotel required $30 million worth of repairs.

Hurricane 'Iniki also caused significant damage to historical sites such as Hanalei Pier, the Haraguchi Rice Mill, and Wai'oli

Rescue ship arrives after tsunami. **Kaua'i Museum**

Home damaged by the 1946 tsunami. **Kaua'i Museum**

Hui'ia Church, which it lifted off its foundations, damaging the precious stained glass windows. All of these sites were later rebuilt or restored.

The word tsunami derives from the Japanese tsu, meaning "harbor," and nami, which means "wave." Tsunamis are caused by earthquakes, landslides, and volcanic eruptions,[2] and have killed more people in Hawai'i than all other natural disasters combined. Since 1837 there have been at least thirteen significant tsunami events affecting the Hawaiian Islands, killing more than 290 people.

The two tsunamis that had the most effect on the Hanalei region occurred in 1946 and 1957. The 1946 tsunami struck on April 1 and killed seventeen people on Kaua'i. It was caused by an earthquake in the Aleutian Islands, an island group 2,400 miles north of the Hawaiian Islands.[3] The first of the waves hit the Hawaiian Islands at six thirty AM[4]

The tsunami altered the course of the Waipā Stream, caused the collapse of the east end of the Waikoko Bridge, and washed away the carp stocked in the Lily Pond in Hanalei town.[5]

On March 9, 1957, another earthquake in the Aleutian Islands generated a tsunami that destroyed more than seventy-five homes along Kaua'i's north shore, including twenty-five of the twenty-nine homes in Hā'ena, and Hā'ena School. The 1957 tsunami also damaged the Hanalei Bridge, requiring the addition of reinforcements that were added in 1959.

Along the beachfront, the tsunami washed the Sanborn home ten feet off its foundation, amazingly causing only minor structural damage.[6] It did damage the Fayé Beach House, however, and knocked out the old Kalihiwai Bridge.

The Old Made New

Princeville

In July of 1968 Harry Trueblood, of Eagle County Development Corporation, bought all but about fifty acres of the Princeville Ranch from a subsidiary of American Factors Ltd (Amfac).[7] The sale included eleven thousand acres of Princeville land and four agricultural parcels of about seven thousand acres each as well as four thousand acres of forest reserve conservation land.[8] Princeville Ranch had just seven employees and two resident workers at the time.

The new owners received approval from the Land Use Commission for urban districting on 995 acres one year later. They dedicated 532 acres to housing and hotel development, leaving the remaining land for a twenty-seven-hole golf course and open space.

As development of the Princeville resort area continued, roads were built and underground utilities installed. In 1971, the Makai Golf Course opened with three nine-hole courses. The Princeville Center opened in 1977, offering twenty-seven thousand square feet of space for rent.

Princeville Hotel Corporation was formed in 1982 with the intent of constructing a major luxury hotel on the east side of Hanalei Bay, at Puʻupōā. In September of 1985 the Sheraton Princeville Hotel opened with three hundred rooms. Development of another golf course, to be named the Prince Golf Course, began a year later on the upper eastern side of Princeville, above the main resort area.

The resort changed hands in 1987, when the Qintex Group of Queensland, Australia, purchased the resort from Princeville Corporation. From 1989 to 1991 an extensive refurbishment took place; a 60,000 square-foot Prince Clubhouse was constructed adjacent to the Prince Golf Course and the hotel was renamed the Sheraton Mirage Princeville. The five-star standard reopened on May 15, 1991.

In June of 1990 the Princeville Corporation was acquired out of bankruptcy by the Japanese real estate development and sales company Suntory Ltd. Suntory became the majority shareholder

(51%), while two other Japanese companies, the banking company Nippon Shinpan & Co. Ltd. and the diversified trading company Mitsui & Co. Ltd., became equal shareholders as minority partners.

They repurchased the resort, and the hotel was officially named "Princeville Hotel." The corporation also continued to operate the Prince and Makai golf courses as well as the Princeville Center and the Princeville Health Club and Spa.

Since the mid-1980s the Princeville Hotel has been managed by Starwood Hotels and Resorts.[9] The hotel was closed for repairs after being severely damaged by Hurricane 'Iniki on September 11, 1992, and reopened over a year later after $30 million of reconstruction work.[10] The hotel's 250-person staff returned to work on October 15, 1993. In May of 1995 the Princeville Hotel was designated "Hotel of the Year" by ITT Sheraton.[11]

Today the community of Princeville is Kaua'i's largest planned resort community, encompassing nine thousand acres. It includes thousands of condominiums, hundreds of homes, a shopping center, the 252-room Princeville Hotel, and the luxurious Princeville Spa, as well as two expansive golf courses rated among the top in the nation.

In 2005 the 9000-acre resort was sold for an undisclosed amount to a Honolulu investment consortium known as Hawai'i Land Development Corporation (now Princeville Associates LLC, a newly formed venture company owned by Jeffrey R. Stone) in partnership with Morgan Stanley Real Estate Funds.[12] In September of 2008, at a cost of more than $60 million, a renovation of the Princeville Hotel began to re-brand the hotel as the St. Regis Resort, Princeville.

The future of the Princeville area remains in flux, with plans in the works for new employee housing, renovations to the Princeville Shopping Center, and new name-brand hotels. Starwood Hotels & Resorts continues to run the Princeville Hotel while also constructing timeshare villas in Princeville for Starwood Vacation Ownership.

Despite the rapid growth of the Princeville area in recent decades, the region still retains a sense of its pristine beauty, with rolling hills that bridge the valleys of Hanalei and Kalihiwai and form a coastal plateau with expansive ocean and mountain views.

Haraguchi Rice Mill

The Haraguchi Rice Mill was the last mill to operate in the Hanalei region, and is now the only remaining rice mill still standing in the state of Hawai'i.[13] The mill was originally constructed of wood and corrugated sheet iron. After Hurricane 'Iwa damaged the structure in 1982, the mill underwent an extensive restoration. Fortunately, just days before the hurricane hit, architectural drawings of the mill were completed by a team of workers with the American Engineering Record, including layout details and exact measurements critical to the authentic mill restoration process.

Concrete cinder blocks were installed for the rice mill's seventy-nine-foot by forty-foot foundation, and an Oregon mill retooled their machinery to provide the unsanded, original-size lumber.[14] The mill's machinery was also refurbished, turning the mill into a historic museum that is now available for educational tours.

In 1992 Hurricane 'Iniki dealt a blow to the Haraguchi Rice Mill.[15] Boone Morrison, an architect and photographer from Hawai'i Island, referred to the original drawings of the rice mill to create a professional blueprint.

Leading the restoration project were Rodney Haraguchi, great grandson of Tomijiro and Ine Haraguchi, the farm's initial founders (see *Chapter 4*), and his wife, Karol. During this second restoration, they refurbished the original Fairbanks-Morse single-cylinder diesel engine.

Rodney and Karol continue the family farming tradition, cultivating about fifty acres of taro with the help of their extended family.

In April 2004, volunteers led by Tomijiro and Rodney's father, William, erected an eighteen-foot-tall yagura (rice bird sentry tower) near the Haraguchi Rice Mill.[16] These sentry towers were once common on local rice fields, and children were often given the job of pulling on a cord attached to tin cans to scare the rice birds away from the fields. The project was an exercise in understanding the skills of old, as the workers used only hand tools and joinery techniques to construct the tower.

Restoring Wai'oli Mission

The Wai'oli Mission area is a historical marker that signifies the early missionary era and the change that would ensue. In 1976 extensive repairs to the historic Wai'oli Mission House were completed and a celebration of the event included a program of Hawaiian hymns and songs.

The Wai'oli Mission has been serving the local congregation continuously since 1834: originally at a meetinghouse structure (no longer standing); from 1841 to 1912 at the first Wai'oli Church (now Mission Hall); and from 1912 to the present day at Wai'oli Hui'ia Church. **Bob Waid**

Three years later, in the summer of 1979, an archaeological excavation of the floor of Wai'oli Mission Hall (the former Wai'oli Church) took place. The church had been constructed in 1841 on the site of a pole-and-thatch meetinghouse built earlier by Hawaiians.[17] Analyses revealed that the area had been used for adze and fishhook construction, and artifacts that were shaped and finished with prehistoric tools as late as 1832.

Also found during the excavation of the church floor were basalt sinkers, woodwork shaped by stone adze, and five separate hearths around which food preparation and consumption was centered.[18] After the archaeological work was completed, repairs of Wai'oli Mission Hall were undertaken.

A restoration of the Wai'oli Mission belfry took place between 1986 and 1987 and included excavating and re-setting the foundation stones, as well as replacing the original 'ōhi'a lehua beams and structural members that had been used to construct the bell tower in

1841.[19] Wood for the restoration came from 'ōhi'a lehua trees that had been knocked down in Kōke'e State Park by Hurricane 'Iwa in 1982. When 'Iniki[20] hit in 1992 the Wai'oli Hui'ia Church was lifted off its foundation, severely damaging the building's structure and the church's precious stained glass windows. An extensive restoration of Wai'oli Hui'ia Church ensued, including replacement of the historic windows with custom-made replicas. Dedication ceremonies for the restored church took place in April of 1994.

Congregational hymns at the Wai'oli Hui'ia Church Sunday service are still sung by the Wai'oli Church Choir in the Hawaiian language. The hymn versions used by the choir singers were originally translated by the early missionaries.

Hanalei Bridge

The Hanalei Bridge, considered the "gateway to Hanalei," is the first of Route 560's seven bridges that accommodate uni-directional traffic. A plan to replace the bridge with a modern, two-lane, concrete structure was proposed by the Department of Transportation in 1974. The Hanalei community rallied for preservation of the bridge, beginning a grassroots movement to save and restore the existing structure.

The cost of repairing and restoring Hanalei Bridge was $442,000. Work included truss reinforcement, replacement of decking and timber stringers, prestressing of floor beams, and painting.[21] On May 24, 1989, a dedication ceremony was held to celebrate the completion of the bridge work.

Improvements had increased the bridge's load limit, but by 1999 bridge inspections identified the need for more repairs, and it was determined that the original Pratt trusses had to be replaced. The Warren trusses, which had been added in 1967, and supported most of the weight going over the bridge, also required replacement.

Repair and restoration work on Hanalei Bridge took place from 2002 to 2003 after a national travel magazine rated the bridge one of the United States' most dangerous. The repair work attempted to replicate the bridge's original truss structure.

A blessing for the restored Hanalei Bridge was attended by United States Senator Daniel Inouye as well as members of the Hanalei Roads Committee who had worked for many years to preserve the historic character of the bridge.[22]

"To the planters in the valley this river is of incalculable value. By ordinary-sized sail-boats it is navigable for three miles above its mouth, and is from one to two hundred feet wide. By means of boats they can send their produce down to any vessel that may be anchored in the harbor awaiting its reception."

—Bates, 1854.[23] **Bali Hai Photos**

Preservation of the Water, Preservation of the Land
Hanalei River and Bay

For many centuries before Western contact, the Hanalei River irrigated the taro fields of Hanalei Valley. During the last two centuries the river waters fed fields of coffee, sugarcane, rice, and many other products, only to again provide water to the thirsty taro today. The river also provides an important community recreational resource enjoyed by kayakers, canoe paddlers, and swimmers.

Many local residents also enjoy fishing from the riverbanks, and local fishermen launch their boats from the Hanalei river mouth. Families from all around Kaua'i gather next to Hanalei Pier at Black Pot Beach Park, a popular spot for picnics, barbecues, and other gatherings of extended family and friends, known as 'ohana.

Hanalei Bay is an important natural habitat for many native species, including honu (sea turtles), nai'a (spinner dolphins), and dozens of species of reef fish. Koholā (humpback whales) occasionally venture into Hanalei Bay, as do various species of manō (sharks), particularly when large fishing nets are set out in the bay by fishing boats.

Also plying the waters of Hanalei Bay are various vessels, including sailboats, one-man canoes, sailing canoes, voyaging canoes, kayaks, fishing boats, and assorted personal watercraft. Dozens of sailboats anchor in Hanalei Bay during the summer months, when the water is generally calm. Many spend the summer in the bay before continuing their journeys across the Pacific.

Hanalei Bay is also the destination site of the Biennial Singlehanded TransPacific Yacht Race (TransPac). The first TransPac took place in 1978 when thirty-three boats sailed from the Golden Gate Bridge toward Hanalei Bay; twenty-two boats finished the 2,120-mile course.[24] The sixteenth race was held in 2008.

> At the present season the anchorage [Hanalei] is safe, but when the N.W. gales blow, a very heavy sea must tumble into the bay. I am informed that a Russian store-ship rode out the season in spite of everything. The anchorage is pretty well covered by a spit, over which there is about nine feet; but there is not sufficient space in bad weather for more than three vessels, although in the present fine season the bay is spacious.
>
> —Captain Edward Belcher of the *Sulphur*, 1837[25]

Today at least three canoe clubs—Hanalei Canoe Club, Nāmolokama Canoe Club, and Kaiola Canoe Club—practice their

Canoes at the start of the 2007 State Championship Canoe Races. **Dave Cunning**

Hanalei Bay during the 2007 State Canoe Races. **Dave Cunning**

paddling skills in the waters of Hanalei Bay. The Hanalei Canoe Club was established in 1973 as an extension of the Hanalei Hawaiian Civic Club. It continues to thrive as an important cultural and community group that trains all age levels in the sport of outrigger canoe paddling, educating the generations about Hawaiian culture and Hawaiian language.

Hanalei National Wildlife Refuge

Hanalei National Wildlife Refuge was designated in 1972 to protect endangered native waterbirds and other wildlife inhabitants of the region. The 917-acre refuge is located just east of the town of Hanalei, extending from the Hanalei Bridge up into Hanalei Valley and along the coastal plain.[26]

The refuge is unique among federal wildlife refuges in that about 120 acres of refuge land are leased to taro farmers, and about 80 acres are used for grazing. Taro farming in Hanalei Valley helps perpetuate the Hawaiian cultural tradition and provides quality wetland habitats for endangered waterbirds.

In 1980 the refuge area was given added protection when it was designated as the Hanalei National Wildlife Refuge Historic and Archaeological District. It was also placed on the National and State Registers of Historic Places.

The Return of Taro

After the decline of the rice industry in the early 1900s, significant taro farming began again in Hanalei. It was initiated by Masato Yokotake in the 1940s and continued by the Tasaka and Morishige families, who primarily planted the lehua maoli variety of taro brought from Waimea.[27]

Upper Hanalei Valley taro terraces were irrigated by a half-mile-long ditch bringing water "through a big rock which is conveniently cracked," observed E.S. Craighill Handy, adding, "the legend runs that Pele sent lightning to split the rock so that the people could get the water down to the fields."[28]

Walter Foss Sanborn also began to grow taro in 1940, in an area of lower eastern Hanalei Valley. The land farmed by Sanborn had been planted in rice for the previous three decades.[29]

With the return of taro farming, a need for mills to turn the corms into poi evolved. Small-scale poi mills began to appear at

Hanalei taro. **Bali Hai Photos**

residents' homes, including the Makas in Hāʻena as well as the Alohiaus and Lotas in Hanalei. Sanborn also maintained a poi mill across the street from his home on Weke Road.[30]

In 1997, 220 acres of taro were farmed in Hanalei, including eight farms on 125 acres within the boundaries of the Hanalei National Wildlife Refuge.[31] Also documented were fifty acres of taro in Waiʻoli Valley, ten to fifteen acres in Waipā Valley, and five to ten acres in Waikoko Valley.[32]

Taro production in the Islands reached its height in 1998, totaling about six million pounds. From 2000 to 2005 taro production decreased from about five million to about three million pounds,[33] and the number of taro farmers decreased from seventy to about fifty. Recent declines in taro and poi production are attributed to pests, diseases, and bad weather; record rains in 2006 caused flooding and significant damage to taro crops.[34]

Kauaʻi currently provides more than 70 percent of all taro grown in the state of Hawaiʻi. More than half of the island's taro is grown in Hanalei Valley. Taro's large, heart-shaped leaves create a scenic patchwork of green fields covering the Hanalei Valley floor.

The Hanalei Watershed Hui

On July 30, 1998, the Hanalei Watershed Hui was established as part of the American Heritage River program under President Bill Clinton.[35] The Watershed Hui protects a sixteen-mile length of the Hanalei River and the twenty-one-square-mile watershed of Hanalei Valley as well as the offshore coral reefs in Hanalei Bay.[36] The Hui also monitors the three neighboring valleys of Wai'oli, Waipā, and Waikoko, which have streams that flow into Hanalei Bay.

The Hui "strives to mālama the ahupua'a (watershed) of Hanalei guided by the Hawaiian principles of mālama 'āina (sustainability and stewardship), pono (integrity and balance), laulima (cooperation), and aloha, especially as it applies to cultural equity and respect."[37] They work in partnership with scientific and other organizations to facilitate research on the watershed.

Hui members gather data on native species and also collect water samples from various sites in Hanalei Bay and along the Hanalei River. Water tests conducted by the Hui in Hanalei Bay have frequently shown high bacterial counts, and thus the Hui continues to work on long-term solutions to reducing contamination from local cesspools, particularly during heavy rains.

The Hui also monitors newly hatched larvae of the native 'o'opu fish, also known as gobies.[38] 'O'opu are born as larvae in freshwater streams then are washed to the ocean, where they develop into mature fish. When they are ready to lay eggs, the 'o'opu swim back upstream, climbing rocks by using specially adapted pelvic fins.

Five 'o'opu species inhabit Kaua'i's north shore streams and rivers: 'o'opu nōpili, 'o'opu nākea, 'o'opu naniha, 'o'opu 'akupa, and 'o'opu 'alamo'o.[39] 'O'opu nākea are the largest of the gobies, reaching up to fourteen inches long, and were once abundant in the Hanalei River. In recent years the 'o'opu nākea populations have severely declined.

As late as the early 1900s, accordng to Frank Kurihara, 'o'opu were considered "delicious [to eat], fried or lawalu'd with ti leaves, or in soups, or dried."[40] Local residents anticipated the first floods of August, when fish "migrated downstream by the hordes."[41]

Ka i'a a ka wai nui i lawe mai ai.
The fish borne along by the flood.
The 'o'opu, which was often carried to the lowlands in freshets.[42]

On May 6, 2003, the Hanalei Heritage River Program received a $700,000 grant from the Environmental Protection Agency for the protection of the Hanalei ahupua'a watershed.[43]

The Waipā Foundation

The lands of Waipā were slated for development in the 1970s, but this was forestalled when local farmers and fishermen began an organized effort to preserve the ahupua'a. The families of David Kawika Sproat, Samson Mahu'iki, and others organized the Hawaiian Farmers of Hanalei, which petitioned the landowner, Kamehameha Schools, for a lease to the valley.[44] When the lease was granted, they began to restore the valley for traditional community use.[45]

In 1994 David Sproat's daughter, Stacy Sproat-Beck, developed a Land Use Masterplan for Waipā and formed the nonprofit (501c3) Waipā Foundation.[46] Today the ongoing activities in the ahupua'a help to sustain the community economically, while providing a living classroom for local children.

Students learn about the native plants and animals, from birds in the mountain forests to the marine life inhabiting the coral reefs in Hanalei Bay; they count native fish, conduct tests on water quality, participate in professionally guided archaeological excavations, investigate the geology of the surrounding mountains and the hydrological cycles of the streams and natural springs, and map the cultural and natural resources of the Waipā ahupua'a.

Other ongoing activities at Waipā include a fishtank aquaculture project as well as a large, organic vegetable/herb garden tended by volunteers who share in the harvest.[47] Native plants are propagated, and a nursery is used to grow tropical flowers.

Teachers and mentors at Waipā include native Hawaiian kūpuna (elders). An integral part of Waipā's program involves the farming of taro, which is milled into poi each week and then provided to community members at a low cost.

Hollywood Comes to Hanalei

Perhaps the most influential factor in bringing Hanalei before the eyes of the world and ushering in a new era of tourism was the region's use as a setting for motion pictures. Beginning in the 1950s, many major films have used the landscape of Kaua'i and the Hanalei area, popularizing the once remote northern shore.

The first major movie to be filmed totally on Kaua'i was *Pagan Love Song* (1950), a Technicolor musical in which Kaua'i represented Tahiti, with some scenes filmed in Hanalei.[48] The film involves a half-American, half-Tahitian Mimi Bennett (Esther Williams), who is ready to leave Tahiti but stays when she meets Hazard Endicott (Howard Keel), an Ohio schoolteacher who has inherited a dilapidated coconut plantation.

The location filming of *Pagan Love Song* was part of a newly developing trend of bringing authentic scenery to the screen. Movies were a popular escape for the millions of GIs returning from World War II.

Bird of Paradise (1951), a Technicolor Polynesian epic, was filmed on Kaua'i and features scenes of Hanalei Bay.[49] The plot centers around a Frenchman (Louis Jordan) who comes to the South Pacific with his friend (Jeff Chandler) seeking peace and tranquility. He falls in love with a local girl (Debra Paget) who must offer herself to the volcano god as a sacrifice to prevent an eruption from destroying the people and their homes. Highlights include hundreds of Hawaiian dancers as well as a memorable landing of a Polynesian voyaging canoe near Hanalei Pier.

In *Miss Sadie Thompson* (1953), the Albert Spencer Wilcox Beach House (Kauikeōlani) on Hanalei Bay represented an island mansion. The film stars Rita Hayworth as Sadie, a nightclub singer with a storied past who travels to New Caledonia (Kaua'i) and encounters some tough U.S. Marines.[50] Sadie leaves the island in a scene filmed at Hanalei Pier.

South Pacific (1958) was one of the biggest box office successes of the 1950s. Filming began in August of 1957 in Hanalei and Hā'ena, which represented French New Caledonia.[51]

Opening scenes of *South Pacific* were filmed near the mouth of the Hanalei River, and the elegant Birkmyre Estate overlooking Hanalei Bay was used as the French planter's home.[52] Numerous other Hanalei scenes are shown throughout the movie.

South Pacific takes place during World War II and involves WAVE officer Nellie Forbush (Mitzi Gaynor). She falls in love with the wealthy Frenchman Emile de Becque (Rossano Brazzi), who is in New Caledonia for a dangerous Navy reconnaissance mission.

Hanalei Bay beneath the peaks of Hīhīmanu, Nāmolokama, and Māmalahoa. **Bob Wright**

Mitzi Gaynor's famous rendition of "Wash That Man Right Out of My Hair" was filmed at Lumahaʻi Beach, just west of Hanalei. The peak of Makana towering over Hāʻena represents the mystical island of Bali Hai. Some scenes were filmed at nearby Makua (Tunnels) Beach. Hundreds of Kauaʻi children, including seventy-four from Hanalei, were hired for a scene filmed in Hāʻena.[53]

One little-known fact about the movie was that its filming was delayed by a tsunami that rocked Kauaʻi's north shore in March of 1957. The tsunami knocked out the old Kalihiwai bridge, stopping trucks bringing heavy filming equipment to the movie sets.

A top-grossing film in the 1970s was a remake of the 1933 version of *King Kong* (1976). The cast and crew stayed at the Hanalei Plantation Hotel and traveled in helicopters to get to the valleys of Kalalau and Honopū on the nearby Nā Pali Coast, which depicted the Valley of Kong.

Perhaps the oldest footage of surfing on Kauaʻi was filmed in 1957 and included the waves of Hanalei Bay. The footage was shot by renowned big wave surfer Greg Noll along with Dewey Weber and other friends. The scenes were released on video in 1992 in *Da Bull—Search for Surf.*

Jurassic Park, directed by Steven Spielberg, was filmed in the summer of 1992 at various Kaua'i locations near Hanalei, including Kapa'a and Kīlauea. Hurricane 'Iniki struck the island on the last day of filming, and is briefly shown in the movie on a computer monitor as a tropical storm in Costa Rica that knocks out power at the dinosaur theme park. After it was released in 1993, *Jurassic Park* became the highest grossing film ever.

Other significant films included *Beachhead* (1954); *Naked Paradise/Thunder Over Hawaii* (1957); *She Gods of Shark Reef* (1958); *Wackiest Ship in the Army* (1961); Elvis Presley's *Paradise, Hawaiian Style* (1965); *Acapulco Gold* (1978); *Seven* (1979); *Behold Hawaii* (1983); *Uncommon Valor* (1983); and *Dragonfly* (2002). These films make use of the natural beauty of Kaua'i, featuring places such as Black Pot Beach Park, Hanalei Pier and Bay, Hā'ena, Moloa'a, and Princeville to represent remote Pacific and South Asian locations, and even, as in *Dragonfly*, Venezuela.

Kaua'i's dramatic backdrops and versatility as a filming location ensure that the movie industry will continue to thrive in the future. Movie stars, such as Pierce Brosnan and Ben Stiller, live on the north shore, and many more are frequent visitors.

Taylor Camp

In 1969 a group of twenty people camped for several months at a beach park in Hāʻena, eight miles west of Hanalei town. They were arrested for vagrancy and fined $1 each. Refusing to pay landed them in jail, and their children were placed in foster care.

Howard Taylor, brother of movie star Elizabeth Taylor, heard the story. An owner of Hāʻena beachfront land, he paid the fines to free the campers and allowed them to live on his property. Thus Taylor camp was born.

On their new plot of land the campers built numerous tree houses, many quite elaborate, cleared space for a large garden, and even constructed a sauna by the beach. The community lived there for nearly a decade before being disbanded by authorities. One by one the tree houses were burned, and eventually all remnants of Taylor Camp were removed.

Today many former residents of Taylor camp continue to live in Hanalei and the surrounding area, where they are business owners, teachers, artists, and other prominent members of the community.

Beneath the Waters

In 1995 the Smithsonian Institution's Dr. Paul Forsythe Johnston used remote sensing equipment to discover the buried location of the sunken wreck of *Haʻaheo o Hawaiʻi* (*Pride of Hawaiʻi*). The shipwreck had remained largely untouched until Johnston began his efforts. Johnston's interest in the wreck had come from his time as a curator at a maritime museum in Salem, Massachusetts, the town where *Haʻaheo o Hawaiʻi* had been constructed in 1816.

The research vessel used for the salvage project was the *Pilialoha* (*Circle of Friends*), captained by Rick Rogers. In July the crew sailed from Haleʻiwa Harbor, Oʻahu, to Hanalei Bay to begin the salvage work. Using old charts as well as modern search techniques, including satellite navigation, the team located the wreck ten feet beneath the sand at the mouth of the Waiʻoli River.

An L-shaped propwash-deflector was used to direct pressure from the *Pilialoha's* prop down onto the seafloor to move sand and uncover artifacts from the wreck. Recovered items included a calabash gourd, a quartered whale's tooth, gold-laced beads, and an ivory ring. Many recovered items might have been part of King Kamehameha II's wardrobe. Though the king wasn't on board during the voyage to Kaua'i, many of his belongings were on the ship when it sank.

Ceramics and tableware from China, fine cabinet glass from France, copper hull sheathing and a black glass liquor bottle from England, and many American-made artifacts, such as a leather holster, a block and tackle (with rope), and musket balls, were found. Other artifacts recovered from the wreck included bronze spikes, porcelain shards, pearlware, glass, bone, iron, ivory, lead piping and a wooden wheel.

Among the Hawaiian artifacts were a folding knife and a two-pronged fork, ballast stones, stone lamps, stone poi pounders, stone anchors, cooking stones, and a cow's tibia bone that had been worked into an awl or meat pick. A pū (triton conch shell) found in the wreckage was likely used as the ship's horn.

During the last days of the 1996 recovery work, large sections of the ship's hull were discovered, but they were left in place due to time constraints.

Another recent shipwreck discovery was the 155-foot U.S. Navy ship *Saginaw*, whose crew members fashioned a rescue vessel from the wreck and sent five men sailing for help. They ended up off the coast of Hanalei, but only one survived.

Marine archaeologists diving in a reef channel at Kure Atoll, about one thousand miles northwest of Kaua'i, discovered the site of the wreck in August of 2003. The divers found a series of metal artifacts, including large iron anchors and heavily encrusted cannons, and, as the *Saginaw* was the only known wreck at Kure to have cannons on board, they helped identify the ship. The ship had wrecked on the reef 133 years earlier.

The twenty-two-foot captain's boat that the five men used to get help is on display at Castle Museum in Saginaw, Michigan. It was this vessel that foundered off Hanalei Bay with the exhausted crew, drifting as far as Kalihiwai before a lone survivor was able to relate the tragic story of the *Saginaw* to authorities, who then sent help to Kure to rescue the stranded crew.

The Boating Controversy

In the 1970s a tour boat industry emerged on Kaua'i's north shore to provide access to the scenic Nā Pali Coast between Kē'ē

Beach on the northwest side of Kaua'i and Polihale on the southwest side. The spectacular coastline is one of the most popular visitor attractions, and is a favorite destination of campers, tour boats, and helicopter sightseeing tours.

Tour companies initially launched their boats primarily from Hanalei Bay and nearby Hā'ena at Makua (Tunnels) Beach. Many companies used the protected waters of the large Hanalei River mouth to service their boats as well as for loading and unloading passengers.

The number of tour boats serving the north shore grew quickly. By the mid-1980s, tour boat owners were increasingly at odds with government agencies and local groups concerned about increases in traffic at beach parks, unenforced permitting regulations, and negative environmental impacts to Hanalei Bay and Hanalei River.

Ambiguity regarding rules, jurisdictions, and permits resulted in numerous lawsuits in the late 1980s. A 1989 ruling by a Third Circuit judge prohibited tour boat activity at the Hanalei River mouth until county permits were acquired by business owners. Tours continued to operate from Hanalei without permits, however, and some boat crews were confronted by protesters who claimed that the commercial boating activities were illegal.

Despite the controversy, the number of daily boat tours and charters continued to increase, and included fishing boats, sailboats, kayaks, catamarans, motorized rubber rafts, and various other vessels that primarily provided tourists with access to the Nā Pali Coast. The legality of boating industry activities was bitterly contested and increasingly contentious. Attempts at mediation by then Mayor JoAnn Yukimura were unsuccessful.

In July of 1991, the Department of Transportation began to enforce the rules against unpermitted boating activities. Eight days later the enforcement was halted, and citations that had been issued were withdrawn.

A series of community meetings orchestrated by Mayor Yukimura resulted in the Hanalei Estuary Management Plan, adopted on September 10, 1992, the evening before Hurricane 'Iniki. Seven commercial boating permits were issued in June of 1993. Illegal boating activity warranted more than one hundred citations, which were given then withdrawn when Mayor Maryanne Kusaka took office in 1994.

During the election season of 1998, Governor Benjamin Cayetano ordered all boat companies to stop running tours from Hanalei Bay and move to official Kauaʻi harbors. In September of 1999 the Department of Land and Natural Resources (DLNR) attempted to stop the final two motorized boat companies from running tours from Hanalei by refusing to reissue state permits, and in response the companies sued the State of Hawaiʻi.

In January of 2000 a circuit judge ruled against the DLNR for not following proper procedures and allowed the two companies to continue their operations. The DLNR immediately began a new process aimed at banning motorized commercial tour boats from Hanalei Bay.

In 2002 the last companies to hold county permits for boat tours from Hanalei went to federal court seeking to block the State's attempt to evict them from Hanalei. A U.S. district judge ruled against the State, saying that "Hanalei Bay and parts of Hanalei River are federal navigable waterways and that the state can't ban commercial boat traffic there."[54] This effectively reversed the earlier proclamation of Governor Cayetano that had brought an abrupt halt to commercial boating from Hanalei in 1998.

While tour boats have largely disappeared from Hanalei waters, the future of the commercial boating industry on Kauaʻi's north shore remains uncertain.

A Pod of Whales in Hanalei Bay

On July 3, 2004, four Kauaʻi Police Department officers and local water safety officers were called to Hanalei Bay to keep beach-goers away from 150 to 200 melon-headed whales congregating near the shoreline.

Melon-headed whales are a relatively small and slender species with a melon-shaped head. They are deep water whales, usually staying at least twenty miles offshore in pods that range in size from about one hundred to five hundred members. Bluish black to dark gray or brown in color, the whales have a white patch on their belly and white lips. Adults reach about nine feet long and weigh up to six hundred pounds, feeding on squid, shrimp, and fish.

The pod of whales had come into Hanalei Bay at about seven AM near Pine Trees Beach, where they swam in a dense cluster very close to shore. Occasionally the whales broke into several pods and

Surfing Then and Now

Surfing has long been a part of Hawaiian history. The sport is mentioned in ancient Hawaiian chants, carved as petroglyphs, and depicted in etchings by European and American artists.

Surfboards, known as papa he'e nalu, were up to 16 feet long and weighed as much as 175 pounds. They were carved from trees with buoyant wood, such as wiliwili, koa, or 'ulu (breadfruit),[55] using a stone or bone adze, and finished with a rough stone called 'ōahi, or granulated coral called pōhaku puna.

To stain the board, the root of a ti plant, pounded bark of a kukui tree, or buds of a banana plant were used. A dark color was also achieved by rubbing the soot from burned kukui nuts into the wood. Kukui oil gave the surfboard a glossy finish.

Today surfboards are made primarily from foam "blanks" that are first shaped to the desired specifications and then finished with coats of liquid resin that hardens. In the last few years, factory-produced surfboards made from epoxy have become increasingly popular.

Many well-known surfboard shapers live in the Hanalei area, including Bobby Allen (BASA), Billy Hamilton (Hamilton Surfboards), Mark Sausen (Papa Sau Surfboards), Ian Vernon (Sunburnt Surfboards), Dick Brewer (Brewer Surfboards), Terry Chung (Terry Chung Surfboards), and others.

Hanalei is a mecca for surfers worldwide, who come to test themselves on the large and challenging waves. Every winter a series of storm systems are generated off of the Asian landmass. As they grow over the Bering Sea, these storms generate enormous swells that propel large ocean waves steadily toward the northern shores of the Hawaiian Islands.

If an experienced local surfer says he surfed Hanalei or The Bay it usually refers to the point break directly out from Hanalei Pier, where a fringing coral reef provides optimal conditions for waves. Names for different areas of that particular break include Futures, Summers, The Point, Flat Rock, and The Bowl.

Along the length of Hanalei Bay are about a dozen other surf spots—Kiddies (near Hanalei Pier), then Pavilions, The Cape, Pine Trees, Grandpas, Middles, Chicken Wing, Waipā, and finally Waikokos, at the far western side of the bay. A few hundred yards offshore, between Pine Trees and The Cape, is a big-waves-only surfing spot called Manalau,[56] often referred to as Monster Mush.

More than a mile offshore on the western side of Hanalei Bay is Queens Reef, and just as far offshore on the eastern side of the bay is Kings Reef. Kings and Queens only break when extremely large swells arrive from the north, usually only a few times a year. When the mountainous waves do arrive, however, the size of these surf breaks rivals any surf spot in the world.

Kings Reef, traditionally known as Aliʻi Reef, is 50 to 70 feet deep with a rock shelf dropping off to about 120 feet.[57] It was first surfed on November 10, 1996, by Titus Kinimaka and Terry Chung, two of Kauaʻi's most renowned local watermen who used a jet ski to tow each other into the massive waves.

The accomplishment of Kinimaka and Chung occurred early in the evolution of the sport of tow-in surfing, which allows surfers to catch waves that are too large and too fast to catch without motorized assistance. In recent years many technological improvements have been made to tow-in surfboards and other equipment that is used to surf giant ocean waves.

Surfing has exploded in popularity during the last decade, with lessons now available at many local beaches and an increasing number of daring surfers exploring Kauaʻi's outside breaks during the biggest of winter swells.

Also increasing in popularity are water sports such as kite surfing, in which the surfer is pulled by a large, parachute-like kite.

Melon-headed whales in Hanalei Bay. **Brenda Zaun**

then slowly rejoined as they all moved slowly eastward along the shore, eventually congregating near Pavilions Beach.

The next day, the Fourth of July, the whale pod remained very near the Hanalei Bay shoreline as marine officials devised a plan to use a string of connected kayaks to nudge the cetaceans out of the bay. The kayaks were hooked together on the beach. Just before this plan was put into action by the National Oceanic and Atmospheric Administration (NOAA) officials, however, a group of local Hawaiian members of the Hanalei Canoe Club suggested a less cumbersome and more natural method of solving the problem.

The plan of the Canoe Club members was to use a long, woven strand of pōhuehue (beach morning glory vine) to gently shepherd the whales from the bay. This hardy native vine grows plentifully along the Hanalei Bay shoreline at the high water mark, and was thought to be a safer and less intrusive method than using kayaks to move the pod out to sea. The vines would also be harmless if run into by the whales.

When the woven strand of pōhuehue was completed it was about six hundred feet long. Canoe Club members used two small boats to lay the strand across the water near the whales, and then very slowly pulled the two ends of the strand seaward to gently nudge the whales out to sea. Within about one hour the whales had gradually moved into slightly deeper waters. The whales then headed for the open sea, to the great joy of all of the rescuers and onlookers.

Tahiti Nui

Bruce Truesdale Marston came from Pasadena, California, and met his wife, Louise, in Tahiti. They built a house at 'Anini, just east of Princeville, because it reminded them of Tahiti, and in the summer of 1964 they opened Tahiti Nui restaurant and lounge in Hanalei.

Tahiti Nui has become known as the north shore's most renowned gathering place, hosting visiting celebrities and featuring local singers, musicians, hula dancing, and the beautiful singing of "Aunty Louise" herself, who was for decades considered the best-known woman on Kaua'i's north shore, and a generous and welcoming host to all who came. Auntie Louise passed away in 2003.

The whale pod had been eerily inactive during the previous day near the shore of Hanalei Bay, but as the whales disappeared toward the horizon many were leaping above the water as if to celebrate their regained freedom. It seemed to be a storybook ending to the near mass stranding. Sadly, the next day one infant melon-headed calf, which was about three feet long, was found dead in Hanalei Bay near Waipā Stream.

The precise cause of the unusual appearance of the melon-headed whales in Hanalei Bay is uncertain, however many attribute the event to the Navy's testing of mid-frequency, active sonar as part of the RIMPAC (Rim of the Pacific) military exercises that take place in Hawaiian waters every two years.[58] A goal of the 2004 sonar tests was to refine the military's ability to utilize high-volume sounds to locate submarines.

The sonar tests involved tracking an underwater torpedo that produced sonar readings similar to a submarine. Military ships were operating sonar periodically during the twenty hours before the whales entered Hanalei Bay, and two of the U.S. Navy ships and four Japanese ships were located nineteen miles off Kaua'i's north shore when the whales appeared.

Two of the military ships reported using their sonar between 6:45 and 7:10 AM, and the whales in Hanalei Bay were first reported around 7:00 AM The Navy was quickly informed of the strange appearance of the whale pod in Hanalei Bay, and within hours their active sonar operations were temporarily suspended as a precaution to protect the marine mammals.

In April of 2006, NOAA scientists concluded that the sonar might have been a contributing cause of the whales congregating in Hanalei Bay. The results of the investigation led to official requests by NOAA for the Navy to adjust their methods in experimenting with the sonar equipment in future RIMPAC exercises.

Connections to the Past

Because of its natural splendor, rich resources, and picturesque charm, Hanalei has long been an idyllic spot for different entrepreneurial ventures. Recently, many local residents have grown concerned about the rapidly increasing development of north shore lands and the consequent loss of public access to beaches and mountain areas. The large increase in the number of vacation rentals on the north shore of Kaua'i has led to a severe shortage of affordable housing and long-term rentals for local residents, while local homeowners have seen huge property tax increases.

Even with the influx of non-resident developers and new landowners, however, the connection Hawaiians keep with their

Hōkūle'a in Hanalei Bay. **Sara Wall**

Puff the Magic Dragon

"Puff, the magic dragon," according to the song's lyrics, "lived by the sea and frolicked in the autumn mist in a land called Honah Lee," leading some people to think the song refers to Hanalei. Indeed it is not difficult to envision the shape of a dragon in the mountains that wrap around the coastline.

The song was written by Peter Yarrow and his Cornell classmate Leonard Lipton, and originally performed by Yarrow's 1960s musical group, Peter, Paul & Mary. Yarrow dispelled the notion of a Hanalei connection, saying it was "serendipitous coincidence."

Yarrow explained that the song was based on a poem by Ogden Nash about a dragon,[59] and that the song was about the loss of innocence.

culture is strong. In recent decades there has been a resurgence in the use of the spoken and written Hawaiian language as well as a renewal of traditional Hawaiian cultural practices. Native groups and others work to restore and preserve native cultural sites, including heiau, fishponds, and whole ahupuaʻa, teaching the keiki (children) techniques and values of their ancestors.

Visits to Hanalei by traditional Hawaiian voyaging canoes and their crews have given further inspiration to the perpetuation of local Hawaiian culture in the region. The *Hōkūleʻa* voyaging canoe has sailed into Hanalei Bay numerous times since it was launched in 1975, including extended visits in June/July of 2005 that were accompanied by the voyaging canoe *Makaliʻi*. From Hanalei Bay the two voyaging canoes sailed to the Northwestern Hawaiian Islands and then returned to Hanalei to offer educational opportunities for local youth.

Over the centuries the Hanalei region has also faced an invasion of non-native plant and animal species. Since Western contact in 1778, many native species have become endangered and extinct, including more than half of all native bird species in the Hawaiian Islands. The loss of any single species imperils the fragile balance of the native ecosystem.

Moon over Makana. **Bob Wright**

The Hanalei National Wildlife Refuge remains a stronghold of conservation, serving as a refuge to several endangered native waterbirds, for example the black-necked stilt, coot, koloa duck, and moorhen. Local conservation efforts have also helped protect threatened and endangered populations of nēnē, albatross, Newell's and wedge-tailed shearwaters, sea turtles, monk seals, and many other native species.

While protecting the region's unique beauty and cultural significance has often proved difficult in the face of powerful commercial interests, new alliances between environmentalists, preservationists, philanthropists, and native groups have led to better planning for future growth.

Five million years ago the island of Kaua'i was born from a fissure in the sea bottom. Growing lush with greenery it transformed into a Pacific paradise, becoming home to thousands of native and endemic species and eventually to voyagers who would settle and begin to create a Hawaiian culture. Utilizing the land's natural resources, the Hawaiians thrived, creating crafts that were at once useful and stunning. They farmed the land and fished the sea to provide for their growing families.

Two centuries ago seafarers and missionary settlers arrived, beginning an era of significant change. The beautiful landscape has continued to be altered over time, serving as host to a multitude of crops including mulberry, sugar, coffee, and rice, and again taro, and the region has been welcoming to all people—adventurers, missionaries, immigrant laborers, and vacationers alike.

While the face of Hanalei and its population continues to change, the heart of the small town remains the same. Longtime residents hold fond memories of the past and strive to preserve the natural resources of the valley and perpetuate the culture of its original inhabitants.

As kūpuna and other cultural practitioners and teachers share their knowledge with younger generations, the greatness of the original Hawaiian settlers is perpetuated. Their work rekindles the love and appreciation the keiki have for the land and the sea, strengthening the connection of the future generations to Hanalei's past and providing them with a solid foundation from which to build their future.

Appendix I

Birds of Hanalei

Native Waterbirds[1]

Aeʻo (Hawaiian Black-Necked Stilt)	*Himantopus mexicanus knudseni*
ʻAlae Keʻoke (Hawaiian Coot)	*Fulica americana alai*
Koloa Maoli (Hawaiian Duck)	*Anas wyvilliana*
ʻAlae ʻUla (Hawaiian Moorhen)	*Gallinula chloropus sandvicensis*
ʻAukuʻu (Black-Crowned Night Heron)	*Nycticorax nycticorax hoactli*

Open Country Birds

Nēnē (Hawaiian Goose)	*Branta sandvicensis*

Migratory Species—Seasonal Residents and Occasional Visitors

Kōlea (Pacific Golden Plover)	*Pluvialis fulva*
Mōlī (Laysan Albatross)	*Diomedea immutabilis*
Koloa Mohā (Northern Shoveler)	*Anas clypeata*
Koloa Māpu (Northern Pintail)	*Anas acuta*
Hunakai (Sanderling)	*Calidris alba*
Green-Winged Teal	*Anas crecca*
Blue-Winged Teal	*Anas discors*
Bufflehead	*Bucephala albeola*
Baikal Teal	*Anas formosa*
White-Faced Ibis	*Plegadis chihi*

Seabirds[2]

ʻIwa (Great Frigatebird)	*Fregata minor palmerstoni*
ʻAʻo (Newell's [Townsend's] Shearwater)	*Puffinus auricularis newelli*
ʻUaʻu Kani (Wedge-Tailed Shearwater)	*Puffinus pacificus chlororhynchus*
Koaʻe Kea (White-Tailed Tropicbird)	*Phaethon lepturus dorotheae*
Koaʻe ʻUla (Red-Tailed Tropicbird)	*Phaethon rubricauda rothschildi*

NATIVE WATERBIRDS

Hawaiian Black-Necked Stilt

Himantopus mexicanus knudseni
Hawaiian Name: Ae'o (One standing tall)
Endemic Subspecies Status:
Endangered Species
Found on Hawai'i, Maui, Lāna'i, Moloka'i,
O'ahu, Kaua'i, and Ni'ihau

Brenda Zaun, USFWS

Often seen in the taro patches of Hanalei Valley, the Hawaiian black-necked stilt is perfectly suited to a wetland environment. The stilt is a wading bird easily identified by its black-and-white forehead, white breast, and long, skinny pink legs that are jointed and bend in the opposite direction of the human leg.[3]

Hawaiian stilts are also known as kukuluae'o, a Hawaiian term that also refers to wooden stilts used for amusement by Hawaiian children in ancient times.

He kukuluā'o.
A stilt.
A thin, long-legged person.[4]

Hawaiian black-necked stilts are wading birds that often gather in groups. They make a chirping sound similar to "kip, kip" or "keek, keek" and use their long beaks to probe the shallow water mud flats for worms, aquatic insects, crabs, fish, and mollusks.

Stilt breeding and nesting season extends from December to August.[5] The stilt builds a nest in a shallow depression in a small mound, often on the banks of taro patches or in low-lying vegetation near the water. The nest is lined with rocks and twigs. The female stilt then lays, on average, four well-camouflaged eggs that incubate for twenty-four to twenty-six days.

Stilt chicks are covered with a downy, tannish brown coat speckled with black. They leave the nest soon after hatching and generally hide under cover until ready to fly. Parents don't feed the chick but instead help them find suitable food sources. Parents sometimes feign injury (a broken wing) in order to draw predators away from the nest and hatchlings.[6]

Brenda Zaun, USFWS

Hawaiian Coot

Fulica americana alai
Hawaiian Name: 'Alae Ke'oke'o or 'Alae Kea
Endemic Subspecies Status: Endangered Species
Found on Hawai'i, Maui, Lāna'i, Moloka'i, O'ahu, and Kaua'i

'Alae ke'oke'o, the Hawaiian coot, is commonly seen inhabiting Hanalei taro patches. A subspecies of the American coot, the Hawaiian coot is about 14 1/2 inches long, and mostly dark gray to black on top with white undertail feathers.[7] The bill is ivory white, and so is the bulbous frontal shield, which is also called the frontal knob.[8] Coots feed on insects, fish, and tadpoles, as well as on leaves and seeds of aquatic plants. Coots don't fly much, though they are sometimes seen flying low over the water. Nesting occurs throughout the year, particularly between March and September, on wetland vegetation or in taro patches where coots use sedges, taro stems, or other aquatic plants to construct nests that may rise and fall with changing water levels.

Coots lay, on average, four to six eggs, which are creamy to tan colored and speckled with black. The eggs incubate for three to four weeks. The coot chick is downy black with a reddish-orange neck and head, and a black-tipped bill. The bird has a baldish appearance due to the absence of down on the crown and forehead. Soon after hatching, the chicks are able to swim.

The largest coot populations are found on Kaua'i, O'ahu, and Maui, with a total population of about two thousand to four thousand birds. Coots are known to fly between the Hawaiian Islands.

Brenda Zaun, USFWS

Hawaiian Duck

Anas wyvilliana
Hawaiian Name: Koloa Maoli (Native duck)
Endemic Subspecies Status: Endangered Species
Found on Hawai'i, O'ahu, Kaua'i; possibly extinct on Maui

The koloa population is estimated at less than 2,500 birds overall, and more than 80% of them are on Kaua'i.[9] Two of the largest koloa populations are found at the Hanalei National Wildlife Refuge and the Alekoko (Menehune) Fishpond.[10]

The koloa is mottled golden brown in color with an olive-colored bill. Male koloa are about twenty inches long while female koloa are about seventeen inches long. Male koloa have a darker head than females, and some females have an orange-tipped bill.

The koloa's secondary wing feathers (speculum) are greenish blue to metallic purple in color with white borders, and the duck's feet and legs are orange. Koloa eat insects, mollusks, and aquatic vegetation. Breeding and nesting occur year round, particularly between December and May, beginning at about one year of age.

Koloa nest in low-elevation wetland areas as well as near mountain streams, river mouths, and taro patches. Koloa use feathers and down to build a well-hidden nest, and then lay from two to ten white to tan-colored eggs.[11] Koloa eggs incubate for about twenty-eight days before hatching, and after about nine weeks the birds learn to fly.

Hawaiian Moorhen
Gallinula chloropus sandvicensis
Also called: Hawaiian Gallinule or Mudhen
Hawaiian Name: 'Alae 'Ula (Red forehead)
Endemic Subspecies Status:
Endangered Species
Found on Oʻahu and Kauaʻi; possibly extinct on Hawaiʻi, Maui, and Molokaʻi

Bob Waid

The Hawaiian moorhen is easily identified by its bright red forehead (frontal shield), and is frequently seen at the Hanalei National Wildlife Refuge.[12] Also called the Hawaiian gallinule, the moorhen is thought to have been quite common throughout the Hawaiian Islands in the 1800s before the population declined rapidly in the early- to mid-1900s.[13]

Hawaiian legend tells of how the 'alae 'ula brought fire from the gods to the Hawaiian people. During the journey, the moorhen was scorched by the flames, giving the bird its red frontal shield. The demigod Māui, seeking to learn the secret of making fire, caught the 'alae 'ula before it could hide.[14]

The adult Hawaiian moorhen is about thirteen inches long, with a black head and neck, and a slate gray to bluish black back that may be somewhat iridescent. The flanks and undertail feathers of moorhen are white, and the bird's red bill has a yellow to light green tip.[15] The feet are not webbed, and the yellowish green legs and feet may show red near the top.

Moorhen are generally shy and secretive, inhabiting freshwater marshes and other wetlands, including taro patches.[16] Moorhen are adept at walking across floating vegetation to feed on mollusks, insects, and aquatic plants such as taro tops and young shoots.

Moorhen courtship behavior includes bowing and arching as well as nibbling. The main breeding period is March through August, though moorhen may breed year round. During breeding season the bird's frontal shield may become enlarged and deeper red in color. A well-hidden nest is built from plants and mud, often on folded reeds.

Moorhen lay from five to nine cream-colored eggs, which are spotted with gray, black, and brown, and incubate for about twenty-two days. The downy moorhen chick has a bright red bill and pale yellow to brown body, and is able to swim soon after hatching. Immature (juvenile) moorhen are olive brown to grayish brown in color.

Brenda Zaun, USFWS

Black-Crowned Night Heron
Nycticorax nycticorax hoactli
Hawaiian Name: 'Auku'u
Indigenous: American continent

The night heron is often seen at the Hanalei National Wildlife Refuge as well as near the mouth of the Hanalei River. Adult night heron are about twenty-five inches long and mostly gray, with yellow legs and a black head, back, and bill.[17] The night heron's wingspan is almost four feet.

Night heron are often seen standing motionless at the edges of lagoons, marshes, canefield ditches, taro patches, and exposed reef areas. They may be heard making a fairly loud "kwok" sound while flying.

When in breeding plumage, the male night heron develops four or five long, white head plumes; the female may have just two or three. These white nuptial plumes grow out from the back region of the bird's head. Immature night heron are streaked with white and brownish rust colors that turn grayish as the bird matures.

Kohāka leo o ka 'auku'u.
The voice of the 'auku'u is heard to croak.
A snooping gossip. The 'auku'u bird lives in the upland and goes to the lowland for fish, often snatching them from people's ponds.[18]

The black-crowned night heron is a solitary wading bird that feeds primarily on crustaceans and fish.[19] The night heron feeds during the night as well as during the day, but is most active at dawn and dusk, looking for prey beneath the water. Breeding occurs around May, when the night heron uses large sticks and twigs to construct a nest in a tree, and then lays two to four bluish green eggs.

OPEN COUNTRY BIRDS

Hawaiian Goose
Branta sandvicensis
Hawaiian Name: Nēnē
Endemic Subspecies Status:
Endangered Species
Found on Oʻahu and Kauaʻi; possibly
extinct on Hawaiʻi, Maui, and Molokaʻi

Bob Waid

Kauaʻi's nēnē population has grown rapidly during the last two decades, and nēnē flocks now inhabit many low elevation habitats, including lower Hanalei Valley, as well as higher elevations, including Kōkeʻe State Park.[20]

The nēnē's ancestors are Canadian geese. They likely first arrived in the Hawaiian Islands after being blown off course or caught in a storm many thousands of years ago. The goose then evolved into a unique Hawaiian species that is now Hawaiʻi's official state bird.

Nēnē are about two feet long, a typical size for geese. The head, face, and the back of the neck (the nape) are black, while the cheeks and the sides of the neck are a light tan color, with a buffy striped pattern (distinct horizontal bands). The bird's lower body has this same light brown color and is striped, but the top of the body is a darker gray or brown.

The nēnē's bill, legs, and feet are black. The webbing between the toes on the nēnē's feet is much reduced compared to the fuller webbing on the feet of its ancestor, the Canadian goose. The nēnē's webbing is an adaptation better suited for walking on high, dry lava flows, a habitat frequented by nēnē on Hawaiʻi Island.

In flight, the sound of the nēnē is something like "ney ney." On the ground, however, nēnē often make a noise more comparable to a cow's moo. Nēnē aren't very shy, and sometimes approach humans.

"Unele! Unele!" wahi a ka nēnē.
"Honk! Honk!" says the goose.[21]

Nēnē nest between October and March, and by the age of two begin laying, on average, four or five creamy white eggs. This ground nesting makes them vulnerable to non-native predators, which is one reason nēnē almost became extinct.[22]

By the age of two, nēnē begin laying eggs, nesting between October and March, and laying on average four or five creamy, white eggs. The mother goose sits on the eggs, which incubate for about thirty days. When the mother leaves the nest she covers the eggs with downy feathers from the nest lining.

During nesting, nēnē adults go through a four- to six-week process called molting, and they cannot fly during this time. The infant chick is able to run around just as soon as its downy feathers dry. The chick's parents provide food for the baby until the hatchling is about ten to twelve weeks old, when the gosling learns to fly.

MIGRATORY SPECIES—
SEASONAL RESIDENTS AND OCCASIONAL VISITORS

The migratory bird species described in this section may be seen in the Hanalei National Wildlife Refuge, except for sanderlings, plovers, and albatross, which are more commonly seen elsewhere in the region.

Sanderlings are often seen along the sandy shoreline of Hanalei Bay, while plovers are seen on the grass lawns of Wai'oli Park or in the yards of local residents. Albatross are rarely seen at the refuge but frequently seen along the ocean cliffs of Princeville and in nearby yards, as well as atop the ocean cliffs that extend toward Kīlauea and beyond.

All of these migratory bird species are considered native to the Hawaiian Islands, though some are considered non-resident migratory birds and only spend a relatively short time in Hawai'i before moving on along their migratory routes.

Pacific Golden Plover
Pluvialis fulva
Hawaiian Name: Kōlea
Migratory: In Hawai'i approximately from September to May

Brenda Zaun, USFWS

Pacific golden plovers are about eleven inches long, weigh about half a pound, and live to about eight years of age. Plovers are dark brown, and spotted with gold on top, but paler on the underside, with a large, dark eye region and a fairly large head relative to their body.

Migrating to the Hawaiian Islands during fall to feed, plovers return north to Alaska for the summer months to lay their eggs. This is similar to the migration pattern of koholā (humpback whales), which also spend their winters in Hawai'i and return north for summer, but whales give birth in Hawaiian waters and feed in their northern habitat, while the plovers feed in the Islands and lay their eggs in the north.

After spending May, June, and July on the Alaskan tundra, plovers head south around August.[23] The plover's non-stop flight between Alaska and Hawai'i may cover more than 3,500 miles but takes less than three days.[24]

Before leaving the Hawaiian Islands in April, the female plover molts into a beautiful beige gold breeding plumage. The male plover gets a "tuxedo" look, with a pure white stripe along the sides of the head and down the neck. The abdomen, breast, cheek, and throat are black.

During its winter stay in the Hawaiian Islands, the plover feeds on insects and other invertebrates, as well as certain flowers and leaves.[25] Plovers are known to return to the same general area each year to feed, and often return to the very same patch of lawn or pasture where they remain throughout the season.[26] Plovers are generally solitary birds during their stay in Hawai'i, often gathering together in large flocks just before they head north. During their long migration, plovers fly at elevations up to twenty thousand feet at speeds of about sixty to seventy miles per hour, and with a tailwind they may exceed one hundred miles per hour,[27] completing the flight to the northern breeding grounds in about fifty to sixty hours.

Once plovers reach their nesting grounds on the Alaskan and Siberian tundra, the male builds a nest lined with lichens and leaves. Plovers typically lay four greenish brown eggs, one every other day. The eggs are incubated by the female at night and the male during the day. Males also share in the duties of caring for the chick.

Less than a month after hatching, the downy goslings and ducklings begin to fledge (learn to fly). In early August the parents leave, and then the chicks follow about one or two months later. Somehow the new generation of plovers finds their way to the remote Hawaiian archipelago thousands of miles away, and then they too repeat the journey each year.[28]

Kōlea kai piha.
Plover, bird of high tides.
The plover feeds along the edge of the sea.[29]

Brenda Zaun, USFWS

Laysan Albatross
Diomedea immutabilis
Hawaiian Name: Mōli
Migratory: In Hawai'i approximately from October to July

Laysan albatross are white, with black on their upper wings and around their eyes, and may be nearly three feet long with a wingspan of up to eighty inches.[30] Adult Laysan albatross weigh from five to seven pounds, making them the largest seabirds in the entire Pacific region.

Adult albatross perform elaborate courtship dances with each other along Princeville's oceanside cliffs and other nearby coastal bluffs. Then they breed, nest, lay their eggs, and nurture their young. The fat and fluffy baby albatross sometimes appear to be even bigger than their parents.

Soon the albatross parents leave, and the young ones must learn to fly on their own. When the fledglings finally head out to sea, they won't return until years later when they are ready to nest.

Laysan albatross sometimes have difficulty taking off for flight unless they can run down a slope or use some other suitable launching area. Once in the air, however, Laysan albatross are superb fliers able to soar for hours without flapping their wings, and sometimes even sleeping while airborne.

Albatross may live for over forty years, and may stay at sea up to five or more years before returning to land to nest. The birds spend the summer months one thousand miles or more from Hawai'i over the waters of the North Pacific. Laysan albatross feed mostly on large squid as well as on the eggs of the mālolo (flying fish). The albatross fish from a sitting position on the water's surface, making them vulnerable to shark attacks.

Laysan albatross usually arrive in the Hawaiian Islands by late October or early November, and stay at their nesting areas until June or July. From their nesting areas the albatross may fly thousands of miles in search of food before returning to feed their young.

Laysan albatross prefer to nest in the same area where they were born, and tend to mate with the same partner for life. The female lays one egg in a nest depression, usually in November or December. The parents alternate tending the egg, which incubates for about two months before hatching.[31] After about 5 1/2 months the chicks fledge.

During albatross nesting season in the Hawaiian Islands, the birds perform bizarre mating dances that include prancing around with their mate and thrusting their beaks skyward along with bill snapping and vocalizations. These courtship displays, as well as the difficulty the chicks have learning to fly, are likely reasons for the nickname "gooney bird."[32]

Northern Shoveler
Anas clypeata
Hawaiian Name: Koloa Mōha
Migratory Waterbird: Winter visitor in Hawai'i

Tom Dove

The northern shoveler is a small duck distinguished by its orange legs and feet, its long and broad, spatulate (spoon-shaped) bill, and a patch of blue on the forewing in both sexes. Northern shovelers are about seventeen to twenty inches long.

The male northern shoveler is dark on top with a white breast and a dark green head. The bill is black on drakes, and brown (bordered with orange) on hens. The bird's sides and belly are rufous colored (reddish, rusty, or chestnut), and the posterior is black.

In autumn, the male northern shoveler may have a fuzzy crescent of white in front of the eye region. Females are mottled brown (sandy) in color with an orange bill, while males have a black bill.[33]

Northern Pintail

Anas acuta
Hawaiian Name: Koloa Māpu
(Wind-blown duck)[34]
Migratory Waterbird: Winter visitor in
Hawai'i (relatively common)

The northern pintail is a relatively common visitor to the Hawaiian Islands, and is distinguished by its long slender neck, long pointed tail, and narrow, brown speculum (secondary wing feathers) with a white border on the rear edge.

The male northern pintail is about twenty-eight inches long and generally grayish in color, with a white breast and dark brown head. A vertical line of white runs up the male's neck and comes to a point on the side of the head.

Female northern pintails are smaller than males, measuring about twenty-one inches long and appearing mottled brown in color with a gray to dark bill. The female's sharp-pointed tail is shorter than the tail of the male. Northern pintails range from the northern parts of the Northern Hemisphere to their wintering grounds as far south as the northern parts of South America, Africa, and India.

Sanderling

Calidris alba
Hawaiian Name: Hunakai (Sea foam)[35]
Migratory Waterbird: Winter visitor in
Hawai'i (approximately from August to
April)

Sanderlings are often seen along the sandy shoreline of Hanalei Bay where they run along the water's edge and dash up and down the beach with each ebb and flow of the breaking waves. As the waves recede, the sanderling pecks away beneath the surface to feed on invertebrates.

The sanderling is about eight inches long, with black legs and a slender, black bill. The bird's winter plumage is gray above, white below, and dark on the shoulder area. When in breeding plumage, the sanderling's breast, back, and head are reddish brown.

Green-Winged Teal
Anas crecca
Migratory Waterbird: Winter visitor in Hawai'i

Tom Dove

The green-winged teal is generally grayish brown, with green wings and a deep green speculum (secondary wing feathers). The belly is white, as are the shoulders, which are seen in flight. Both male and female green-winged teal measure about 14 1/2 inches long.

The male green-winged teal has a brown to chestnut-colored (or rusty-colored) head with a green streak behind the eye (postocular). Near the green-winged teal's shoulder is a vertical bar of white. Female green-winged teal are speckled brown in color with a light stripe of white above the eye. The bird's legs and bill are gray.

Green-winged teal range from the northern parts of North America to their wintering grounds as far south as Central America and the West Indies.[36]

Blue-Winged Teal
Anas discors
Migratory Waterbird: Occasional winter visitor in Hawai'i

Tom Dove

The blue-winged teal is a small duck measuring about 15 1/2 inches long, with a blue-black bill, a blue patch on the forewing, and a brown breast spotted with black. The blue-winged teal has a longer bill than the green-winged teal.

The male blue-winged teal has a gray head with a crescent of white on the face, curving in front of the eye, and a dark posterior flanked with white. The feet and legs are orange. Both sexes have a pale blue patch on the forewing. Female blue-winged teal are more of a mottled brown color.

Blue-winged teal range from Canada to the southern United States during their summer breeding season, and winter as far south as Argentina.

Bufflehead
Bucephala albeola
Migratory Waterbird: Occasional winter visitor in Hawai'i

Tom Dove

Bufflehead are occasional visitors to the Hawaiian Islands, and are sometimes seen in the Hanalei National Wildlife Refuge.

Both male and female bufflehead are relatively small, measuring about fourteen inches long. Most bufflehead seen in the Islands are females, which are darker in color (dusty brown) than males. Females also have a white spot on the cheek (white ear patch), and have a smaller bill than the male.

The bufflehead in flight reveals a large, white wing patch, which is smaller on the female than the male. The male bufflehead is predominantly white with a black back and relatively small, stubby bill. The head has a patch of white that makes the bird look somewhat like it is wearing a white bonnet. The head's black region may show glossy purple green.[37]

Baikal Teal
Anas formosa
Migratory Waterbird: Occasional winter visitor in Hawai'i

H. Douglas Pratt

Another occasional visitor to Hanalei is the baikal teal, which is about seventeen inches long. The male baikal teal has a cream colored, circular pattern on its cheeks, while the female is distinguished by a white spot near its bill. The male's eyebrow stripe (supercilium) is continuous over the eye, while the female's eyebrow stripe is broken by the eye region.

White-Faced Ibis
Plegadis chihi
Migratory Waterbird: Occasional winter
visitor in Hawai'i

Brenda Zaun, USFWS

The white-faced ibis is occasionally seen amidst the taro fields of the Hanalei National Wildlife Refuge. When not in breeding plumage (e.g., when in the Hawaiian Islands), the white-faced ibis is dark colored with dark gray legs, a glossy green body, gray facial area, and pale streaks along the neck area. The bill is down-curved, and the iris is red (or brown when the bird is a juvenile).

In breeding plumage, the ibis's red face area is bordered with white feathers, and its body is chestnut colored. The white-faced ibis breeds in the western region of North America.

SEABIRDS

Great Frigatebird
Fregata minor palmerstoni
Hawaiian Name: 'Iwa (Thief)[38]
Also called: Man O' War

Eric VanderWerf

Often seen flying over Kaua'i's north shore, the great frigatebird has a forked tail, bent wings, and a wingspan that may exceed seven feet, making it appear somewhat like an ancient pterodactyl in flight.[39]

Despite the frigatebird's large wingspan and a body length averaging forty-three inches, frigatebirds usually weigh less than three pounds. Females are black with some white feathers on the upper breast and throat, while males have all black feathers.[40] Female frigatebirds are generally bigger than males.

He 'iwa ho'ohaehae nāulu.
An 'iwa that teases the rain clouds.
A beautiful maiden or handsome youth who rouses jealous envy in others.[41]

Male frigatebirds have an inflatable red pouch of skin under their throat. They often blow up this throat (gular) pouch like a balloon, usually when they are near a colony of birds and want to get a female's attention. In breeding season the males gather together and show off their puffed-up red throat pouches.

Frigatebirds can glide for several hours with very little effort, often soaring at heights above five hundred feet, the highest of any of Hawai'i's seabirds. This soaring ability is particularly helpful to frigatebirds because they have very little webbing between their toes and don't land on the water if they can avoid it. Frigatebirds also lack oil glands to waterproof their feathers, and they don't dive beneath the ocean's surface for fish as some other seabirds do.

Frigatebirds sometimes dive extremely fast through the air, and may engage in sharp, spiraling turns. They are probably the most acrobatic of all of Hawai'i's seabirds, and may chase and dive down upon red-footed boobies, shearwaters, and other seabirds to force them to drop or disgorge their food. Then with agility and speed the frigatebird swoops down and catches the food before it hits the water. This food piracy explains how the frigatebird got its Hawaiian name, 'iwa, which means "thief."

In addition to stealing food from other seabirds, frigatebirds fly low over the water and use their long, hooked bills to grab floating food, including squid, fish, newly hatched sea turtles, and even mālolo (flying fish).

Frigatebirds are migratory, traveling between their nesting areas and places where food is more plentiful. Most frigatebird nesting occurs on the Northwestern Hawaiian Islands.[42] Frigatebirds are biennial breeders (nesting every other year), beginning at about five years of age.[43]

Females lay one white egg around March or April, and both male and female frigatebirds take turns incubating the egg. After about 1 1/2 months, the frigatebird chick hatches and is soon covered with white, downy feathers.[44] Frigatebird chicks are fed by the adults about every eighteen hours. The chick stays in the nest about 4 1/2 months before growing adult feathers and fledging, which usually occurs in October.

Brenda Zaun, USFWS

Newell's (Townsend's) Shearwater
Puffinus auricularis newelli
Hawaiian Name: 'A'o
Endemic Subspecies Status:
Threatened subspecies.
Found on Kaua'i, O'ahu, and Hawai'i

The Newell's shearwater has a black back, a white breast, and is about thirteen inches long with a wingspan that may exceed three feet. Newell's shearwaters breed on the Hawaiian Islands from April to November, flying to their nesting colonies each day at dark and leaving again before dawn.

The sound of the Newell's shearwater is a repeated "ah-oh," which explains their Hawaiian name, 'a'o. The sounds of the birds above the colonies at night have been described as similar to the sounds of crying babies, mules, or even ghoulish laughter.

He 'a'o ka manu noho i ka lua, 'a'ole e loa'a i ka lima ke nao aku.
It is an 'a'o, a bird that lives in a burrow and
cannot be caught even when the arm is thrust into the hole.
Said of a person who is too smart to be caught.[45]

Newell's shearwaters spend about six months over the eastern tropical Pacific before returning, usually in April, to their mountain nesting sites, which are often located in areas dense with uluhe ferns.

Newell's shearwaters often skim close to the surface of the ocean and then plunge into the water to catch fish or squid they spot from the air.[46] Webbed feet allow the Newell's shearwater to kick off from the water's surface.[47]

H. Douglas Pratt

Wedge-Tailed Shearwaters
Puffinus pacificus chlororhynchus
Hawaiian Name: 'Ua'u Kani
Indigenous (migratory)

The most commonly seen Hawaiian seabird offshore of the main Hawaiian Islands is the wedge-tailed shearwater. Brownish gray and about eighteen inches long, the wedge-tailed shearwater has a pointed beak, wedge-shaped tail, and a wingspan of about three feet. Birds in the "light phase" (most Hawaiian wedge-tailed shearwaters) are dark on top but whitish colored underneath.

Wedge-tailed shearwaters nest in ground burrows, which are small little caves dug about two to three feet into the hillside. The shearwaters begin preparing their nests in April and lay a single white egg in June. Each parent sits on the egg for about ten days at a time as the other parent feeds at sea.

The shearwater chick hatches after about fifty-two days, usually in August. The parents share the duties of feeding partly digested food (regurgitated squid and fish) to the nestling. About two weeks before the chick fledges, the parents leave. During this time the chicks must survive on their own stored fat until they learn to fly and can seek food on their own.

Wedge-tailed shearwaters are often called "the moaning birds" because they make strange wailing or crying sounds when they are settled in their colonies, particularly at dawn and dusk.[48] Like Laysan albatross, wedge-tailed shearwaters return to the same location where they were born to lay their eggs.[49] The chicks hatch in July or August, and after about 3 1/2 months the chicks fledge.[50]

RESCUING SHEARWATERS

In autumn, the fledgling Newell's shearwaters on Kaua'i's north shore leave their colonies and head for the sea, where they begin feeding on their own for the first time. During this maiden journey the birds often become confused by bright lights near roadways and other areas. This causes the birds to become disoriented and land, making them vulnerable to predators such as cats and dogs, and other hazards including cars.

Local residents are encouraged to rescue stranded shearwaters and leave them in small, protected cages provided at "aid stations." Hanalei's aid station is located near the Hanalei Liquor Store.[51] Birds left at the aid stations are picked up each morning by state and federal wildlife biologists.[52]

Brenda Zaun, USFWS

White-Tailed Tropicbird
Phaethon lepturus dorotheae
Hawaiian Name: Koaʻe Kea

Red-Tailed Tropicbird
Phaethon rubricauda rothschildi
Hawaiian Name: Koaʻe ʻUla

Tropicbirds are often seen gliding over Kaua'i's north shore, particularly near the Kīlauea National Wildlife Refuge and along the Nā Pali Coast. Their long, thin bodies effortlessly soar high above the ocean and over the mountain valleys.

The red-tailed tropicbird and the white-tailed tropicbird are both almost all white in color, but the red-tailed tropicbird has a red bill and red tail feathers while the white-tailed tropicbird has a yellow bill and white tail feathers. Both species dive into the water as deep as ten feet to catch fish and squid, and tropicbirds may give a loud, scream-like sound while in flight.

Ke koaʻe iho ia, he manu lele no ka pali kahakō.
That is the tropicbird, one that flies at the sheer cliffs.
Said of a person who is hard to catch.[53]

The red-tailed tropicbird has a forty-four-inch wingspan and is about thirty-nine inches long, compared to the thirty-six-inch wingspan and twenty-seven-inch length of the white-tailed tropicbird. Red-tailed tropicbirds also have two long, red tail feathers as well as black feathers around their eyes. White-tailed tropicbirds have black eye stripes, long, white tail feathers, and black bars across their wings and back.[54]

Tropicbirds are extremely graceful in flight, but awkward on land due to their fully webbed feet. Breeding extends from March to October.

Red-tailed tropicbirds are known for their elaborate displays of courtship during flight, sometimes repeatedly circling each other in an upward and

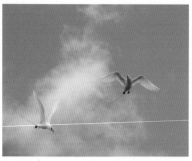 

Tropicbird courtship display. **Brenda Zaun, USFWS**   Tropicbird chicks. **Brenda Zaun, USFWS**

backwards flight motion. A tropicbird engaged in this backward flight appears a bit like it is rowing a boat, and may be nearly stationary in the wind during this elaborate courtship dance, which usually lasts less than ten seconds.

The red-tailed tropicbird lays its eggs on the ground, usually under a shrub, beach vegetation or a rock overhang. The white-tailed tropicbird may nest inland and along the coastline, and lays its egg on a crater wall or on a ledge on a steep cliff face. The chicks of both birds are fully feathered after about six weeks, and by about two months of age they learn to fly.

Ancient Hawaiians utilized feathers from both the red-tailed and white-tailed tropicbirds to make royal feather standards called kāhili, symbols of chiefly rank consisting of feather clusters attached to long poles.[55]

'Au i ke kai me he manu ala.
Cross the sea as a bird.
To sail across the sea. Also applied to a hill that juts out into
the sea or is seen from far out at sea.[56]

Appendix II

Polynesian-Introduced Species

The following plants and animals were brought to the Hawaiian Islands by the early Polynesian settlers on their voyaging canoes, and were an integral part of traditional Hawaiian culture.

Polynesian-Introduced Animals

ʻĪlio (dogs)	*Canis familiaris*
Moa (chickens)	*Gallus gallus*
Puaʻa (pigs)	*Sus scrofa*

Polynesian-Introduced Plants

ʻApe (Elephant's Ear)	*Alocasia macrorrhizos*
ʻAuhuhu	*Tephrosia purpurea*
ʻAwa (Kava)	*Piper methysticum*
ʻAwapuhi Kuahiwi (Shampoo Ginger)	*Zingiber zerumbet*
Ipu (Bottle Gourd)	*Lagenaria siceraria*
Kalo (Taro)	*Colocasia esculenta*
Kamani (Alexandrian Laurel)	*Calophyllum inophyllum*
Kī (Ti)	*Cordyline fruticosa*
Kō (Sugarcane)	*Saccharum officinarum*
Kukui (Candlenut)	*Aleurites moluccana*
Laukahi (Native Plantain)	*Plantago species*
Maiʻa (Banana Plant)	*Musa species*
Milo (Portia Tree)	*Thespesia populnea*
Niu (Coconut Palms)	*Cocos nucifera*
Noni (Indian Mulberry)	*Morinda citrifolia*
ʻOhe (Bamboo)	*Schizostachyum glaucifolium*
ʻŌhiʻa ʻAi (Mountain Apple)	*Eugenia malaccense*
ʻŌlena (Turmeric)	*Curcuma longa*
Pia (Polynesian Arrowroot)	*Tacca leontopetaloides*
ʻUala (Sweet Potato)	*Ipomoea batatas*
Uhi (Yam)	*Dioscorea alata*
Piʻa (Yam)	*Dioscorea pentaphylla*
Hoi (Yam)	*Dioscorea bulbifera*
ʻUlu (Breadfruit)	*Artocarpus altilis*
Wauke (Paper Mulberry)	*Broussonetia papyrifera*

Timeline of the History of Hanalei

c.4000 BC   Ancient mariners in voyaging canoes migrate outward from the Southeast Asian mainland, eventually inhabiting hundreds of islands, including islands of Polynesia.[1] By 1200 AD these ancient voyagers settle nearly every habitable island over some ten million square miles of the Pacific Ocean.

c.2500 BC   A shallow marine bay fills the area that is now Hanalei's coastal plain. The bay begins a seaward regression.[2]

c.300–1000[3]   Polynesian voyagers sailing double-hulled voyaging canoes from the Marquesas Islands about 2,500 miles to the southeast become the first settlers of the Hawaiian Islands.[4] They bring with them pigs, chickens, dogs, and more than two dozen species of plants that provide material for food, clothing, cordage, and many other uses.[5]

c.1200   A second major wave of immigrants to the Islands, this time from Tahiti, conquer and dominate the earlier Marquesan settlers.[6]

c.1200[7]   Taro is farmed in Hanalei Valley in large, irrigated pondfields known as lo'i kalo (taro patches). Networks of 'auwai (irrigation channels) bring water to the taro. Agricultural terraces are also cultivated on the surrounding hillsides.

c.1300   Contact with southern Polynesia ceases or severely diminishes, and Hawaiians no longer complete long-distance, open-ocean voyages. A unique Hawaiian culture continues to evolve.[8]

1778   **January 18:** British Captain James Cook, on a voyage of discovery for England, and in command of the HMS *Discovery* and HMS *Resolution*, comes in sight of O'ahu and then Kaua'i and Ni'ihau.[9]
     On January 19, Cook anchors his ships off the mouth of the Wailua River, and barters nails and pieces of iron for water, pigs, fowl, plantains, sweet potatoes, and taro corms. On January 20, Cook goes ashore for the first time at Waimea Bay on Kaua'i's southwest side.

c.1780 Birth of Kaumuali'i, the future ruler of Kaua'i, to Kā'eokūlani and Kamakahelei.

1810 King Kamehameha I meets Kaua'i's King Kaumuali'i in Honolulu, where Kaumuali'i signs a treaty ceding Kaua'i to Kamehameha to avoid war. Kaumuali'i agrees to place Kaua'i and Ni'ihau under Kamehameha's control and pledges him allegiance. This act unites all the islands under a single ruler. Kaumuali'i remains as high chief of Kaua'i and Ni'ihau.

1815 **January 31:** The Russian ship *Behring* becomes stranded at Waimea Bay. The ship's cargo of sealskins is taken to Makaweli by King Kaumuali'i, causing the Russian-American Company (the owner of the ship and its cargo) to send Georg Anton Schäffer to retrieve the cargo or seek appropriate payment.

1816 Kaumuali'i signs a document with Georg Anton Schäffer that puts Kaua'i under the protection of the Russian Empire, though neither Schäffer nor Kaumuali'i has the authority for such an agreement. In exchange for the ship *Lydia*, Schäffer is given Hanalei Valley.[10]

1816 **November:** Lieutenant Otto von Kotzebue arrives in Hawai'i on the Russian Navy brig *Rurik* and repudiates the activities of Schäffer, informing Kamehameha that Schäffer and Kaumuali'i do not have the support of the Russian Emperor. Problems come to a head in December when Hawaiians kill a Russian and set fire to buildings near Fort Alexander above the Hanalei rivermouth.[11]

KING KAUMUALI'I
(c.1780-1824)

Parents: Kā'eokūlani (father) and Kamakahelei (mother)
Grandparents: Kekaulike and Holau (parents of Kā'eokūlani)
Son: George P. (Prince) Kaumuali'i (Humehume)
Grandchildren: Queen Kapi'olani, Virginia Kapo'oloku Po'omaikelani, and Esther Kinoiki Kekaulike (children of Kūhiō and Kinoiki)
Queen: Deborah Kapule (Kekaiha'akūlou)
Summary of Life of Kaumuali'i:
• Paramount ruler (king) of Kaua'i
• Ceded the island of Kaua'i to King Kamehameha I in 1810, allowing King Kamehameha I to declare Hawai'i one nation
• Supported Russian occupation (led by Georg Anton Schäffer) of Kaua'i in 1816
• Pledged his allegiance to King Kamehameha II (Liholiho) on September 16, 1821, at Waimea, Kaua'i, and accepted Liholiho's sovereignty
• Taken prisoner by Liholiho on September 16, 1821, and taken to O'ahu
• On October 9, 1821, Kaumuali'i married kuhina nui (premier) Ka'ahumanu, former queen and favorite wife of King Kamehameha I

1824	**April 5:** The *Haʻaheo o Hawaiʻi* (*Pride of Hawaiʻi*), the ship of the Hawaiian monarchy, becomes shipwrecked offshore of the mouth of the Waiʻoli River in Hanalei Bay. Built in 1816 in Massachusetts and measuring one hundrd feet long on its deck, the ship was originally named *Cleopatra's Barge* and cost about $50,000 to build and another $50,000 to furnish (see *1995*).

1831 **August 27:** Richard Charlton, the British consul for Hawaiʻi in Honolulu, secures a twenty-year lease from Kauaʻi's Governor Kaikioʻewa for a portion of Hanalei from the eastern side of Hanalei Valley to Kalihiwai. With about one hundred head of cattle, Charlton begins Kauaʻi's first cattle ranch.[12]

1832 Native Hawaiians at Waiʻoli erect a large pole-and-thatch building for use by missionaries during their visits to the area.

1834 **April:** The pole-and-thatch building at Waiʻoli burns down.

1834 **August 21 & 22:** Reverend William Patterson Alexander and family sail a double-hulled canoe belonging to Governor Kaikioʻewa for eight and a half hours from Kauaʻi's Waimea Bay along the Nā Pali Coast at night.[13] In the morning they arrive at the Waiʻoli river mouth in Hanalei Bay. The Alexanders are accompanied to Waiʻoli by seventy-five people, including David Papohaku from the church of Father Whitney at Waimea.[14]

1834 Missionary William Alexander erects a cookhouse at Waiʻoli using coral limestone blocks[15] from the shallows near the mouth of Waipā stream in the foundation, the front steps, and the chimney (this cookhouse later becomes part of the Waiʻoli Mission House—see *1840*). Initially about seven hundred people attend worship at the Waiʻoli meetinghouse.[16]

1834 Joel P. Dedman, a neighbor of the Alexanders, receives a grant of land from Kaikioʻewa for the cultivation of sugarcane.[17]

1835 Missionaries estimate the population of the Haleleʻa district at 3,107 people.[18]

1836 Reverend William Alexander begins acquiring native ʻōhiʻa lehua timber from the mountains behind the Waiʻoli mission for a Western-style frame house.

1836 **October:** Missionary Hiram Bingham visits the Alexanders at Waiʻoli. In November, the frame of the new Mission House is erected.

c.1836 Englishman Captain Kellett, known for his long, white hair, arrives in Hanalei and becomes Hanalei's pilot of the port. Kellett later constructs a house on a bluff known as Lanihuli, which overlooks the ocean near the mouth of the Hanalei River.

1836–1844	Charles Titcomb leases ninety acres of land on the Hanalei River from Kamehameha III for silk production, including an extensive cocoonery. By 1840 about one hundred thousand mulberry trees are growing, enough to feed five hundred thousand silkworms imported from China and America.[19]
1837	The new Waiʻoli Mission House is completed. The two-story, four-room, Western-style, timber-framed structure becomes home to the Alexanders.
1837	Edward Johnson and his wife Lois arrive at the Waiʻoli mission from New Hampshire to help Reverend Alexander direct the Waiʻoli mission schools and begin a school for older boys. Also in 1837, winds destroy the missionary meetinghouse at Waiʻoli.[20]
1838	**January 27:** The framing and thatching is completed on a forty-foot by twenty-four-foot schoolhouse at Waiʻoli. A Western-style, wood-framed home is built for Reverend and Mrs. Johnson, who teach at the Waiʻoli mission station.[21]
1839	Seven acres of sugarcane are planted at Waiʻoli to raise money to build a church and schoolhouse.
1840s	Throughout the 1840s the valleys of Hanalei and Waiʻoli produce an abundance of fruits.[22] Coffee soon becomes a dominant crop, and cattle ranching also becomes significant. Taro is still grown, but its acreage decreases due to lower consumption and traditional food production and a tragic decline in the native population.
1840	The Alexanders are visited at Waiʻoli by members of the Wilkes Expedition.[23]
1840s	Hubertson's Store, Hanalei's first trading store, is built near the Hanalei river mouth and run by an Englishman named Hubertson.
1840–1841	Richard Charlton, the British Consul in Honolulu, has about one hundred head of cattle on his Hanalei cattle ranch. The beef is considered the finest available.
1841	**November:** A new Western-style, timber-framed Waiʻoli Church meetinghouse is built using logs of native ʻōhiʻa lehua.[24]
1842	**September 8:** Frenchman John Bernard and British subject Godfrey Rhodes obtain a fifty-year government land lease in Hanalei Valley to begin the Hanalei Coffee Plantation, the Islands' first commercial coffee plantation.[25] The lease is for ninety acres on the east bank of the Hanalei River and sixty acres on the west side of the river.

1843	Reverend George B. Rowell arrives at the Waiʻoli mission station to replace Reverend William Alexander, who goes to Maui's Lahainaluna Seminary.[26] Church membership at Waiʻoli is 180, up from 27 in 1837.[27] More than 400 Haleleʻa youth attend mission schools.[28]
1843	A church bell for the Waiʻoli Church arrives from Boston to be placed in the Waiʻoli belfry.
1844	Charles Titcomb abandons his attempt to build an industry of silk production in Hanalei because of insect pests, high winds, labor problems, and a drought. He begins a coffee plantation using children of the missionary-run Select School at Waiʻoli to tend to the thousands of coffee plants.[29]
1845	**April 18:** Frenchman John Bernard leaves Honolulu for Kauaʻi on the schooner *Paalua*, which sinks a few hundred yards offshore of Hanalei Bay on April 19, 1845, in a heavy squall, killing Bernard and several others.[30]
1845	**June 16:** The hundred-acre Hanalei Valley estate of Frenchman John Bernard is bought by John K. Von Pfister and Godfrey Rhodes, and becomes known as the Rhodes & Co. Coffee Plantation.[31] A coffee mill is built just above the current site of the Hanalei Bridge (not erected until 1912). Rhodes also builds a two-room stone house called Kikiula on the hill above the ridge. Kikiula later becomes known as the Princeville Plantation House and then the Princeville Ranch House, and is home to a succession of Princeville Plantation managers.
1845	Captain Jules Dudoit, the first French consul to Hawaiʻi, buys the lease to the Charlton Ranch lands. After retiring from the consulship, Dudoit moves to Hanalei where he exports butter and beef, and sells beef to whaling ships.
1846	**July 15:** American Protestant missionaries Abner and Lucy Wilcox board the schooner *Emelia* and sail to Hanalei from Oʻahu to serve at the Waiʻoli mission station for the next twenty-three years.
1848	In association with the government, American Joseph Gardner grows cotton at Waiʻoli, and runs a cotton and woolen cloth mill with a loom and several spinning wheels.[32] Gardner is placed in charge of all government sheep.
1850s	More than one hundred thousand coffee trees grow in Hanalei Valley on coffee plantations. Charles Titcomb's coffee mill consists of a mule turning a perpendicular post fitted at the top with a horizontal cog wheel that turns a flay wheel connected by bands to the milling machinery.

1851   Archibald Archer and Gottfried Wundenberg plant tobacco at Limunui on the banks of the Hanalei River. Prospects for their crop and other attempts to grow tobacco appear favorable for about two years before a cutworm devastates the tobacco crop in Hanalei Valley.

1853   **March 14:** Scotsman Robert Crichton Wyllie, the minister of foreign affairs for the Hawaiian Kingdom, pays $1,300 for government (crown) lands leased to the Rhodes & Co. Coffee Plantation in Hanalei Valley. The importation of Chinese laborers and the end of a period of drought help restore coffee production to profitable levels until a blight poses a new threat.

1853   The *Akamai,* an interisland steamer formerly known as the *SB Wheeler,* makes its first regular run between Kauaʻi and Oʻahu. The 106-foot-long, 114-ton side-wheeler takes on a cargo that includes fourteen thousand pounds of coffee from the Rhodes & Co. Coffee Plantation.

1855   **September 13:** Robert Crichton Wyllie purchases Godfrey Rhodes' business interest in his coffee plantation for $8,000. Gottfried Frederick Wundenberg moves from Honolulu to Hanalei to oversee the plantation.

1856   King Kamehameha IV and his wife, Queen Emma, visit Kauaʻi as part of a "Royal Progress" through the Hawaiian Islands.[33]

1857   Wild cattle around the port of Hanalei number in the thousands. The beef packing industry of earlier years no longer exists due to an inability to bring the product to market.

1860   Waiʻoli mission statistics estimate the district's population at 1,641, down from 3,107 in 1835.[34] During the 1800s, measles and whooping cough epidemics as well as other foreign diseases[35] take many lives in Hanalei and throughout the Hawaiian Islands. The native population of the Islands at this time is only 69,800 people, and continues to decline from about 300,000 at the time of first Western contact (1778).[36]

1860   King Kamehameha IV and his wife Queen Emma visit Kauaʻi with their two-year-old son, Prince Albert Kauikeaouli. The royal family stays at the Hanalei estate of Robert Crichton Wyllie, the minister of foreign affairs for the Hawaiian Kingdom.

   To honor Prince Albert, Wyllie changes the name of his estate to Princeville Plantation, and makes the young prince the estate's intended heir. Tragically, Prince Albert passes away in 1862 at the age of four, and then the following year his father, King Kamehameha IV, passes away at the age of twenty-nine.

1861	Robert Crichton Wyllie processes sugarcane at a mule-powered mill at his Hanalei estate, and in 1862, he completes construction on the Hanalei Sugar Mill on the east bank of the Hanalei River just downriver from the Hanalei Bridge. The mill has a 110-foot smokestack and includes $40,000 worth of machinery purchased from Glasgow, Scotland, making it the most modern and productive sugar mill in the Hawaiian Islands.
1862	Louise Johnson begins Halele'a's first English school, the Hanalei English School, which becomes a public school in 1881.
1863	Robert Crichton Wyllie harvests his first crop of sugar. His mill eventually becomes the center of a small but busy factory village that includes a post office, storage buildings, camphouses, and a butcher shop.
1863	The Sandwich Islands Mission becomes independent, and is no longer supported by the American Mission Board. As part of the missionaries' pensions, the Wai'oli Mission House is deeded to Abner Wilcox.
1864	**October 3:** A Roman Catholic chapel is dedicated on the western bank of the Hanalei River near the rivermouth. A tall and slender, wooden church belfry was built on the church site around 1900 by Father Sylvester, who had long served the Hanalei area.
1865	**October 19:** Robert Crichton Wyllie, the owner of the Princeville Plantation, passes away. His nephew and heir, Robert Crichton Cockrane, arrives in Hawai'i from Waltham, Illinois to learn the sugarcane business from manager John Low.
1869	Upon a return visit to their original home in Connecticut, Wai'oli missionaries Abner and Lucy Wilcox both contract malarial fever just a few days after arriving, and pass away within one week of each other.
1870s–1960	Rice becomes the dominant agricultural product in Hanalei, first cultivated by Chinese and then by Japanese and Filipino immigrants. By 1882 Hanalei Valley is almost completely cultivated in rice.
1874	**March 17:** Newly elected King Kalākaua arrives in Hanalei on the monarch's royal tour of the Hawaiian Kingdom on the steamer *Kilauea*, greeted by a royal twenty-one-gun salute. The "guns" are actually large logs of 'ōhi'a lehua that are bored out and packed with gunpowder.[37]
1879	Five Chinese farmers become the first Chinese to lease land from the Princeville Plantation, leasing forty-two acres[38] of Hanalei Valley land for $15/acre/year.[39]

1880	An established Chinese rice factoring company, the Chulan company, leases three hundred acres of Hanalei Valley land from the Princeville Plantation for $20/acre/year.
1880	Princeville Plantation employs two hundred laborers and has nine hundred breeding stock, four hundred head working stock, and one hundred fifty steers. About two hundred acres of rice grow in Hanalei Valley and about one hundred acres of sugarcane are cultivated on the upper slopes.
1881	**September 23:** Princess Regent Liliʻuokalani, the future queen, arrives by ship at Hanalei Bay. The next day, she travels to Kīlauea to commemorate the Kīlauea Sugar Corporation's purchase of a railroad engine and twenty-four railroad cars to carry sugarcane. Princess Liliʻuokalani strikes two hard blows to drive in the ceremonial first spike.[40]
1884	The Chinese population of Hanalei is 459, increasing to 689 by 1896.[41]
c.1890	The former residence of Mr. and Mrs. Edward and Lois H. Johnson at Waiʻoli, originally built near the Waiʻoli Mission House, is moved east, closer to the ocean to a site across from the current Hanalei Pavilion and adjacent to the Wilcox estate.
1892	The first Hanalei Pier is built of wood on the eastern side of Hanalei Bay near the mouth of the Hanalei River.
1892	Hanalei and Waiʻoli Valleys produce 750 acres of rice, of the 7,321 total acres grown in the Hawaiian Islands. Mokulēʻia in Oʻahu is the second-largest rice producing area in the Islands, with 738 acres in cultivation, followed by Waikīkī, with 542 acres planted in rice.[42]
1893	At least five rice mills operate in the Hanalei region, including one near the Hanalei River about midway between the Hanalei Bridge and Hanalei Town.[43]
1894	The Hanalei Sugar Mill is shut down by C. Brewer & Co.
1895	Albert Spencer Wilcox, the son of pioneering Waiʻoli missionaries Abner and Lucy Wilcox, secures complete ownership of the Princeville Plantation and converts much of the land into a cattle ranch.
c.1895	A bridge is constructed over the Hanalei River, replacing a hand-pulled ferry. A steep wagon road leads down to the bridge and ends at Hanalei, beyond which there is only a trail (see *1912*).

1895   Eric Knudsen writes in his journal: "Rice fields and taro patches covered the flat bottom lands as far as the eye could see...many Chinamen were working in the fields."[44]

1899   Kauikeōlani (the Albert Spencer Wilcox Beach House), is built near the shoreline of Hanalei Bay and becomes the home of A. S. Wilcox and his wife Emma Kauikeōlani Napoleon Mahelona.

1909–1919   Joseph Hughes Moragne, Kaua'i's first county engineer, helps to create the "Belt Road" around Kaua'i, including the road from Hanalei to Hā'ena.

1910   Walter Foss Sanborn builds the first Western-style "beach house" directly bordering the beach in Hanalei.

1912   The Hanalei Bridge is erected over the Hanalei River at the bottom of the hill descending into Hanalei Valley. The new Pratt-truss steel bridge replaces the previous iron-truss bridge, erected around 1895 just upriver from the site of the new bridge.

1912   A replacement pier is constructed on Hanalei Bay. The new Hanalei Pier, built to meet the needs of Hanalei's thriving rice industry, is constructed using reinforced concrete.

1912   Wai'oli Hui'ia Church is built by Sam, George, and Albert Wilcox in honor of their parents, Abner and Lucy Wilcox.[45]

1914   Charles, Elsie, and Mabel Wilcox, and their parents Samuel and Emma Wilcox, along with Ethel Damon, buy five adjoining beachfront lots in Hanalei at an auction. Mabel and Charles plan a house known as Mahamoku ("island of peace"), which is built by Sam Itchioka of Līhu'e.

1914   The telephone directory lists eight general merchandising stores (seven Chinese-owned) as well as twelve Chinese rice-planting companies in the Hanalei region.[46]

1915   Norwegian Hans Peter Fayé, the nephew of prominent sugar planter Valdemar "Kanuka" Knudsen, builds a home fronting Hanalei Bay.

1915   Renowned author Jack London (1876–1916) attends a lū'au in Niumalu with Walter Foss Sanborn, and later drives to Hanalei Bay to board a steamer back to Honolulu.

1919   The 110-foot smokestack of the Hanalei Sugar Mill is torn down, and the bricks are sold to the Kīlauea Sugar Company.

1921   Elsie Wilcox, Mabel Wilcox, and Lucy Etta Wilcox Sloggett, granddaughters of Wai'oli missionaries Abner and Lucy Wilcox, undertake a complete and extensive restoration of the Waiʻoli Mission House and Waiʻoli Mission Hall (the former Waiʻoli Church).

1926   The Territory of Hawaiʻi constructs a new schoolhouse at Waiʻoli.

1928   At a cost of $150,000, a 3,558-foot tunnel is built through rock to divert water into the Hanalei Tunnel from the Kaʻāpoko tributary of the Hanalei River.[47]

1929   Electricity becomes available in Hanalei from the Wainiha Power Plant, built in 1908 to provide power to McBryde Sugar Company in ʻEleʻele.[48]

1930   The Haraguchi Rice Mill is built on the west bank of the Hanalei River, just upriver from the Hanalei Bridge, and on the site where another mill, the Man Sing (million success) Mill, had previously stood before it burned down in 1930. Man Sing sold his rice mill to the Haraguchis in 1924.

1930s   At least four rice mills operate in the Hanalei region, including the Hiramoto Mill (formerly Hee Fat Mill) at Waipā; the Ching Young Mill in Hanalei Town; the Nakatsuji Mill (formerly Hop Chong Wai Mill, managed by Ah Hoy) just east of the Waiʻoli Bridge; and the Haraguchi Mill, on the site of the old Man Sing Mill just upriver from the Hanalei Bridge.[49]

1934   A lūʻau is held to celebrate the Waiʻoli Mission Centennial.

1946   April 1—A tsunami kills seventeen people on Kauaʻi and causes extensive damage in the Hanalei region, including the collapse of Waikoko Bridge.

1952   The Waiʻoli Mission House is incorporated as a museum.

1955   St. Williams Catholic Church is constructed in Hanalei town at the intersection of Route 560 and Mālolo Road after a land trade between the Catholic Church and Gaylord Parke Wilcox. The former language school building is moved to a lot on the Hanalei Bay shoreline that was once the site of the Sloggett Beach House.[50]

1957   March 9: A tsunami destroys more than seventy-five homes on Kauaʻi's north shore and damages Hanalei Bridge.

1966   A parsonage is built near Waiʻoli Huiʻia Church.

1968   July: Harry Trueblood of Eagle County Development Corporation, a Denver-based subsidiary of Consolidated Oil and Gas Company, purchases all but about fifty acres of the Princeville Ranch from a subsidiary of American Factors Ltd. (Amfac), including about eleven thousand acres of Princeville land, seven thousand acres of agricultural land, and four thousand acres of forest reserve conservation land.[51]

1968   Princeville owners receive approval from the Land Use Commission for urban districting on 995 acres. In the 1970s the development of a major resort area begins.

1972   Hanalei National Wildlife Refuge is established on 917 acres in Hanalei Valley.

1973   Three Waiʻoli mission structures are placed on the National Register of Historic Places: the Waiʻoli Mission House (built from 1834–1837); the Waiʻoli Mission Hall (the former Waiʻoli Church, built in 1841); and the Waiʻoli Huiʻia Church (built in 1912).

1973   The Hanalei Canoe Club is established as an extension of the Hanalei Hawaiian Civic Club. The State Championship Regatta is held in Hanalei Bay, and Hanalei Canoe Club takes first place.

1977   The Princeville Center opens, offering twenty-seven thousand square feet of space for rent.

1978   Thirty-three boats sail 2,120 miles from California's Golden Gate Bridge to Hanalei Bay in the first annual Singlehanded TransPacific Yacht Race. Twenty-two boats finish the race.

1979   Archaeologists excavate the interior floor of the 1841 Waiʻoli Mission Hall (the former Waiʻoli Church). After the excavation, extensive repairs are undertaken to stabilize the building.

1982   Princeville Hotel Corporation is formed to construct a major luxury hotel at Puʻupōā on the shoreline of the east side of Hanalei Bay. The three hundred-room Sheraton Princeville Hotel opens in September of 1985. The development of the Prince Golf Course begins in 1986.

1987   The Qintex Group of Queensland, Australia, purchases the Sheraton Princeville Hotel. In 1989, construction begins on the sixty thousand square-foot Prince Clubhouse adjacent to the golf course. In 1991 the hotel is extensively refurbished, upgraded to a five-star standard, and renamed Sheraton Mirage Princeville.

1992   **September 11:** Hurricane 'Iniki makes a direct hit on Kauaʻi. More than 70% of Kauaʻi's homes are damaged and 1,421 homes are completely destroyed, including 279 homes in Princeville. The hurricane causes more than $3 billion in property damage on Kauaʻi, and the Princeville Hotel requires $30 million in repairs.

1995   The Smithsonian Institution's Dr. Paul Forsythe Johnston uses remote sensing equipment in Hanalei Bay to discover the buried location of the wreckage of *Ha'aheo o Hawai'i* (*Cleopatra's Barge*), the Hawaiian monarchy's former ship, which sank in 1824. Archaeological excavation of the wreck occurs during the summers of 1995 and 1996.

1998   **July 30:** President Bill Clinton formally designates the Hanalei River as an American Heritage River, making it one of just fourteen rivers nationwide to receive the Heritage designation, and the only tropical waterway to receive the designation. On May 6, 2003, the Hanalei Heritage River Program receives a $700,000 grant from the Environmental Protection Agency toward the protection of the Hanalei ahupua'a watershed.[52]

2005   The nine thousand-acre Princeville Resort is sold for $200 million to a Honolulu investment consortium known as Hawai'i Land Development Corporation in partnership with Morgan Stanley Real Estate Funds.[53] The sale includes the Princeville Hotel along with the resort's two golf courses, the Princeville Tennis Club and Pro Shop, Princeville Health Club and Spa, the Princeville Shopping Center, and other north shore lands.

2008   **September:** The Princeville Hotel begins a renovation costing more than $60 million to re-brand the hotel as the St. Regis Resort, Princeville, opening in 2009.

Complete List of Sources

The footnotes referred to in this text may be seen at *www.hawaiianencyclopedia. com*

Note: In the following list of sources, many Hawaiian words are lacking proper diacritical marks. This is due to the fact that all sources are cited exactly as published, and not altered to conform to proper spelling and punctuation. In the text of this book, however, all Hawaiian words (other than in cited titles or quotes) conform to proper Hawaiian spelling, including diacritical marks (e.g., glottal stop ('okina) and macron (kahakō)).

Abbott, Isabella Aiona. *Lā'au Hawai'i: Traditional Hawaiian Uses of Plants.* Honolulu: Bishop Museum Press, 1992.

"A Brief History of the Wai'oli Hui'ia Church." *Wai'oli Hui'ia Church Bulletin,* 2003.

"A Brief History of Tour Boats on the North Shore of Kaua'i." *Environment Hawai'i,* December 1997.

Adams, Wanda. "Hanging Out in and Around Hanalei." *Honolulu Advertiser,* April 6, 2003.

———. "Road to Hanalei an Experience in Itself." *Honolulu Advertiser,* April 6, 2003.

Akaka, Daniel K. "Akaka Welcomes White House Designation of Hanalei River as an American Heritage River." Press release, July 30, 1998.

Alexander, James M. *Mission Life in Hawaii; Memoir of Rev. William P. Alexander.* Oakland, CA: Pacific Press Publishing Co., 1888.

Alexander, Mary C. *Notes of the Early Life of William Patterson and Mary Ann Alexander* (1834-1843). Līhu'e: Kaua'i Historical Society, 1934.

Alexander, Mary Charlotte. *William Patterson Alexander: In Kentucky, the Marquesas, Hawaii.* Honolulu: privately printed, 1934.

Alexander, William DeWitt. "Private Journal of a Tour of Kauai (Written by William DeWitt Alexander, when a boy of sixteen, in 1849)." Read to the Kauai Historical Society, May 8, 1933.

Shakespeare, William. "Scene II." *Antony and Cleopatra.* http://the-tech.mit.edu/ Shakespeare/cleopatra/cleopatra.2.2.html.

Athens, Stephen J. *Prehistoric Pondfield Agriculture in Hawai'i: Archaeological Investigations at the Hanalei National Wildlife Refuge, Kaua'i.* Honolulu: Department of Anthropology, Bernice P. Bishop Museum, 1983.

"At Home in the Islands: Graham Nash Builds Our House on Hanalei Bay." http:// www.islander-magazine.com/nash.html.

Au, Laurie. "200 Small Whales Linger in Kauai's Hanalei Bay." *Honolulu Star-Bulletin*, July 4, 2004.

"Autopsy Finds Melon-head Whale Died of Starvation. *Garden Island*, July 29, 2004.

Berg, Carl. "Mud Deposits Affecting Hanalei Coral." *Garden Island*, September 24, 2007.

Billig, Pérez Billig. "Waipā: A Living Ahupua'a." *Spirit of Aloha*, November/ December 2002.

Bingham, Hiram. *A Residence of Twenty-One Years in the Sandwich Islands.* Hartford: Hezekiah Huntington, 1848.

Bird, Isabella L. *Six Months in the Sandwich Islands.* 1875. Reprint. Honolulu: University of Hawaii Press for Friends of the Library of Hawaii, 1964.

Blaich, Beryl. Notes on file regarding Sanborn beach house, based on information from Janet Sanborn, Alan Sanborn, January 5, 1987. Kaua'i Historical Society.

Borg, Jim. "Genetic Research Offers Intriguing New View of Polynesian Migrations." *Hawaii Magazine*, February 1997.

Bovard Studios, Inc. "Stained Glass Windows: Great Restoration Stories." http:// www.bovardstudio.com/customers/architects_restoration_engagements_ great_stories.aspx.

———. "Stained Glass Windows: Windows for the Soul." http://www.bovardstudio. com/gallery/windows_for_the_soul_pages.aspx?pg=066-Waioli-Huiia-Church.html.

Calhoun, R. Scott, and Charles H. Fletcher. "Measured and Predicted Sediment Yield from a Subtropical, Heavy Rainfall, Steep-sided River Basin: Hanalei, Kauai, Hawaiian Islands." *Geomorphology* 30 (1999): 213-226.

"Ching Young Village History Page." http://www.chingyoungvillage.com/history. htm.

Choo, David K. "Agriculture Poi Story." http://www.hawaiibusiness.cc/hb82001/ default.cfm?articleid=10.

Clark, John R. K. *Beaches of Kaua'i and Ni'ihau*. Honolulu: University of Hawaii Press, 1990.

Conrow, Joan. "Haraguchi Rice Mill Site of Yagura-raising Effort." *Garden Island*, April 13, 2004.

———. "Kauai Man Sounds 164-year-old Royal Conch: The Shell Was Recovered from King Kamehameha II's Sunken Royal Yacht in Hanalei." *Honolulu Star-Bulletin*, December 6, 2002.

———. "Picture Perfect?: The Changing Face of Hanalei." *Kaua'i Business Report*, May 2003.

———. "Taro-Birds-Trouble." Honolulu Star-Bulletin, April 1, 1996.

Cook, Chris. "Hanalei Road Listed on National Register of Historic Places." *Garden Island*.

———. "Kaua'i Surfers Conquer King's Reef at Hanalei." *Garden Island*, November 29, 1996.

———. "Louise Marston of Tahiti Nui: 1928-2003." Garden Island, October 12, 2003.

———. "New Book Tells Story of Waimea's Russian Fort from Hawaiian Perspective." *Garden Island*, May 26, 2002.

———. "No Hanalei Link for Folk Song 'Puff the Magic Dragon.'" *Garden Island*, July 25, 2004.

———. *Princeville's History*. Honolulu: 2002.

———. "Robeson, Wilcox Honored for Preserving Hanalei Bridge: Statewide Historic Hawai'i Foundation Conference Opens." *Garden Island*, May 15, 2003.

———. *The Kaua'i Movie Book: Films made on the Garden Island*. Honolulu: Mutual Publishing, 1996.

Cooper, George, and Gavan Daws. *Land and Power in Hawaii: The Democratic Years*. Honolulu: University of Hawaii Press, 1985.

Culliney, John L. *Islands in a Far Sea: Nature and Man in Hawaii*. San Francisco: Sierra Club Books, 1988.

Curtis, Paul. "Nishii Returns to Princeville Corporation: Yasuno Announces Retirement." *Garden Island*, April 20, 2003.

Damon, Ethel M. *Koamalu: A Story of Pioneers on Kauai and of What They Built in That Island Garden.* vol. 1. Honolulu: privately printed, 1931.

———. *Letters from the Life of Abner and Lucy Wilcox, 1836-1869.* Honolulu: privately printed, 1950.

Davies, Theo. *An Account of the First Visit to the Island of Kauai in September 1860.* Transcription from the original journal written in longhand on board S. S. Ariel, on the Atlantic, August 22,1862.

Day, A. Grove. *History Makers of Hawaii: A Biographical Dictionary.* Honolulu: Mutual Publishing, 1984.

Dickey, Lyle A. "Hanalei Place Names." Read at the meeting of the Kauai Historical Society, October 22, 1934.

"DNA Tests Trace Polynesians to China Origins." *Honolulu Advertiser*, August 11, 1998.

Donohugh, Donald. *The Story of Kōloa: A Kaua'i Plantation Town.* Honolulu: Mutual Publishing, 2001.

Dorrance, William H., and Francis S. Morgan. *Sugar Islands: The 165-Year Story of Sugar in Hawai'i.* Honolulu: Mutual Publishing, 2000.

"EPA Grant to Help Evaluate Hanalei Waters." *Honolulu Advertiser*, June 2, 2003.

Evenhuis, Neal L., and Lucius G. Eldredge, eds. "Records of the Hawaii Biological Survey for 2000." Bishop Museum Occasional Papers nos. 68, 69. Honolulu: Bishop Museum, 2002.

Flinn, John. "Destination Hawaii." *San Francisco Examiner*, September 6, 1998.

Fogel, Robert William. "The Phases of the Four Great Awakenings." http://www.press.uchicago.edu/Misc/Chicago/256626.html.

Fox, Bob. "The Wilcox Beach House at Hanalei Beach." Kaua'i Historical Society.

Frommer's. "A World of Travel Experience." http://www.frommers.com/destinations/kauai/0011021993.html.

Frostad, Shon. "Where are the O'opu? It's About the River." *Hanalei Heritage River* 1, no. 5 (January 2001).

Fujimoto, Dennis. "Haraguchi Rice Mill Receives Young Bros. Grant." *Garden Island*, August 14, 2003.

———. "Melon-head Whales Depart Hanalei Bay Thanks to Reverse Hukilau." *Garden Island*, July 5, 2004.

Gima, Craig. "Whale's Body Found Near Hanalei Bay: The Melon-headed Calf Is Packed in Ice Prior to a Necropsy." *Honolulu Star-Bulletin*, July 6, 2004.

Gomes, Andrew. "Stone Bids for Hanalei Resort: Ko Olina Developer Expected to Take On Kaua'i's Princeville." *Honolulu Advertiser*, July 15, 2004.

Gradie, Jonathan C., et al. "Airborne Multispectral Imagery for Quantifying Suspended Sediment Plumes: Hanalei Bay, Kauai." http://ltpwww.gsfc.nasa.gov/ISSSR-95/airborne.htm.

Hanalei Cottage. "Hanalei Fire station—Statement of Historical and/or Architectural Significance." http://hanalei-house.com/hancott.html.

"Hanalei Hawaii Resource Guide." http://www.pe.net/~rksnow/hiscountyhanalei.htm.

"Hanalei Heritage River: Hui Watershed Action Plan—Our Mission Statement." http://www.hanaleiriver.org/hhrinfo/wateractionl.html.

"Hanalei House." http://hanalei-house.com/hanhouse.html.

"Hanalei House and Cottage: Your Special Hideaway." http://hanalei-house.com.

"Hanalei Poi Company." http://www.hanaleipoi.com/pages/about.html.

"Hanalei Poi Company—Our Poi Mill." http://www.hanaleipoi.com/pages/mill.html.

"Hanalei River Program Awarded $700,000." *Garden Island*, May 7, 2003.

"Hanalei's Beautiful New Church Edifice." *Garden Island*, October 29, 1912.

"Hanalei School: Hanalei School History and General Information." http://www.aloha.net/~winny/history.html.

"Hanalei School History." http://www.hanalei.k12.hi.us/hist.html.

"Hanalei Surf Online: The One Lane Bridges of Hanalei, Kauai." http://www.hanaleiurf.com/hanalei_bridges.htm.

"Haraguchi Rice Mill Hosts Free Workshop on Traditional Timber Framing April 5-9." *Kaua'i Business Report*, April 2004.

"Hawaiian Culture, Hawaiian History, and Interesting Facts About Kauai and Hanalei." http://www.hanaleibayresort.com/hanaleibay/facts.html.

Hawaii's Birds. Honolulu: Hawaiian Audubon Society, 1993.

Hayworth, Phil. "Stone Plans Changes at Princeville." *Garden Island*, November 16, 2004.

———. "The Future of Princeville: New Owners Say Community, Market to Lead Development." *Garden Island*, July 18, 2004.

Hazlett, Richard W., and Donald W. Hyndman. *Roadside Geology of Hawai'i*. Missoula, MT: Mountain Press Publishing Company, 1996.

Helen Kapililani Sanborn Davis: Reminiscences of a Life in the Islands, as told to Maili Yardley. Honolulu: Native Books, 2000.

"Historic Register Application Statement of Historical and/or Architectural Significance." n.d.

Historic Waioli Hui'ia United Church of Christ. "Informational Brochure." n.d.

"History of the Historic Bed and Breakfast." http://www.historicbnb.com/history.html.

"Holocene History of Sediment Deposition and Stratigraphy on the Hanalei Coastal Plain, Kauai, Hawaii (Abstract)." http://www.soest.hawaii.edu/GG/STUDENTS/calhoun/abstract.html.

"Hoopulapula Haraguchi Rice Mill—Hawaii Museums Association Database." http:www.hawaiimuseums.org/mc/iskauai_hoopulapula.htm?nowritefs.

"Island Incentives: Princeville and North Shore." http://www.islandincentives.com/pub/places/kauai-north.html.

"Human DNA Analysis Points to African Origin: Study Performed on Complete Genome." *Honolulu Advertiser*, December 7, 2000.

Joesting, Edward. *Kauai: The Separate Kingdom*. Honolulu: University of Hawaii Press, 1984.

Johnson, Steve. "Summary of Restoration of Waioli Belltower, 1987." Kaua'i Historical Society.

Johnston, Paul Forsythe. "Hanalei Redux—A Shocking Find." http://www.si.edu/i+d/redux.html.

———. "Hanalei Redux—Next year?" http://www.si.edu/i+d/redux.03.html.

———. "Hanalei Redux—The Real Work Begins: Details in the Lab and at the Desk." http://www.si.edu/i+d/redux.02.html.

———."Do they really pay you that?" http://www.si.edu/i+d/ship.arc.html.

"Kauai Harbor House: History." http://kauai-harborhouse.com/history.html.

"Kauikeōlani Estate: Hanalei Plantation Cottages." http://www.hanaleiland.com/pages/kaui_floorplan.htm.

"KauaiNetwork.org—Rural Champions—The Waipa Foundation." http://kauainetwork.org/waipa.html.

Kaufman, Mark. "Navy Sonar Exercises Under Fire Over Potential Effects on Whales: Hanalei Impacts Felt All the Way to Washington." *Garden Island*, July 12, 2004.

Kayal, Michele. "The Power of Poi: Hanalei Chilled Product Gaining Market Appeal." *Honolulu Advertiser*, January 1, 2001.

King, Josephine W. "Reminiscences of Hanalei, Kauai." Presented at the Kauaʻi Historical Society, April 26, 1917.

Korn, Alfons L. *The Victorian Visitors; An Account of the Hawaiian Kingdom, 1861-1866*. Honolulu: University of Hawaii Press, 1958.

Krauss, Bob. "Pacific Migration Theory Disputed: Polynesians May Be from Indonesia." *Honolulu Advertiser*, July 18, 2000.

Krauss, Bob, and William P. Alexander. *Grove Farm Plantation: The Biography of a Hawaiian Sugar Plantation*. Palo Alto, CA: Pacific Books, 1965, 1984.

Kubota, Gary T. "Poi Takes a Pounding." *Honolulu Star-Bulletin*, July 7, 2002.

Kurihara, Frank H. *Hanohano Hanalei*. Skyline Designs, 1996. Bishop Museum Archives (MS Doc. 303).

"Lease of Waiʻoli Land to William P. Alexander by King Kamehameha III, (1841)." Kauaʻi Historical Society.

"Lease—Kamehameha III To William P. Alexander. 1841." Translation. Kauaʻi Historical Society

"Lumahaʻi Hula." Kimo Alama, Keaulana Collection. Bishop Museum Archives.

Lydgate, J. M. "The Wreck of the Saginaw: Notes on Halford's Story. From memories of S. W. Wilcox, A. S. Wilcox and Mrs. S. B. Deverill, mainly." May 22, 1914.

"Record of Guests. Kr. Oni O. Mahamoku." Kauaʻi Historical Society.

"Maritime Archaeology in Hawai'i: Cleopatra's Barge—The Pride of Hawai'i." http://www.captainrick.com/archaeology.htm.

Matisoo-Smith, E., et al. "Patterns of Prehistoric Human Mobility in Polynesia Indicated by mtDNA from the Pacific Rat." *Anthropology* 95 (December 1998): 15145-15150.

Matsunaga, Mark. "Scientists Still Fish for Migration Answer: Canoes Ready to Test Theory of the Fishhooks." *Honolulu Advertiser*, April 16, 1995.

"Mechanics Needed to Restore Rice Mill Engine" *Kaua'i Business Review*, March 2003.

Moffat, Riley M., and Gary L. Fitzpatrick. *Surveying the Māhele.* Honolulu: Editions Limited, 1995.

MSN Entertainment. "Acapulco Gold (1972) Overview." http://entertainment.msn. com/Movies/Movie.aspx?m=504466.

———. "Beachhead (1954)." http://entertainment.msn.com/Movies/Movie. aspx?m=45046.

———. "Bird of Paradise (1951)." http://entertainment.msn.com/Movies/Movie. aspx?m=492076, 3/29/2003.

———. "Miss Sadie Thompson (1953)." http://entertainment.msn.com/Movies/ Movie.aspx?m=41578.

———. "Naked Paradise (1957)." http://entertainment.msn.com/Movies/Movie. aspx?m=64076.

———. "Pagan Love Song (1950)." http://entertainment.msn.com/Movies/Movie. aspx?m=127725.

———. "Paradise, Hawaiian Style (1966)." http://entertainment.msn.com/Movies/ Movie.aspx?m=489765.

———. "Seven (1979)." http://entertainment.msn.com/Movies/Movie. aspx?m=45762.

———. "She-Gods of Shark Reef (1958)." http://entertainment.msn.com/Movies/ Movie.aspx?m=110899.

———. "South Pacific (1958)." http://entertainment.msn.com/Movies/Movie. aspx?m=465308.

———. "The Wackiest Ship in the Army (1961)." http://entertainment.msn.com/ Movies/Movie.aspx?m=54495.

————. "Uncommon Valor (1983)." http://entertainment.msn.com/Movies/Movie. aspx?m=84985.

"National Register of Historic Places—Hawaii (HI), Kauai County." http://www. nationalregisterofhistoric places.com/HI/Kauai/districts.html.

"Navy Admits to Sonar Use Prior to Beaching." *Kauai Island Monthly*, September 10, 2004.

"New Church is Dedicated." *Garden Island*, October 22, 1912.

"New Top for Hanalei Bridge." *Garden Island*, February 9, 2003.

"North Shore Kauai: Hanalei Valley Lookout." http://www.kauai-hawaii.com/north/ hanalei_vl.html.

"North Shore Kauai: Waioli Mission House." http://www.kauai-hawaii.com/north/ waioli_mh.html.

O'Malley, Anne E. "Not Your Run-of-the-mill Education: Students Visit Historic Hanalei Rice Mill." *Kauai Island Monthly*, May 14, 2004.

Orazio, Carl, principal investigator. "Survey of Organic Chemical Contaminants in Water, Sediment and Biota of the Hanalei River, Island of Kauai, Hawaii, December, 2001." Final Report CERC-8335-FYO3-31-01, Columbia Environmental Research Center, November 12, 2002.

Peterson, Roger Tory. *Western Birds: A Field Guide to Western Birds*. 3rd ed. Boston: Houghton Mifflin Company, 1990.

Pichaske, Pete. "Smithsonian to Excavate King Kamehameha II's Sunken Yacht: The Team Leader Says Artifacts Could Offer Insight Into Hawaiian Culture In The Early 1800s." http://www.holoholo.org/reporter/kamyacht.html.

Piercy, LaRue W. *Hawaii's Missionary Saga: Sacrifice and Godliness in Paradise*. Honolulu, HI: Mutual Publishing, 1992.

"Post Office in Paradise: Kauai Postmarks, Part 1—Anahola to Koloa." http://www. hawaiianstamps.com/iskauai1.html.

Pratt, Douglas, Phillip L. Bruner, and Delwyn G. Berrett. *A Field Guide to the Birds of Hawai'i and the Tropical Pacific*. Princeton: Princeton University Press, 1987.

"Princeville and North Shore." http://www.islandincentives.com/pub/places/kauai-north.html.

"Princeville Corporation Finalizes Sale of Land." Garden Island, September 14, 2003.

"Princeville Ranch." *Na Leo 'O Princeville*, Summer 2003.

"Princeville Resort: A Place to Stay." http://www.princevillecom/sta/index.html.

"Princeville Resort: Destination Princeville." http://www.princevillecom/dest/dest_pv.html.

"Press Release for Preservation News." *The Hanalei Project*: 1000 Friends of Kauai, June 6, 1989.

Pukui, Mary Kawena. *'Ōlelo No'eau: Hawaiian Proverbs & Poetical Sayings*. Honolulu: Bishop Museum Press, 1983.

Pukui, Mary Kawena, and Samuel H. Elbert. *Hawaiian Dictionary*. Revised and enlarged edition. Honolulu: University of Hawaii Press, 1986.

Pukui, Mary Kawena, Samuel H. Elbert, and Esther T. Mookini. *Place Names of Hawaii*. Revised and expanded edition. Honolulu: University of Hawaii Press, 1974.

"Recreation.gov: Hanalei NWR." http://www.recreation.gov/detail.cfm?ID=(1417).

"Renovated Hanalei Bridge Officially Blessed." *Garden Island*, November 9, 2003.

"Report of the Committee on the Support of Mr. Wilcox and the Waioli Select School, 1861." Grove Farm Archives.

"Report of the Superintendent of Public Instruction to the Governor of the Territory of Hawaii from December 31, 1902 to December 31, 1904."

"Report of Waioli Select School." [ca. 1848-49]. Grove Farm Archives.

"Report of Waioli Select School, 1859 & 60." Grove Farm Archives.

"Report of Waioli Select School From July 16th, to May 12th, 1863." Grove Farm Archives.

"Restoration: Hana Hou!" *Ho'opulapula Haraguchi Rice Mill News*, Winter 2001.

Riznik, Barnes. "Overview of Historic House Museums and Parks in Hawai'i: Changing Ideas of Preservation and Interpretation." http://crm.cr.nps.gov/archive/19-8/19-8-13.pdf.

———. "Waioli Mission House: Hanalei, Kauai."

———. "Kaua'i, Hawai'i: Grove Farm Homestead and Waioli Mission House, 1987."

Riznik, Barnes, and Robert J. Schleck. "Waioli Mission House, Grove Farm Homestead. Proposal, Waioli Church Belfry." August 13, 1985.

Robinson, Robby. "History of the Singlehanded TransPacific Yacht Race." http://www.sfbaysss.org/transpac96/tphist.html.

Schleck, Robert J. "The Wilcox Quilts in Hawaii. Kaua'i, Hawai'i: Grove Farm Homestead and Waioli Mission House, 1986."

Shapiro, Lisa, M.A., and William A., Shapiro, M.A. "Archaeological Investigations of Hanalei National Wildlife Refuge, Hanalei, Island of Kaua'i, May, 1995."

Soboleski, Hank. "History Makers of Kaua'i: Abner and Lucy Wilcox." *Garden Island*, October 7, 2001.

———. "History Makers of Kaua'i: Georg Anton Schaffer." *Garden Island*, April 22, 2001.

———. "History Makers of Kaua'i: H.P. Fayé." *Garden Island*, March, 29, 2003.

———. "History Makers of Kaua'i: Mabel Wilcox." *Garden Island*, June 24, 2001.

———. "History Makers of Kaua'i: Queen Emma." *Garden Island*, March 17, 2002.

———. "Jack London & Kaua'i: The Famous Author's Stay with Reverend Lydgate in 1915." *Kaua'i*, v2 (October 2003).

Sommer, Anthony. "Hanalei Bay Yields Royal Treasures: Divers Find a Section of King Kamehameha II's Sunken Yacht—And Not a Moment Too Soon." *Honolulu Star-Bulletin*, July 26, 2000.

"State Must Pay Hanalei Legal Fees of $100,000: Three Tour Operators Celebrate a Federal Court Ruling that Keeps Their Businesses Afloat." *Honolulu Star-Bulletin*, August 28, 2003.

"State of the River 2001: Hanalei American Heritage River." http://www.epa.gov/rivers/sor/sorhanalei.pdf.

"Structurae: Hanalei River Bridge (1912)." http://www.structurae.de/en/structures/data/str00935.php.

TenBruggencate, Jan. "Groups Urge Navy to Reduce Sonar Harm to Whales." *Honolulu Advertiser*, July 15, 2004.

———. "Hanalei Braces for Boats." *Honolulu Advertiser*, May 15, 2002.

———. "State Planning to Restore Hanalei Bridge." *Honolulu Advertiser*, October 23, 1999.

————. "Whale Dies After Pod Returns to Sea. Carcass of 3-foot Infant Washes Ashore at Hanalei." *Honolulu Advertiser*, July 7, 2004.

"The Legacy of a Young Hawaiian Prince." *Na Leo 'O Princeville: A publication of Princeville Corporation & Princeville Utilities Company, Inc.*, Spring 2003.

"The Reader's Companion to American History: Second Great Awakening." http://college.hmco.com/history/readerscomp/rcah/html/ah_077700_ secondgreata.htm.

"The Wade Residence—Hanalei, Kauai." Kaua'i Historical Society.

Tsutsumi, Cheryl Chee. "Where Movies Spun their Magic." *Honolulu Star-Bulletin*, March 28, 2003.

"Uncommon Valor." http://apolloguide.com/mov_revtemp.asp?CId=3264.

University of Hawai'i Botany Department. "Hawaiian Native Plant Genera." http:// www.botany.hawaii.edu/faculty/carr/natives.htm.

U.S. Department of the Interior, National Park Service. Sanborn Beach House: National Register of Historic Places. n.d.

————. *Waioli Church—National Register of Historic Places: Statement of Architectural and Historical Significance.* n.d.

————. *Waioli Mission District—National Register of Historic Places: Inventory— Nomination Form.* n.d.

U.S. Fish & Wildlife Service. "Threatened and Endangered Species System (TESS), Listings by State and Territory as of 7/20/2002." http://ecos.fws.gov/ servlet/TESSWebpageUsaLists?state=HI.

U.S. Fish & Wildlife Service, Pacific Islands. "National Wildlife Refuges: Kaua'i National Wildlife Refuge Complex—Hanalei NWR." http://pacificislands.fws. gov/wnwr/khanaleinwr.html.

Vorsino, Mary. "Whales Herded Farther Offshore by Volunteers: Kayaks and Canoes Were Used to Move the Animals Out to Sea." *Honolulu Star-Bulletin*, July 5, 2004.

Wagner, Warren L., and Derral R. Herbst. "Electronic Supplement to the Manual of the Flowering Plants of Hawai'i." http://rathbun.si.edu/botany/ pacificislandbiodiversity/hawaiianflora/supplement.htm.

Wagner, Warren L., Derral R. Herbst, and S.H. Sohmer. *Manual of the Flowering Plants of Hawai'i.* Rev. ed., vols. 1 and 2. Honolulu: University of Hawai'i Press; Bishop Museum Press, 1999.

"Waimea's Russian Fort Is Worth a Stop." Kaua'i Beach Press, 2001.

"Waioli Mission House—Hawaii Museums Association Database." http://www. hawaiimuseums.org/mc/iskauai_waioli.htm?nowritefs.

"Waipa Foundation." http://www.waipafoundation.org.

"Whale Carcass Found in Hanalei: Yearling to be Flown to California for Necropsy, Tests to Determine Cause of Death." *Garden Island*, July 6, 2004.

Whitney, Henry M. *The Hawaiian Guide Book for Travelers*. 1875. Reprint. Rutland, VT: Tuttle, 1970.

Wichman, Frederick B. *Kaua'i: Ancient Place-Names and Their Stories*. Honolulu: University of Hawai'i Press, 1998.

Wilcox, Carol. "Albert Spencer Wilcox Beach House, Statement of Historical And/ Or Architectural Significance." Kaua'i Historical Society, 1978.

———. *Sugar Water: Hawai'i's Plantation Ditches*. Honolulu: University of Hawai'i Press, 1996.

———. *The Kauai Album*. Lihu'e: Kauai Historical Society, 1981.

Wilcox, Elsie H. "Hanalei in History." Paper read before the Kauai Historical Society, April 26, 1917.

Wilcox, Elsie Hart, compiler. "A Record of the Descendants of Abner Wilcox and Lucy Eliza Hart Wilcox of Hawaii, 1836-1950." Honolulu, 1950.

"William Haraguchi: A Living Treasure for Life-long Commitment to Agriculture." *Garden Island*, June 26, 2002.

Wilson, Christie. "Hanalei Project to Enhance Refuge View." *Honolulu Advertiser*, July 8, 2003.

Wright, Anna S. Wundenberg. Personal letter, 1921. Kaua'i Historical Society.

"Yacht excavation: Research Report No. 85, Summer 1996: Excavation of historic oceangoing yacht to begin this summer off Kauai." http://www.si.edu/opa/ researchreports/9685/9685ship.htm.

"101 Things to Do Magazines: 101 Things to Do in Hawaii—35: Kick Back in Hanalei." http://www.101things.com/Magazines?Hawaii/kauai/Activities/All/35.

"2000 Family Business of the Year Awards: Less than 25 employees. WT Haraguchi Farm, Inc." http://www.cba.hawaii.edu/quarterly/CBAQ25-1-01.pdf.

Index

Other Kaua'i Books by Mutual

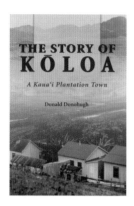

The Story of Kōloa
A Kaua'i Plantation Town
by Donald Donohugh

A plantation town's detailed history, based on both oral and written accounts, written by a long-time resident. Much of Kaua'i's history impacted Kōloa.

Trim Size: 6 x 9 in.
Page Count: 304 pages
Retail: $18.95 softcover; $22.95 casebound
ISBN-10: 1-56647-449-3 • ISBN-13: 978-1-56647-449-8 (soft)
ISBN-10: 1-56647-507-4 • ISBN-13: 978-1-56647-507-5 (case)

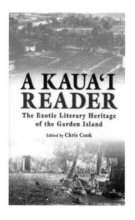

A Kaua'i Reader
The Exotic Literary Heritage of the Garden Island
Edited and with contributions by Chris Cook

Legendary characters, myths, tales, historical accounts, and modern day vignettes of the Garden Island, including Ni'ihau. Modern accounts include Hurricane Iniki, Frank Sinatra's near-drowning on Kaua'i, and two contemporary surf stories.

Trim Size: 5 x 7¾ in.
Page Count: 400 pages
Retail: $13.95 softcover
ISBN-10: 1-56647-832-4
ISBN-13: 978-1-56647-832-8

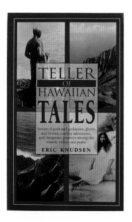

Teller of Hawaiian Tales
by Eric Knudsen

Sixty campfire yarns tell of gods and goddesses, ghosts and heroes, cowboy adventures, and legendary feats among Kaua'i's valleys and peaks.

Trim Size: 4¼ x 7 in.
Page Count: 272 pages
Retail: $6.95 mass market
ISBN-10: 0-935180-33-8
ISBN-13: 978-0-935180-33-6

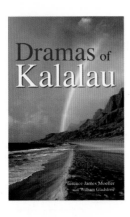

Dramas of Kalalau
by Terence Moeller

Here are stories of people who have hiked the trail along Na Pali Coast—accounts of adventure, achievement, humor, spirituality, and survival.

Trim Size: 5 x 7 in.
Page Count: 192 pp
Retail: $13.95 softcover
ISBN-10: 1-56647-827-8
ISBN-13: 978-1-56647-827-4

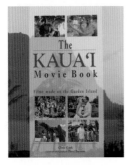

The Kaua'i Movie Book
Films Made on the Garden Island
by Chris Cook; landscape photography by David Boynton

Beautiful, lush Kaua'i is a favorite filming locale for Hollywood, having served as outback Australia, Fantasy Island, the misty domain of King Kong, Peter Pan's Never-Never Land, and Vietnam on film. Its white-sand beaches, verdant valleys, and breathtaking Nā Pali Coast have attracted filmmakers since 1933. *The Kaua'i Movie Book* is the definitive guide to movies filmed on the Garden Isle. Organized geographically, it covers everything from blockbusters like *Raiders of the Lost Ark* to documentaries, foreign films, and surf movies. Includes a guide to movie locations, index, at-a-glance movie facts, and over 300 full-color photographs.

Trim Size: 8½" x 11"
Page Count: 128 pages (with over 300 color photos)
Retail: $27.95 hardcover; $22.95 softcover
ISBN-10: 1-56647-141-9 • ISBN-13: 978-1-56647-141-1 (hard)
ISBN-10: 1-56647-129-X • ISBN-13: 978-1-56647-129-9 (soft)